EMPLOYMENT FUTURES

Employment Futures

Reorganization, Dislocation,
and Public Policy

PAUL OSTERMAN

New York   Oxford
OXFORD UNIVERSITY PRESS
1988

Oxford University Press

Oxford New York Toronto
Delhi Bombay Calcutta Madras Karachi
Petaling Jaya Singapore Hong Kong Tokyo
Nairobi Dar es Salaam Cape Town
Melbourne Auckland

and associated companies in
Beirut Berlin Ibadan Nicosia

Copyright © 1988 by Oxford University Press, Inc.
Published by Oxford University Press, Inc.,
200 Madison Avenue, New York, New York 10016

Oxford is a registered trademark of Oxford University Press

Library of Congress Catalog-in-Publication Data
Osterman, Paul.
Employment futures.
Includes index.
1. Manpower planning—United States. 2. Manpower policy—
United States. 3. Industrial relations—United States. I. Title.
HF5549.2.U5077 1988   331.11'0973   87-31459
ISBN 0-19-505279-X

9 8 7 6 5 4 3 2 1

Printed in the United States of America
on acid-free paper

For Susan, Rachel, and Michelle

PREFACE

This book deals with labor markets and public policy, and explores several recent developments, both in the external environment and within firms. Although these developments may appear unconnected, I contend that either they are linked by economic forces or they can be fruitfully joined by creative public policy. The book touches on four main themes: the dislocation of laid-off workers, the reorganization of work within firms, the persistent problems of low earnings and poverty, and the possibilities of an expanded and aggressive public policy to deal with these problems.

The battering the American economy has received in recent years has exposed a central weakness in the labor market: it does a poor job of providing employment in other firms or industries for experienced adult workers who are laid off. This difficulty contrasts with the considerable success of the labor market in generating jobs and finding employment for increased numbers of younger and women job entrants. However, experienced adults who are laid off endure extremely long periods of joblessness, and those who do find work must often take substantial wage cuts. These facts are at the heart of much of the current concern about dislocated workers and plant closing legislation, but they point to deeper issues: the appropriate level of security that should be provided by the labor market, and whether a useful role for public policy exists.

Employment security has broad importance beyond the situation of those people directly dislocated, because it is at the heart of another issue facing the labor market: the organization of work within firms. An observer attempting to predict the evolution of employment practices would be struck by two very different tendencies. New technologies and the realities of heightened competition are forcing firms to innovate, but responses differ. Some firms seek to transform their work structures by broadening jobs and gaining a more committed labor force. A key element in this strategy is increased employment security. Other firms attempt to force change in internal practices by aggressive concession bargaining or work force reduction through layoffs. In effect, employment practices have reached something of a crossroads since the different models compete. Which pattern will come to dominate and become the new American model is unclear, but in this book a strong case is made that the former is preferable.

Although the committed labor force and the employment security approach is preferable, it is difficult for firms to guarantee high levels of security. The most common strategy reduces the core labor force and attempts to absorb fluctuations with a growing group of peripheral—temporary, part-time, or contract—employees. While this may succeed in specific instances, the overall impact simply redistributes insecurity. In any case, the strategy is inherently limited and few companies have found a way to go much beyond it. Here there is the potential for developing an active public employment policy that not only does a more effective job of assisting displaced workers, but also, by making the external labor market less threatening, helps effect the transformation of work organization within firms. This may seem utopian, but in a lengthy discussion of European approaches we show that in several nations employment policy plays a role similar to that advocated for the United States.

There are additional benefits to such a policy. The impulse toward protectionism would be reduced were an effective employment policy able to reduce the risks of job loss.

In fact a recent upsurge of interest in employment policy has occured, both in terms of programs for dislocated workers and in other arenas, such as employment assistance for welfare recipients. Indeed, it is at the bottom end of the labor market that employment policy traditionally has been concentrated. There is good reason for this because the problems of low earnings and poverty remain substantial. Unfortunately, narrowly targeted programs aimed exclusively at the poor have delivered unsatisfactory results largely because they stigmatize clients. This observation also argues for expanding the scope of employment policy and developing a system that addresses a variety of needs: those of skilled experienced workers, of the economically disadvantaged, and some of the human resource concerns of firms.

In recent years themes in this book have not been fashionable in either academic economics literature or public discourse. This may be changing and my hope is that the book will interest (both academic and general) audiences concerned with public policy, human resource professionals within companies, and anyone interested in gaining a general understanding of how labor markets have evolved in this country.

In working on this book I have received assistance from many people. Some helped with the research, especially in matters concerning European labor markets and employment policy. For this I am grateful to Patsy Buchmann, Anne Heald, Alan Larsson, Annika Ohgren, and Per Silenstam. Cay Stratton hired me to help administer the Job Training Partnership Act in Massachusetts, and I learned a great deal from her and from the experience. The following people read portions of the manuscript (several on the list read it in its entirety, sometimes more than once!), corrected errors, and pointed me in better directions: Katherine Abraham, Gordon Berlin, Anders Bjorklund, Clair Brown, Peter Cappelli, Bill Dickens, Peter Doeringer, Susan Eckstein, Bernie Elbaum, Gosta Esping-Anderson, Steven Hamilton, Harry Katz, Tom Kochan, Sar Levitan, Bob McKersie, Michael Piore, Gunter Schmid, Werner Segenberger, Bill Spring, Judith Tendler, Lester Thurow, and Eskil Wadensjo.

When I began the book I was employed by Boston University and am grateful for the sabbatical support I received. The Industrial Relations Section of the M.I.T. Sloan School, where I teach now, provided much assistance, and I thank Tom Kochan, Bob McKersie, and Michael Piore. The German Marshall Fund got me started by financing a research trip to Europe and while the money was important so was the guidance of the Fund's project officer, Anne Heald. The Ford Foundation supported me while I wrote the book; I am grateful for the assistance and for Gordon Berlin's suggestions.

CONTENTS

EMPLOYMENT FUTURES

1

Introduction

The past decade has been an uneasy one for the American labor market because of a series of paradoxes. The market produced an explosion of job growth; contrary to some opinions, most of these jobs have been of high quality. Yet at the same time unemployment seems uncomfortably high, poverty rates have not declined, and workers who lose their jobs because of plant closings and large-scale layoffs have considerable difficulty finding new work. Firms are also torn in several directions. In some enterprises a series of innovations have emphasized cooperation and worker commitment. Other companies are following a path of employer militancy and forced concessions. Even in firms that offer the bulk of their work force good secure jobs, a growing minority of employees is found in less desirable part-time and temporary positions.

This book offers an interpretation of these developments that discusses the evolution of work within firms. The book then uses that interpretation to explore the possibilities of an active public employment policy and to ground that exploration in a theory of labor market functioning. The ultimate argument is that a broad understanding of the interaction of developments inside and outside the firm can provide a coherent interpretation of the developments just outlined and explain why the market seems to be moving in several directions at once. With such an understanding, we can think creatively about the scope of public policy.

The Issues at Stake

As the foregoing implies, we want to understand and tie together four topics: unemployment and dislocation, poverty and low earnings, the organization of work within the firm, and employment policy. What is the state of play with respect to each of these concerns?

Unemployment and Dislocation

Two characteristics of unemployment are controversial and of concern. First, the unemployment rate has been drifting steadily up; each business cycle ends with a higher unemployment rate than the previous one. Expectations for the economy have deteriorated accordingly. In the 1960s a 4% unemployment rate was considered "full employment"; today the concensus would be 6% or more.

The worsening of unemployment is partially due to increased macroeconomic caution as policymakers exercise restraint to avoid inflation. However, this cannot be the entire explanation since, even after controlling for capacity utilization (a measure of economywide demand), there is an upward unemployment trend.[1] Equally inadequate is the common explanation that the problem is due to an influx of unemployment-prone youth and other inexperienced workers. Even accepting, for the sake of argument, the implicit normative weighting of different groups' unemployment, the arithmetic does not work out.[2]

An increasingly worrisome component of unemployment is the problems faced by so-called dislocated workers. These are typically experienced and skilled employees who lose work because of plant closings or large-scale layoffs. These layoffs might be triggered by technological change, shifting product demand, or international trade imbalances. The rocky economy of the past decade has raised sharply the visibility of this group and induced a range of policy efforts such as the Trade Adjustment Assistance Act, the dislocated workers training programs funded under the Job Training Partnership Act, and several union-management job security and training agreements. Although the popular image associates this group with blue collar union workers, nonunion blue collar and white collar employees increasingly face similar difficulties.

Is worker dislocation really a problem? Are the costs associated with job loss transitory or permanent? Why does the labor market not reabsorb these workers smoothly? These are the questions that we will address in Chapters 2 and 3. These questions are particularly important, because we want to tie the answers to an understanding of employment policy within firms and the scope of public policy. However, the answers we give—that unemployment is very costly and is linked to a series of market failures—are controversial in the economics profession.

For people whose formative experience was the Great Depression (and this includes the economists and other social scientists who dominated debate through most of the postwar period), there would be no question about the nature or impact of unemployment. Joblessness was a costly evil and obviously had adverse consequences for those experiencing it. However, in recent years this view has been strongly challenged. A "new view" of unemployment has emerged, one that characterizes the nature of unemployment in a manner that minimizes its consequences and, in a complementary manner, attributes the existence of unemployment itself either to voluntary decisions by those affected or to government programs that provide incentives to remain unemployed. The spirit of the new view is illustrated by the subhead of a recent article examining whether unemployment in one period was correlated with subsequent unemployment; the subhead posed the research question as "The Persistence of Unemployment Behavior."[3]

A good summary of this new view is provided by Martin Feldstein.

[The] picture of a hard core of unemployed people unable to find jobs is an inaccurate description of our economy and a misleading basis for policy. A more accurate description is an active labor market in which almost everyone who is out of work can find his usual type of job in a relatively short time . . . the duration of unemployment is quite short. Even in a year like 1971 with a very high unemployment rate, 45% of those unemployed had been out of work for less than five weeks . . . job losses account for less than half of total unemployment . . . the remainder are those who voluntarily left their last jobs, are reentering the labor force or never worked before.[4]

In brief, unemployment is not that much of a concern because it is short and often voluntary. If correct, this perspective poses a major challenge to both the conventional view of unemployment and to those who believe that public policy can, or should, be deployed.

As it turns out, the new view has been largely discredited by subsequent research. This work can be summarized as follows.

It is true, as the new view claims, that most unemployment periods are short. However, paradoxical as this may seem, most people who are unemployed are in the midst of long unemployment spells. Put differently, over a period of time—say a year—there are many unemployment periods, most of which are short. Hence the typical unemployment period is short. However, by virtue of their very shortness, these periods do not count for much in generating the overall unemployment rate and, if we were to sample all the people who were unemployed at a point in time (say today), they would, on average, be in the midst of long unemployment periods. The reason is that people with short unemployment periods would be less likely to appear in our sample. As one of the researchers in this area has pointed out, these distinctions correspond to the difference between life expectancy at birth and life expectancy of a given population. The former is shorter than the latter because the calculation includes many people who die young; by contrast, if we sample the population today, the typical person is in the midst of a longer life cycle. Akerloff and Main estimated that the typical unemployment period in 1978 lasted 6.3 weeks (a relatively short time), but that the typical person who was unemployed at any point in the year was in the midst of a period that would last 26.2 weeks.[5] This means that most unemployment is generated by long spells of prolonged joblessness.[6]

These calculations suggest that in one sense the new view is correct, but it is also irrelevant to the issue as most people understand it. There are many short spells of unemployment, but the people who experience them account for little aggregate unemployment and, by virtue of the shortness of their spells, are not representative of a sample of the unemployed at any point in time. If we think about the problems of the unemployed as a group and ask about their experience, we find that the typical person is in the midst of a lengthy unemployment period. We also find that a relatively small group of people account for much of the problem.

The heavy concentration of unemployment and its persistence also cast considerable doubt on the view that the bulk of joblessness results from voluntary search behavior or from people idly waiting to be called back to a prior job. There are additional reasons to be skeptical of the search theory explanation. The behavior of the unemployed is not consistent with the notion that they are investors speculating their lost wages from unemployment against possible higher wages in better jobs that they hope to get. The unemployed seem to search among many firms, yet most take the first job they are offered. In a 1976 survey of individuals who were in the midst of unemployment spells lasting four weeks or more, nearly 60% had contacted six or more employers; however, only 10% of those unemployed had turned down the first job they were offered, a finding replicated in other research.[7] Furthermore, it is generally possible to search for a new job without quitting and risking unemployment; in fact, quit rates are inversely related to the unemployment rate not positively correlated, as would be expected if high unemployment were caused by people quitting to search for new jobs.[8]

It is true, of course, that when people become unemployed they do search for work, and it may be possible to model their search strategies in cost/benefit terms. However, to conclude that search behavior is the key to understanding unemployment is illogical. If, on a ship at sea, some process generates a number of people to be thrown overboard, another process selects the particular individuals, and the victims, once in the ocean, swim for shore, it would be logically possible but hardly sensible to understand the death rate among the ship's population in terms of swimming ability. The earlier processes are clearly of prior importance.

In summary, it seems most fruitful to think of unemployment as having a double character. For many people it is a brief break in their careers; for others it represents a considerably more difficult period. Most of the people who are unemployed at a given point in time fall into the latter category.

Low Earnings

If unemployment and worker dislocation are one reason to be concerned with labor market performance, then the persistence of low earnings among a substantial fraction of the labor force is another. Indeed, the traditional goal of employment policy has been to raise the earnings of those below the poverty line. Our intention is to broaden the scope of employment policy but, in doing so, we do not want to lose sight of this traditional constituency. Indeed, it is our contention that by making employment policy more inclusive it can better serve those most in need.

Chapter 2 devotes considerable care to estimating the magnitude—the fraction of the labor force—suffering from problems of persistent low earnings. The chapter and the book do not however enter the debate about the causes of low earnings. A great deal of scholarly effort over the past 20 years has gone into such analysis. The question of race is central to any such discussion. Although the economic situation of minorities has improved relative to that of whites over most of the postwar period, it remains inferior and, indeed, deteriorated in the 1980s.[9] This fact, combined with undoubted evidence of past discrimination and the fact that Title VII antidiscrimination legal cases continue to be won in substantial numbers,[10] suggests that discrimination remains a serious concern. Other researchers, however, argue for the "declining significance of race" and suggest that the aggregate data on the deteriorating position of blacks mask the large role that social class plays.[11] In this view the black population is divided between a middle class whose labor market situation closely resembles that of whites and an underclass trapped in a cycle of poverty. The problem is to understand what perpetuates the underclass.

Race looms large but is not the only explanation of low earnings. A substantial body of economics literature directs our attention to "human capital," the education and training of the poor, and suggests that the solution lies in efforts to augment skills and motivation. By contrast, a minority of the profession would argue for a dual labor market interpretation of labor market disadvantage and claim that hiring barriers of firms providing good jobs (so-called primary firms), combined with efforts by low-wage secondary labor market employers to maintain an adequate labor supply, can explain poverty by emphasizing the behavior of firms rather than the characteristics of individuals. Finally, it is possible to develop a number of specialized explanations, such as the problems of teenage pregnancies and single parents.

It is obvious that there is no shortage of explanations. It is also clear that no explanation can easily carry the day. For example, proponents of the racism argument have to explain why the earnings distribution has worsened during the period when racism, though not eradicated, has diminished. Social class theorists, on the other hand, must confront evidence that at each level of education, from high school dropouts to college graduates, blacks continue to have higher unemployment rates and usually lower earnings than whites. Human capital theory sounds plausible until we notice (as will be described in Chapter 5) that programs seeking to upgrade education and skills have had little success in raising earnings. If dual labor market theory is not just another way of restating the racism argument, it must explain why barriers between the segments persist, since plausible explanations (other than racism) are hard to find.

These debates are interesting and important, both as intellectual explorations and as guides to policy. Indeed, one can obviously argue that until we "understand" the problem, policy formulation is unwarranted. Although the argument is plausible, this book will not follow it, but will deal instead with policy at the level of "systems," not programs. At the programmatic level we want to know whether to put our resources into educational remediation, pregnancy counseling, or other interventions. These important decisions should be taken with care and can be informed by the debates reviewed previously. However, a major point of this book is that a collection of such programs cannot succeed on a large scale if isolated from the mainstream of the private economy, that is, if they are part of a separate antipoverty effort. Before we can deliver programs we must create a system that gives the programs, of whatever kind, a chance to succeed. This point, elaborated at length later, does not depend on an explanation of low earnings. Instead, it relies on an argument about how employment policy fits in with other features of the labor market. Our discussion of low earnings is intended to convince the reader that an employment policy is necessary, that there is a problem to be solved, a need to be addressed. The discussion of the solution will turn on a different set of evidence and arguments.

Shifts in the Organization of Work

In the past decade there have been many efforts to reorganize work practices within firms; there has been even more discussion, often confused, of the need to do so. We interpret these developments in the context of changes in the pattern of internal labor markets. The term "internal labor market" is shorthand for the administrative rules and personnel practices that firms use to structure work. These rules cover hiring, training, promotion, job classification, and wage setting. In both union and nonunion settings and for both white and blue collar workers, these rules are in flux. In many union settings employers are seeking to enlarge job content and build greater worker commitment through a variety of devices such as quality circles, expanded training, and employment security programs. Indeed, the personnel literature is full of new ideas and programs aimed at expanding employee involvement and participation in the enterprise. Yet, paradoxically, in similar settings but in a very different spirit, employers are aggressively seeking wage concessions and forced work rule changes, and are often laying off workers. The coexistence of these two tendencies causes confusion about the direction of work. The changes are not limited to blue collar employment. White collar work has traditionally been more secure, but that may be changing as numerous large firms cut back on their staffs. This raises the question of whether the traditional premises of white collar work are stable. Taken together, it is apparent that internal labor markets are in a period of flux, but it is not easy to discern or understand the main lines of change.

Stable patterns for blue and white collar internal labor markets emerged in the wake of World War II and, until recently, the only intellectual challenge has been to describe and rationalize those rules. Because those rules were implicitly viewed as permanent, little effort was devoted to understanding why and how they change. It is now apparent that a theory of change is necessary. This in turn requires an understanding of what choices are available to firms and what considerations shape their choices. Although pieces of such a theory are in the literature, it would be hard to argue that they have been pulled together coherently to shed light on the often contradictory developments now underway. This book attempts to fill this gap.

Employment Policy

It is apparent that a major goal of this book will be to describe and understand the developments just outlined with respect to dislocation, poverty, and the evolution of internal labor markets. Another objective is more activist. The problems of worker dislocation and poverty obviously have strong normative components, and it would be desirable to generate policies that hasten transitions and ease the economic hardship. However, there is also a case to be made for public policy with respect to internal labor markets. We will argue that one of the main alternatives currently in the "arena" has a series of advantages both for the stakeholders (management and employees) of firms and for the broader economy. However, a series of difficulties exists in disseminating this model and making it broadly attractive. Hence, both because of dislocation and because of concerns about the evolution of internal labor markets, it seems desirable to consider the role of employment policy in the economy. For reasons that will become clear (having to do with the linkage between the problems of internal labor markets and the nature of dislocation), our discussion of employment policy emphasizes training and placement activities.

Interest in an active employment policy has waxed and waned in the postwar period. In the late 1950s and early 1960s a strong faction of labor economists argued that technical change worsened unemployment by rendering some skills obselete (this was termed "structural unemployment"),[12] and several legislative initiatives, such as the Area Redevelopment Act and the Manpower Development and Training Act, were enacted. However, this argument was roundly opposed by the mainstream of the profession, which held that economic growth and well-functioning labor markets would combine to solve the "problem." This view was seemingly vindicated by the low unemployment of the middle to late 1960s. The earlier programs were therefore transformed into antipoverty efforts and their intellectual foundation became human capital theory. The central idea of human capital theory was that poverty was caused by inadequate levels of education and training. Markets were assumed to work well if people brought with them appropriate levels of skill. The upshot was programs, initiated during the War on Poverty and consolidated in later federal training policies, aimed at providing poor people with remedial education and skill training. However, these enthusiasms also passed. The training programs were at least partially discredited both by their generally poor results and by the broader political attack on the welfare state. Human capital theory survived and still flourishes, but the persistence of low earnings in the face of substantial educational and training investments makes it difficult to accept standard explanations of poverty. Today the structural diagnosis is being revived in the form of concern with dislocation caused by trade, technology, and capital flight. However, although the diagnosis may be similar to that of the past, there has been no satisfactory attempt to provide an intellectual explanation of why market adjustment fails to mitigate the problem.

Each of these waves of concern created a set of institutions and ideas that are still with us in part. Structural unemployment is one of the "categories" of unemployment that are regularly presented to undergraduate and even graduate students.[13] It sits in uneasy relation to more "modern" notions of unemployment, which tend to describe joblessness as flowing from voluntary search behavior by the unemployed, but the idea has proved durable. Human capital theory continues as the central paradigm of modern labor economics and many (though fewer than before) still believe that low income can be explained in these terms.[14] The training institutions created during the War on Poverty have been retained, in sharply diminished dimensions, and now deliver services very similar to those of the past under the aegis of the Reagan Administration's Job Training Partnership Act. Even the current interest in dislocated workers, inchoate as it is, created programs such as the Trade Adjustment Assistance Act, which provides relocation and training assistance. This confused mixture is leavened with institutions whose origins precede World War II: vocational education, which was institutionalized in the early twentieth century, and the U.S. Employment Service, created during the New Deal.

The Perspective of This Book

This book explores three difficult and, in many ways, puzzling issues: the problems of experienced workers who are dislocated and cannot find comparable new employment; the dilemmas facing firms as they respond to shifting economic conditions by trying to change the organization of work; and the appropriate role of employment policy. We also address the problems of low-income workers and argue that by understanding the broader labor market, we can better meet their specific problems.

At the core of our analysis is a set of ideas concerning the nature and evolution of work arrangements within firms. We interpret the dislocated worker problem or, more generally, the difficulties experienced workers face in finding new employment in light of the hiring and promotion practices of most firms. These hiring practices are such that the bulk of hiring occurs at the bottom rungs of job ladders, and incumbents with seniority are protected from fluctuations in labor demand. Union contracts provide this kind of protection for their members, but similar practices exist in many nonunion blue collar industries and in many white collar settings as well.

This general pattern worked well when the economy was relatively stable and whatever adjustment that was required could be shouldered by plentiful supplies of new entrants. However, in recent years the economy has become much more variable and uncertain, and shifting demographics have increased the fraction of the labor force composed of relatively inflexible adult workers. The consequence is increased dislocation and adjustment problems.

The book also argues that the widespread confusion in the workplace flows from two competing views of how work rules should be restructured to contend with the shifting environment. The differences center on the degree of internal flexibility management enjoys regarding job classifications and worker assignments and in differences in the extent of employment security each model provides. In order to gain more internal flexibility greater levels of employment security are necessary. Changes in technology and in product markets have shifted the balance between the two alternatives, and it is increasingly desirable for firms to opt for the high flexibility/high security alternative. However, in blue collar work employers face serious difficulties in making the transition, while in white collar settings—where employment security and flexibility has been the rule—it is growing harder to maintain past practices. One problem is that firms feel more unable to offer a high level of employment security. Another difficulty is that employees perceive the external labor market to be a dangerous place and are reluctant to alter work practices that have provided a degree of job protection in the past.

This argument implies that problems of worker dislocation and internal labor market evolution are linked. This linkage emerges because the problem of dislocation and market adjustment is exacerbated by internal labor market structures (i.e., hiring and promotion patterns), because employee fear of the consequences of dislocation makes change in internal labor market patterns difficult, and because firms believe that the cost of providing employment security may be too high. Most of the current discussion about labor market adjustment and worker dislocation fails to make these connections. If the argument in this book is convincing, it represents a new perspective on the problem.

Methodologically, our perspective places this book in the tradition of economic analysis that has sought to take institutions seriously and show how and why a theory of institutional evolution is necessary to generate a satisfactory understanding of economic evolution. As such, our work is a blend of economic, sociological, and political reasoning (it is also a blend of interviews and statistics). Research of this sort has, of course, been done before, but it does represent a minority position in the social sciences and particularly in economics. Whatever the broader merits of such a perspective, we would argue that it is essential for understanding employer decision-making in the context of bureaucratic institutions and the interplay of those decisions with market forces.

The material in this book also represents something of a minority view with respect to the formulation of employment policy. A classic statement of the "American approach" to employment policy can be found in Richard Lester's *Manpower Planning for A Free Society*, a book written at the beginning of the 1960's surge of training programs. Lester wrote:

> The key concepts and recommendations in this book can be applied to America's manpower problems without any basic change in the existing institutional structure or any interference in individual freedoms . . . in a free society manpower planning aims to enlarge job opportunities through the power of informed choice. . . .[15]

The consequence of this philosophy is that American programs aim to provide individuals with information and skills but are not integrated in any substantial way into the human resource calculations or industrial relations strategies of firms. In the jargon of the economics profession, employment policy operates largely on the supply side of the market. Even those efforts—such as Public Service Employment, New Careers, and the like—which were demand-side (or job creation) efforts, emphasized government jobs, not a significant interaction with the private market economy.

At its best this perspective leads to a set of labor market preparation and information efforts. In addition, in the 1960s and early 1970s a group of com-mitted academics and policy advocates produced an impressive and high-qual-ity body of work covering both the philosophy and tactics of employment pool-icy.[16] However, in other hands this view too often became a rationale for programs that were irrelevant to labor market participants. In either case, we later dem-onstrate that the actual performance of programs based on this philosophy is disappointing.

Set against this orientation is an alternative view in which employment pol-icy is designed to interact with the private calculations of the key labor market actors. Here we seek to build up a theory of employment policy by under-standing what openings are provided by the actual problems that confront firms and workers in the labor market. We want to ground our theory of employment policy in a theory of internal and external labor market evolution. To be sure, demographic shifts, individual attributes, and labor supply are important, but only as one set of building blocks in a broader theory. Unlike human capital theory, we do not focus only on labor supply (changing people), and unlike the view represented by Lester, we do not take a passive stance toward private institutions. That is, we seek to understand first how key employer policies affect labor market outcomes. Then we examine variations and trends in these policies. On the basis of this understanding, we search for policy alternatives that encourage, reenforce, and diffuse the employer policies that have the most favorable labor market consequences.

Specifically, we try to use our analysis of the tensions in internal labor market development as firms attempt to redesign work to show how an em-ployment policy can contribute to a resolution of the dilemmas employers face. It is our view that if an employment policy can be useful, it will be used and, as such, will be more effective than past efforts and will garner broader political support. This will in turn make it a more efficacious device for the welfare of its traditional constituency—poor people—because the programs will be suf-ficiently broad based that they will no longer stigmatize. The basic point, how-ever, is that our theory holds that public policy must be grounded in an insti-tutional understanding of private economic structures and organizational policies.

Plan of the Book

Chapter 2 lays out some of the facts that underlie our concern with labor market performance. Working with several data sources, we first examine the Amer-ican record of job creation. We then turn to a major theme of the book—worker dislocation and labor market adjustment—and attempt to document the extent of dislocation and how successful or unsuccessful the labor market is in reem-ploying laid-off workers. To motivate further the subsequent discussion of em-ployment policy, we also examine how widespread the problem of persistent low earnings is. Chapter 3 outlines a model that helps explain why the labor market seems to do poorly in finding comparable work for experienced em-ployees who are laid off. That model rests on an interaction of internal labor market practices and supply conditions in the labor market. The chapter argues that a combination of technological and demographic trends will worsen the already difficult problems of readjustment.

Chapter 4 shifts attention from individual data and directly addresses the firm's internal labor market. We describe the alternatives firms face today as they consider how to organize work and discuss the costs and benefits of these alternatives. We then apply this analysis to recent events, particularly the confusion alluded to earlier. In conducting this analysis we pay special attention to the technological and product market developments that have undermined the previous internal labor market patterns for white and blue collar employees and outline what we see as the major new alternatives. The chapter closes with our argument that firms are facing a difficult choice that has broad public and private implications. The question is whether or not employment policy can help shape the direction of those choices.

Chapter 5 traces the history and performance of U.S. employment policy and reaches a pessimistic conclusion about current institutional capacities. We inquire whether it is possible to conceive of an alternative structure for employment policy that holds more promise. To explore this question, we turn, in Chapter 6, to comparative research and examine the employment policies of Sweden and Germany. Our argument is not that we should adopt any particular program or model from these nations. The point is that in both countries public employment policy interacts with the private calculations of firms and unions and hence plays the kind of integrated role that we think is lacking here. In other words, the public employment policy in both nations assists firms by encouraging more supple and flexible internal labor markets. By being useful to firms, the policy is given the opportunity to accomplish other objectives such as assisting persons in labor market difficulty. Therefore, although we may not be interested in the specifics of Swedish and German policy, we can document and learn an important general lesson.

In Chapter 7 we first summarize our argument and then draw some implications for U.S. policy. The aim of the policy conclusion is to point to some broad strategic directions that seem useful. However, in addition to these ideas about policy, this book will also accomplish its intended goal if it helps convince the reader that understanding the interaction among markets, institutional structures and organizational policies, and public policy offers an interesting and useful way to conduct analysis.

Chapters 2 and 6 have appendices that elaborate on some of the themes in the chapters. These appendices are intended only for readers interested in greater detail and can be skipped without any loss of continuity.

2

Growth, Dislocation, and Poverty: The Dimensions of the Problem

In this chapter we begin to assess the state of the American labor market. We are, however, not aiming to deliver a final grade. The economy is too large and complex for any summary judgment to make sense or be useful. Instead, our ambition is more limited; we hope to pinpoint those areas where the labor market performs well and those with problems and use this mapping to identify the scope of public policy.

The most fundamental requirement for a well functioning labor market is that jobs be available. How good these jobs are, how they are allocated to potential workers, and how well they match the skills and locational preferences of those workers are all important questions but, before these topics become interesting, there must first be job generation.

It is precisely on the issue of job generation that the optimists make their strongest case. The performance of the American economy over the past decade and a half has indeed been remarkable. Table 2.1 provides data on job creation between 1971 and 1981. These years were choosen in order to provide comparable beginning and end points: in 1971 the Federal Reserve Board index of capacity utilization stood at 79.8, while in 1981 it was 80.2. Another advantage of using the 1981 end point is that it is the last year with economic conditions similar to those of the early 1970s in which the census occupational definitions remain unchanged. In Table 2.2 we bring the data up to date by examining job growth for the 1982–86 period. Both tables are limited to nonagricultural jobs held by people 20 years old or more. In that sense they understate total job growth over the period, but we avoid being misled by special circumstances in the youth and agricultural labor markets.

Looking first at the 1971–81 period, the enormous increase in jobs, at the rate of nearly 2 million per year, is evident. Furthermore, this growth occurred during a period in which the economy experienced two major oil shocks and the deepest recession since the Great Depression.

Beyond the sheer numbers, several other important characteristics of the job growth stand out. Two-thirds of the new jobs were held by women, a development that clearly reflects their rising labor force participation (between

1971 and 1981 the labor force participation rate of married women rose from 40.6% to 50.5%). However, male employment also grew impressively, increasing by nearly 16% over the period.

Table 2.1 Job Growth, 1971–81

| | Men | | Women | |
Occupation	Number of New Jobs (000)	Percent of Growth	Number of New Jobs (000)	Percent of Growth
Professional	2144	31.2	2820	24.2
Managers	1014	14.7	1568	13.4
Clerical	219	3.1	4296	36.9
Sales	550	8.0	629	5.4
Crafts	1703	24.7	384	3.2
Operators	395	5.7	459	3.9
Laborers	186	2.7	210	1.8
Private household service	1	0.0	−336	−2.6
Other service	652	9.4	1609	13.8
		100		100

Source: Calculated from *Employment and Earnings.* Employment data are limited to nonagricultural occupations and to individuals age 20 and older. In 1971 total employment was 43,582,000 for men (age 20 plus and nonagricultural) and 26,687,000 for women. In 1981 the respective figures were 50,450,000 and 38,335,000.

Table 2.2 Job Growth, 1982–86

| | Men | | Women | |
Occupation	Number of New Jobs (000)	Percent of Growth	Number of New Jobs (000)	Percent of Growth
Executive, administrative, managerial	785	16.2	1271	23.0
Professional	492	10.2	863	15.6
Technicians	133	2.8	209	3.8
Sales	683	14.1	1106	20.0
Administrative support	235	4.9	1008	18.2
Service	478	9.9	805	14.6
Precision, craft, repair	1311	27.1	308	5.6
Operators, assemblers, inspectors	156	3.2	−55	−0.01
Transportation operators	290	6.0	82	0.01
Handlers, cleaners, helpers, laborers	270	5.6	2−77	−0.01
Total	4833	100	5502	100

Source: Calculated from *Employment and Earnings.* Employment data are limited to nonagricultural occupations and to individuals age 20 and older.

The second notable characteristic of the growth is that, judging by the occupational distribution, the quality of the new jobs seems quite high. Occupational classes as broad as these one-digit groups can be deceptive since, within a category, say sales work, one can find the Fuller brush man and the IBM mainframe salesperson. Nonetheless, these classes provide a useful first cut. For men, what might be termed the three top categories—professionals, managers, and craft workers—accounted for over 70% of all job growth, despite the fact that these fields made up just over 53% of employment in 1971. The weight of male employment therefore shifted toward these good jobs. Women's employment growth was less concentrated in good jobs, just as their base employment in 1971 was less favorably distributed. Even so, the direction of growth was positive. While professional, managerial, and craft jobs accounted for 22% of their 1971 employment, these occupations accounted for nearly 41% of growth.

The 1982–86 period demonstrates a continuation of the earlier trends. Job growth is even more impressive, gaining 10 million over 4 years. Furthermore, the growth was again weighted toward high-quality occupations. If we take as the "best" jobs the four categories executive/administrative/managerial, professional, technicians, and precision/craft/repair, then these accounted for 56.2% of job growth for men, although in 1982 they represented only 49.3% of total employment. For women these same four occupations provided 48% of job growth, although in 1982 they were only 28.8% of employment. For both men and women, then, the good jobs provided more than their share of job growth and, hence, the overall distribution of jobs ranked by quality was improving.

It is important to dwell on the quality as well as the magnitude of job growth because of the confused nature of the discussion concerning the evolution of job quality in America. Some commentators claim we are becoming a nation of fast-food chains and emphasize labor force projections that the occupations responsible for the greatest future job growth will be janitors, cashiers, and salesclerks. The record of the recent past, which we have just reviewed, simply does not support such pessimism. We will also see later that what we know about the characteristics of new technologies also suggests moderately optimistic conclusions concerning job quality (although more sober ones concerning the employment levels).

Another line of analysis examines trends in income and earnings. Here evidence and interpretation is more complex. It is important to keep in mind our question: Is the job content of the economy shifting in the direction of more low-skilled work and to jobs that pay or provide working conditions substantially below the average? Is a typical new job along these dimensions, near the average, better than average, or worse than average?

In answering this question it is important to distinguish (as many do not) between three developments: declining average levels of earnings, a worsening distribution of annual income, and a shift in the direction of more low-wage or low-quality jobs. The third of these concerns—a possible worsening in the job content of the economy—is the focus of our discussion, but it is often confused with the other two concerns.

In the past decade and a half, the level of earnings (i.e., the average earnings of a typical worker) has stagnated because of a slack economy, weakening union power, and employer militancy. This trend is undeniable and is a serious source of concern. It does not mean, however, that there are more "bad" jobs than there used to be. The average has gotten worse and the entire distribution of jobs has shifted downward. However, the common understanding of a bad jobs is one that is bad relative to others in the economy. For example, a bad job might be one that earned less than 50% of the median wage. A deterioration in the average wage does not necessarily change the distribution of jobs around that average. Everyone may be worse off but the number of bad jobs (in the sense of jobs at the bottom of the distribution) has not increased. This may seem merely a play on words but in fact is crucial for understanding the trends in hiring or training requirements. For example, skill levels needed to do a job and hence to get hired may rise even as the wages of that job stagnate. Confusing the two issues does not help find solutions to the problem of falling earnings.

The second development concerns the distribution of family income, which has become less equal in recent years. In part, this is due to demographic developments and family composition, but labor market developments also play a significant role.[2] Among these labor market developments is a proliferation of part-time work, and indeed, many of these jobs are low quality in the sense we mean. However, an additional major source of the worsening income distribution has been the high unemployment of recent years and declining labor force participation of disadvantaged groups. These are serious concerns and we will take them up later in the chapter. However, it does not aid understanding to confuse them with the job quality issue.

It is hard to discern clear evidence that job quality—measured as a relative concept—has worsened, other than the increase in part-time work. As we have seen, most of the new jobs created in recent years have been high quality, at least as measured by their occupational distribution. Furthermore, other analysts who have examined wage distributions over time find no evidence that they have become less equal or that the trend is moving in the direction of a larger fraction of low-wage employment.[3]

To summarize, slack labor markets and reduced worker bargaining power have reduced average earnings and also worsened the distribution of annual income. These are major problems and this book addresses them. It does not help matters, however, to also argue that the economy is moving toward more low-skilled work. In fact, the opposite is occurring, and we must understand this if we are to devise effective solutions to real problems.

The Dark Lining

It is apparent from the evidence on job creation that the U.S. labor market has performed exceptionally well by this measure. What, then, is there to concern us? There are three sources of concern. First, despite the good record of job growth, unemployment rates have remained high. Second, for many workers job loss has long-term, adverse consequences. That is, the labor market does a poor job of reabsorbing people who are dislocated by economic change. Third, a substantial number of people have persistently low earnings, earnings that are too low to support themselves or their families.

The remainder of this chapter analyzes these three issues. Our major emphasis will be on the problems of dislocation and the capacity of the labor market to reemploy job losers. This focus follows from our interest in understanding the evolution of the "mainstream" labor market and how developments both inside and outside the firm set the stage for employment policy. Indeed, Chapters 3 and 4 develop an extensive argument concerning how the facts documented in this chapter can be understood by considering technology, shifting demographics, and the internal labor market system of employers. However, it is important to remain aware of the special problems of low-income workers. Indeed, at the conclusion of the book we demonstrate how an employment policy with a broad base can serve poor people better than the narrowly targeted efforts of the past. Hence the concluding section of this chapter documents the extent of low earnings in the labor force.

The Impact of Unemployment

The postwar record with respect to unemployment has not been satisfactory. The unemployment rate has drifted steadily up, ending each business cycle at a higher level than before. This trend is only partially explained by reduced stimulus stemming from fears of inflation or by the changing composition of the labor force. Even after controls are introduced to account for these explanations, the long-term trend suggests a worsening in unemployment.[4]

Regardless of its cause, high unemployment is obviously a matter of concern because of lost output and lower income levels. However, we want to ask a different question: Is there any evidence from the experience of the unemployed that joblessness poses a *labor market policy* problem as opposed to a purely macroeconomic problem?

The point of this distinction turns on the consequences of unemployment to individuals. If unemployment was only a macroeconomic concern, in effect we would live in a world of repeated lotteries. In each period the given number of jobs (determined by macroeconomic policy) would be allocated by some random rule and the remainder of the labor force would be unemployed. In the next period a new lottery would be held, again with the number of jobs determined by that period's macroregime. In this environment our policy focus would be on how the number of jobs was determined.

In the alternative scenario, which is the one that poses labor market policy issues, people in an identifiable group are repeated losers. Instead of the jobs being given out randomly if the losers in one period were also the losers in the next, we would be concerned not only with the process that determined the number of jobs but also with the method for allocating those jobs. This is determined by the set of institutions and behavioral rules that we refer to by the shorthand term "labor market." The second situation—a world of repeated losers—poses the question of whether we should seek to change those rules, that is, whether we should have a labor market policy concerned with unemployment. All of this is not to say that macroeconomic questions lose their importance (they obviously do not), but only that labor market policy issues also become significant.

This discussion becomes important when we consider the consequences of unemployment. In the first world, the purely macroeconomic environment, if an individual loses his or her job we would not expect that to have long-term consequences. Put differently, if we were to draw a sample several years after the fact (e.g., after the upturn following the job loss), we should not be able to distinguish those who had lost their jobs from those who did not. On the other hand, if after the job loss the people who lost their jobs seem to remain permanently at a disadvantge, there is cause for concern. Our shorthand for this will be the term "adjustment." If the labor market works well after a shock that causes job loss, with sufficient time for the business cycle to play itself out, various adjustment mechanisms should function to restore the relative economic position of those who lost work.

The foregoing provides a useful first cut at our distinction between a labor market and a macroproblem. However, we need to refine the analysis a bit further, since it is not realistic to expect that there never be any adverse consequences of unemployment. To make sense of the material that follows, we need to think through what patterns we would expect to find in the data if the market was adjusting "well" and what we would expect if there were problems. Consider, for example, the arguments of those who believe that wages in many industries are too high because of union pressure or long-standing oligopolistic product markets that reduce competitive pressure. In this view the unemployment itself is caused by inappropriate wages and we should expect, indeed, even welcome, wage loss upon reemployment. Others might claim that job loss is related to employers learning about worker quality and that the next employer, observing the "signal" of a layoff, will offer a lower wage.

What, then, are the possibilities? One consequence of job loss is simple inability to find another job. For individuals who are unemployed for a short period of time this might be attributed to search behavior or to an inappropriately high expected wages. However, as the unemployment spell lengthens, this explanation becomes implausible. Any number of possibilities stand out, including that the person's skills—specific human capital—are no longer in demand, geographic mismatch and immobility, or hiring practices of firms that mitigate against taking on older, experienced workers. In Chapter 3 we will develop our interpretation of the problem, but in all of these cases most observers would agree that market adjustment is a problem. A well-functioning labor market should include mechanisms to reemploy people who lose their job due to shifting product market demand.

Whether reemployment "should" occur at the previous wage is less clear. In standard economic theory in a labor market with no specific human capital or institutional features such as unions, the answer is yes, if the other characteristics of jobs (safety, cleanliness, etc.) remain the same or are controlled for. However, such a labor market bears little resemblence to reality. Once we step outside this world economic theory offers little guidance about what the proper new wage should be.[5] However, we do have some tools for thinking about the question. The following discussion will, therefore, be imprecise but helpful.

It seems useful to distinguish among three possibilities. First, wage loss might follow from earnings on the previous job that were inappropriately high in the sense that some major imperfection (e.g., a sheltered industry that simply passed on wage increases to consumers) led to the initial high wage. In this case one may regret the personal suffering caused by the drop in living standards (and perhaps provide some transition assistance) and agree that although the drop is due to a malfunction in the economy, the labor market itself is probably doing well. Similar conclusions may be reached concerning individuals who are personally problematic (lazy, insubordinate, unambitious), lose jobs for these reasons, and are unable to find another employer who overlooks these qualities. This suggests that in the data analysis we want to find ways to control as best as we can for personal characteristics.

The third case is one in which demand for a particular set of skills diminishes, resulting both in layoffs and difficulty in finding comparable work. What would one expect of a well-functioning labor market in such a circumstance? It seems reasonable that an individual should be able to build on his or her skills and learn new ones that lead to reemployment. One might expect some wage loss as compensation to the next employer for the training. However, if the wage loss is very substantial, either because training is very "expensive" or because the new job is far below the old one in the earnings distribution, this raises serious questions. Although there is no agreed-on standard against which to judge this case, it seems reasonable to believe that in a well-functioning labor market experienced workers who change jobs because of shifts in the demand for skill should not have to accept wage reductions that require discontinuous reduction in levels of well-being. To the extent that the structure of demand requires such changes, the burden should fall at the entry level through changes in the allocation of young workers. Granting that this conclusion is as much a matter of judgment as "science," we will maintain it throughout this chapter. In later chapters we will argue that there are also efficiency reasons for reaching this conclusion: the unwillingness of workers who face such risks to accept change in the work place.

Throughout the discussion that follows we will try to employ the data to distinguish among the various interpretations just outlined. In the end we will have to accept some ambiguity, both because of the limitations of the data and because conclusions about success or failure of adjustment mechanisms partly turn on value judgments. However, we will press the data as hard as possible.

Finding New Employment

An excellent source for examining these issues in detail is a special survey conducted in January 1984 as part of the regular Current Population Survey. Members of that sample were asked if, at any time from 1979 through the time of the survey, they had lost their job due to either a plant closing, slack work, or the abolition of their position or shift. If the answer was yes, these people were asked a series of questions about the character of the job they had lost (if more than one job had been lost, they were asked about the job on which they had the longest tenure) and their experiences during the period from the time of that job loss until the survey date.[6]

When an individual loses a job due to plant closings or layoffs, what are the chances of becoming reemployed? The answer depends on three considerations: the length of time since the job was lost, the performance of the labor market (the demand side), and the individual's goals and behavior (the supply side). In Table 2.3 we examine the employment status of job losers after controlling for the most important of the conditioning variables. We divide the sample by the two demographic categories that are the most important determinants of labor supply: age and sex. We also look separately at people who had lost their job within a year of the survey (i.e., had lost their job in 1983 or the first month of 1984) and those who had lost their job sometime between 1979 and 1982 (i.e., more than a year prior to the survey).

This table tells a striking story. A remarkably large percentage of people who lose their jobs fail to find new ones. If we look at prime age—men (26–55) who had lost their job over a year prior to the survey (and hence have had lots of time to find new work)—only 75% are working. The unemployment rate for this group is 19.9% (the unemployment rate is calculated by dividing the number unemployed by the sum of those unemployed and working). For prime-age women, only 63.5% are working. For both groups the unemployment rates are understatments, since many of those out of the labor force pre-

Table 2.3 Employment Status in January 1984 of Job Losers by When Job Lost and Age

	Lost Job 1983–84			Lost Job 1979–82		
Age	20–25	26–55	56+	20–25	26–55	56+
Percent of Males:						
Working	49.3	50.2	23.5	75.9	75.2	43.1
Unemployed	43.8	44.3	58.5	18.4	18.9	23.4
Out of labor force	6.7	5.4	17.9	5.6	5.7	33.3
Percent of Females:						
Working	46.4	44.0	24.8	60.8	63.5	38.3
Unemployed	37.4	38.6	50.5	13.9	14.5	11.5
Out of labor force	16.1	17.3	24.5	25.1	21.9	50.0

Source: January 1984 Current Population Survey.

sumably are job seekers who have become discouraged and stopped looking. To provide a basis for comparison, it is important to note that data from the same survey (the January 1984 Current Population Survey) show that for the same age group of men who had not experienced a layoff the unemployment rates was 3.3%; for women of the same age group who had not experienced a layoff the unemployment rate was 4.7%.

Much the same lesson is apparent throughout the table. For all groups the unemployment rates are strikingly high. People who lose their jobs clearly experience a great deal of difficulty in becoming reemployed. Finally, it is worth noting the magnitude of the problem. In January 1984, 1,418,586 people had lost their jobs at least a year ago and were still unemployed. In addition, some fraction of the additional 1.4 million unemployed who had lost their jobs less than a year ago could be expected to join the long-term group.

There are several directions in which it is worthwhile to probe a bit deeper into these patterns. First, one might ask whether the problem is merely one of a few hard-hit industries. The late 1970s and early 1980s saw a precipitous decline of employment in the older smokestack industries, especially auto and steel. Are we observing here the special problems of those industries or is it a more general phenomenon?

To answer this question we recalculated the data separately for those who were and those who were not employed in auto or steel.[7] This does not modify the results to any substantial extent. Among the entire sample of job losers, those who had been employed in auto or steel accounted for 6.8% of the men and 2.3% of the women, shares that are larger than their representation in the labor force as a whole but that do not dominate the sample. Among the prime-age male group who had lost their job a year ago or more, 24.2% of the non-auto/steel group was not working at the time of the survey compared with 30.6% of the auto/steel group. For the youngest group (20–25) there is very little difference in the two samples, and what there is goes in the opposite direction: 24.3% of the non-auto/steel group are not working compared with 18.7% of the auto/steel group. Finally, for the oldest group (age 56 plus), 55.1% of the non-auto/steel group are out of work compared to 76.1% of the auto/steel group. In short, workers who had been employed in auto and steel were worse off (except for the youngest group) as a result of layoffs than workers employed elsewhere, but the non-auto/steel workers nonetheless also experienced very substantial difficulties in finding employment.

Another possible explanation and partial mitigation of these findings is that what we are really observing is that people who lose their jobs do not actively search for new work but instead wait, hoping for recall. This would be particularly true in unionized settings that maintain formal seniority-based recall lists, but it could also be an issue elsewhere due either to informal understandings or simply to strong worker attachment and highly specific skills.

If behavior of this sort explained our observations, reemployment rates should be especially low among workers with substantial job tenure, since these are the employees with the greatest stake in maintaining their former attachments. By contrast, those with little tenure should be willing to seek employment else-

Table 2.4 Employment Status In January 1984 by Tenure on Lost Job (for those who lost their jobs 1979–82)

	0–1 Years Tenure	*2–3 Years Tenure*	*4–5 Years Tenure*	*6+ Years Tenure*
Percent of Males:				
Working	74.3	75.4	75.9	64.3
Unemployed	18.7	18.0	18.4	21.8
Out of labor force	6.8	6.5	5.6	13.7
Percent of Females:				
Working	60.4	63.9	64.3	52.2
Unemployed	13.8	12.9	14.5	15.8
Out of labor force	25.7	23.1	21.0	31.9

Source: January 1984 Current Population Survey.

where. To examine this, we classified people into four tenure classes: those who had been at their lost job for a year or less, those who had been there 2 or 3 years, those with 4 or 5 years' seniority, and those with greater than 5 years. In Table 2.4 we examine the employment status for those in each tenure class. The table is limited to those who had lost their job at least a year prior to the survey.

It is apparent that there is some relationship there along the lines expected but that the relationship is very weak. Even among men with a year or less of job tenure, over 25% were without work a year or more after losing their job, and the comparable figure for women is 29.5%. These data make it difficult to argue that the overall finding of substantial and persistent joblessness subsequent to layoff is caused by a concentration of high-tenure workers waiting recall. Furthermore, the conclusion drawn from this table is not changed when we add additional controls for age or when we examine those who lost their job less than a year prior to the survey.[8]

The Situation of Job Finders

It is apparent that large numbers of people are simply unable to become reemployed over a reasonable time period. This alone should be a source of considerable concern. What about those who did find work? How do their new jobs compare with those they left?

In Table 2.5 we examine the situation of those who *found* jobs (hence, some represented in the previous tables are excluded here), and we classify this sample into four groups: those whose wages (after adjusting for inflation) in the current job are 25% or more less than in the job they had lost; those whose wages in the current job are between 10 and 25% less than the earlier job; those whose current wages are plus or minus 10% of the earlier wages; and those whose wages are 10% or more above the old job.

The impact of layoffs varies considerably. It is clear that the losers (the two loss categories taken together) outweigh the winners: for the sample as a

Table 2.5 Relationship Between Current Earnings and Earnings on Lost Job

Age	Men			Women		
	20–25	*26–55*	*56+*	*20–25*	*26–55*	*56+*
Percent who:						
Lost more than 25% of earnings	29.4%	33.4%	34.4%	26.9%	30.8%	54.3%
Lost 10 to 24% of earnings	10.0	13.5	17.5	18.5	14.5	13.6
Remained 10% plus or minus of earnings	24.4	24.3	29.3	20.5	20.6	12.9
Gained more than 10% of earnings	36.0	28.7	18.6	34.0	34.0	18.9

Source: January 1984 Current Population Survey. Sample is limited to individuals who experienced layoffs at some point between 1979 and 1984 and who were reemployed at the time of the January 1984 interview. Earnings for current and lost jobs are in constant dollars and are weekly earnings.

whole, 45% of the men and 47% of the women are losers compared with 30% and 33% respectively, as winners. At the same time, for both sexes we cannot overlook the 30% of the sample whose earnings in the new job were higher than in the old one. The conclusion, then, has to be that on balance a layoff is costly even for those who did find work, but that a nontrivial minority gain.

One might wonder whether earnings losses of this magnitude are transitory. That is, do the losses merely represent the initial difficulty of regaining one's footing, or are they symptoms of a more permanent labor market problem? Table 2.6 explores this, and the results demonstrate that while the fraction experiencing earnings loss is slightly reduced for those who were laid off over a year ago, the reduction is marginal and the basic pattern remains. This implies that for most job losers there is little catch-up effect and that the losers are most probably on a permanently lower earnings trajectory. In effect, they have

Table 2.6 Relationship Between When the Job is Lost and Subsequent Earnings Reductions (for those who found jobs)

	Males aged:			Females aged:		
	20–25	*26–55*	*56+*	*20–25*	*26–55*	*56+*
Lost Job More Than a Year Ago:						
Percent experiencing earnings loss of 25% or more	32.1	34.8	31.3	25.6	32.3	59.9
Lost Job Less Than a Year Ago:						
Percent experiencing earnings loss of 25% or more	21.4	28.3	47.3	30.5	24.5	31.3

Source: January 1984 Current Population Survey. Sample is limited to individuals who experienced layoffs at some point between 1979 and 1984 and who were reemployed at the time of the January 1984 interview. Earnings for current and lost jobs are in constant dollars and are weekly earnings.

been knocked down several steps and will remain behind (this finding is confirmed in two ways in the appendix to this chapter with a different analysis employing an alternative data set and with more sophisticated statistical techniques with the same data set).

As we noted, the foregoing estimates of earnings loss are based on a comparison of the individual's wages on the earlier and later jobs. There are several ways in which this procedure is too simple. First is the assumption that the lost job is the proper criteria against which to judge the loss. Earnings loss might have occured even in the absence of layoffs if the workers were employed in slow growing and troubled firms. To control for this we should ask about the earnings of similar individuals who had not lost their job and compare the earnings of the laid-off group to their more fortunate brethern.

A second issue concerns unmeasured characteristics of the job losers. A strong skeptic would attempt to undermine the previous findings by pointing out that the people who lose their jobs may in some substantial but unobservable way be less productive than others in the labor force. If an employer has any discretion concerning whom to layoff or which plant to close, the choices may be made in a manner that targets the worst employees. Alternatively, more able people who find themselves in a potential layoff or plant-closing situation may search for and find work before the actual event. In either case, the subsequent difficulties experienced by the unemployed group may reflect not the impact of unemployment itself but some degree of individual disadvantage.

These arguments are difficult to accept as explaining the magnitude of the problems experienced by those laid off. Employers in most unionized and many nonunionized settings do not have discretion concerning whom to layoff in large-scale reductions. Furthermore, only a small fraction of all job separations are "for cause."[9] Nonetheless, the argument must have some merit, and it is worthwhile to assess whether alternative statistical procedures that control for these unmeasured characteristics lead us to alter our findings.

Testing the alternative explanations involve somewhat more complicated statistical procedures than those employed thus far. For this reason the analysis is relegated to the appendix to this chapter. The bottom line, however, is straightforward. The findings presented are robust. Job loss followed by reemployment is associated with substantial earnings loss, even after more elaborate statistical controls are introduced.

The Correlates of Adjustment Problems

We have seen that there is substantial risk associated with job loss. The chances of not finding a new job are very high; if a new job is located, the odds are good that the job will pay substantially less than the prior job. In our sample 38.4% of laid-off workers were "losers," meaning that they either had failed to find a new job or had found one but with earnings 25% or more below the prior job. If we limit the sample to those who were laid off a year or more prior to the survey, the percentage of the sample that were losers remains high at 32.9%. These figures are, in fact, underestimates of the problem because we have not counted labor force withdrawal in the loser category, and an additional substantial fraction of the sample experienced an earnings loss of under 25%, but still enough to hurt.

What can we say about who are the losers and who are not? If we can learn about the correlates of adjustment problems, this may give us an initial clue concerning what features of the labor market stand in the way of recovery from job loss. Hence, although we will focus, by necessity, on the characteristics of the people, we are equally interested in making inferences about the impact of institutions on the adjustment process.

As noted, we will define a loser as someone who has either failed to find a new job or found one that pays 25% or more below the lost job. In Table 2.7 we examine the personal (or what might be termed the "human capital") characteristics of these losers. (This table shows the relationship among several personal characteristics and the chances of a laid-off worker becoming a loser. It *does not* deal with the question of who is laid off in the first place.)

Several characteristics stand out.

1. Women who are laid off are less likely to be losers than are men: 41% of men fall into this category compared to 34% of women. Since in

Table 2.7 Characteristics of "Losers"

A. Percent losers by sex

Men: 41.9
Women: 34.0

B. Percent losers by educational attainment

	Less Than High School	High School Degree	Some College	College Degree or More
Men	51.5	51.1	41.1	26.7
Women	41.2	30.4	34.0	26.7

C. Percent losers by race

White   36.4
Other   50.7

D. Percent losers by tenure category on last job

	0–1 Years	2–3 Years	4–5 Years	6+ Years
Men	39.4	38.5	41.2	47.4
Women	33.2	31.6	37.2	37.8

Source: January 1984 Current Population Survey tape. "Losers" are those who had been laid off and either were unemployed at the time of the survey or who were employed in jobs that paid 25% or more less (in real terms) than the prior jobs. The sample is limited to nonagricultural workers. The table should be read as follows: 34.0% of all women in the January 1984 Current Population Survey who had been laid off sometime in the past 5 years were losers by our criteria; 36.4% of all whites in the survey who had been laid off sometime the past 5 years were losers by our criteria; of men with 0 to 1 years of tenure who were laid off, 39.4% were losers, and so on.

most other aspects of economic activity women are sharply disadvantaged relative to men, this finding suggests that there is something different about the kinds of jobs that women and men hold that accounts for this difference. However, the magnitude of the difference is not substantial, and it weakens considerably in the more complete analysis in the appendix to this chapter.

2. Blacks who are laid off are more likely to be losers than are whites: for example, among males, of those who lost their jobs 39% of whites were losers compared to 54% of blacks;

3. Better education reduces the chance of a laid-off worker becoming a loser. For both men and women a college degree almost cuts in half the chances of falling into this category compared to a high school dropout. However, below college level, while there is still some association between education level and outcome, the difference is sharply reduced.

4. There is some relationship between tenure and the chances of being a loser in that high-tenure people are more at risk. However, the differences are not very great. This is presumably the result of the fact that high tenure would have two offsetting effects: to the extent that it brings with it higher skills and more knowledge of the labor market, it should increase the chances of finding a new job. However, to the extent that it is associated with large firm-specific investment in skills, it will make the person more likely to await a recall and will also increase the chances that the next job will involve an income loss.

These findings concerning the relationship between personal characteristics and outcomes from job loss are a mix of the surprising and unsurprising. It is not news that blacks fare worse than whites in the labor market nor that the better educated do better than others. However, it is somewhat unusual to learn that women have better results than men and that the weak relationship between tenure and loser status is contrary to the conventional view that it is the long-tenure worker who is most (if not exclusively) at risk from dislocation. However, these simple correlations do not tell us why the particular patterns exist (i.e., what lies behind them). A partial step in this direction is possible if we examine the relationship among industry, occupation, and outcome.

Table 2.8 explores these relationships. The occupational classifications are collapsed into two categories, blue and white collar, while the industry variables are grouped into three categories, manufacturing, construction, and other. The first portion of the table still works with our loser variable. However, we are also interested in the correlates of earnings loss for those who do find work, so in the second portion of the table we limit the sample to job finders. For these people we have created a new variable, "same," which captures whether their new industry is the same as the one in which they had previously worked. For many of these people this might reflect a return to the same firm but, since we lack direct information on this, a more conservative interpretation is that they stayed in the same industry (requiring that the new occupation also be the same as the old one would be inappropriate, given that in many situations

Table 2.8 Relationship Between Industry and Occupation and Consequences of Job Loss

A. Percent losers by industry and occupation

	Manufacturing		Construction		Other	
	Blue Collar	White Collar	Blue Collar	White Collar	Blue Collar	White Collar
Men	45.9	30.9	46.0	31.7	40.5	31.9
Women	40.2	32.2	—	—	38.7	28.9

B. Relationship between returning to the same industry or firm and earnings loss: percent experiencing earnings loss of 25% or more

	Same		Not Same	
	Blue Collar	*White Collar*	*Blue Collar*	*White Collar*
Men	18.5	18.4	43.3	27.2
Women	17.7	20.8	40.4	29.8

Source: January 1984 Current Population Survey tape. "Same" industry/firm is measured by a match on the three-digit occupation codes.

individuals recalled even to the same firm would be required to start off in a lower occupation in the job ladder).

It is apparent from Panel A of Table 2.8 that the key relationship is that blue collar workers are more likely to have difficulty than white collar employees. It is occupation, not industry, of prior employment that seems key. That is, regardless of industry, laid-off blue collar workers have a higher probability of remaining unemployed or experiencing an earnings loss than do white collar employees, whereas within each occupational category it does not make much difference in which industry one had worked. Furthermore, these patterns are consistent for men and women.

This suggests that there is something about the way in which blue collar work is organized that makes employees more susceptible to suffering adverse consequences from unemployment. Of course, the problem may be with blue collar workers, who are, on average, less educated and mobile than white collar employees. When we controlled for educational category (in unreported tables), the key break was at high school. For individuals with a high school degree or less, the blue collar/white collar distinction loses force, while the differences remain sharp for those with at least some college. This highlights the crudeness of our classification scheme: many low-level jobs classified as white collar have more in common with blue collar work in terms of the structure of career ladders and the chances for mobility than with higher-level white collar employment.

Panel B of Table 2.8 examines only those who found new jobs and asks whether people who return to the same job or same industry experience less of an earnings loss than those who do not. Twenty-five percent of the men and 16% of the women returned to the same job/industry, a fraction that does not vary substantially by occupational grouping. Put differently, industry or firm attachment seems roughly the same for white and blue collar work. The major finding is that for blue collar work individuals who do return to the same firm/industry are much better off than those who have to make a change. For both men and women, roughly 18% of "returners" experience a loss compared to over 40% of nonreturners. In fact, the effect is so powerful for blue collar workers that within the returner group the gap between white and blue collar work is wiped out. Equally striking is the contrast with the white collar pattern. For white collar workers there is only a modest payoff to returning to the same firm/industry. What this does, then, is reenforce the earlier observation that the organization of work, either in terms of the distribution of firm specific skills or the organization of the hiring process, has a major impact on the pattern of adjustment that follows job loss.

An important question is whether the impact of returning to the same job/industry is so significant because of the firm-specific training (human capital) that is lost unless the same job is retained, or whether it is due to some other failure in the labor market's reemployment mechanisms. An example of the latter (indeed, the point we will press in Chapter 3) is that the common pattern of restricting hiring to the entry level makes it very difficult for unemployed experienced workers to find jobs in different firms comparable to the ones they lost. It is hard to distinguish rigorously between the specific human capital and the hiring pattern explanations, but it is important to try to do so because the specific human capital story implies that the subsequent earnings losses are more grounded in efficiency considerations while the alternative tends to point us more in the direction of market or institutional imperfections.

One way of testing the two explanations is to see whether the relationship between earnings loss and return to the same job/industry holds even for people who had little tenure in their prior job. These individuals are less likely to have substantial investments in firm-specific human capital; therefore, if the impact of returning to the same firm/industry is as before, we can more confidently attribute its effect to factors other than specific human capital. The relevant data are presented in Table 2.9. As is apparent, there is some merit to the specific human capital argument. For example, for those who did not return to the same firm/industry, the percent who were losers increases with tenure level. At the same time, however, it is also clear that the specific human capital argument cannot be the whole story. Even within the low-tenure groups the "same" variable performs much as before. For example, among those with up to a year of tenure, the percent who were losers is 13.6% for male returners but 31.8% for male nonreturners. Hence we have strong reason to believe that the "same" variable is capturing an important characteristic of the adjustment and hiring patterns of the labor market.

The foregoing analysis could be criticized because it essentially looks at two or three variables at a time, failing to control for other influences. For example, in looking at the impact of whether staying in the same job/industry makes a difference, we did not control for the possibility that there is a difference in the educational attainment of movers and stayers, and this might be what is driving the process. In order to allay these concerns, Part 2 of the

Table 2.9 Percent Experiencing Earnings Loss of 25% or More by Occupation, Tenure on Lost Job, Sex, and Same Firm/Industry

| | Blue Collar | | | | | | | |
| | 0–1 Years Tenure | | 2–3 Years Tenure | | 4–5 Years Tenure | | 6+ Years Tenure | |
	Same	Not Same	Same	Not Same	Same	Not Same	Same	Not Same
Men	13.6	31.8	16.0	43.9	32.6	45.3	10.3	58.8
Women	13.5	35.6	26.7	39.9	15.2	47.5	18.3	50.9

| | White Collar | | | | | | | |
| | 0–1 Years Tenure | | 2–3 Years Tenure | | 4–5 Years Tenure | | 6+ Years Tenure | |
	Same	Not Same	Same	Not Same	Same	Not Same	Same	Not Same
Men	10.0	19.9	12.6	26.8	18.3	28.9	35.5	41.4
Women	19.5	27.1	22.9	26.3	20.6	33.2	19.5	43.1

Source: January, 1984 Current Population Survey. Data on those employed in construction are omitted because of the low level of firm-specific tenure in that industry.

appendix of this chapter contains more sophisticated models. These do not change in any substantial way the findings described here. In short, our conclusion is that personal characteristics such as education or job specific training do play a role in influencing whether job loss is followed by reemployment at comparable wages. However, equally if not more important are institutional features of the labor market: whether a person is a blue collar or low-level white collar employee (versus the more successful upper-level white collar workers who tend not to be losers) and whether the person is forced to look for work outside the firm or industry in which they had worked before. The importance of these institutional variables suggests that in much of the labor market adjustment difficulties are built into labor market structure and that if we want to improve the outcomes purposive action may be appropriate.

Low Earnings

Since the War on Poverty was declared in the middle of the 1960s, the central goal of job training has been to assist those whose earnings fall below a minimum level. Thus in most although not all programs, eligibility depends on low earnings. A central theme of this book is that such narrow targeting is a mistake for two reasons: the problems that public policy should address are much broader and, in any case, programs that narrowly focus on poor people stigmatize them and consequently are ineffective. Nonetheless, people at the bottom of the income distribution remain, and should remain, a central constituency for employment policy. In this section we ask about the dimension of the problem.

The emphasis here is on low earnings, not low income. People receive income from many sources other than work: dividends and interest, alimony, pensions, and government transfer payments. For poor people the major source of unearned income is government transfer programs. These programs represent an alternative to labor market policy: the philosophy behind the American version of the welfare state has been to permit the labor market to generate whatever distributional outcomes flow from market processes and then compensate the losers through transfer programs. In fact, these programs are indeed minimal: in 1980 (prior to the recent cutbacks) total cash assistance programs for the nonelderly poor totaled under $20 billion. If these funds were spread evenly over the total population below the poverty line, they would average $50 per poor person per month. In fact, they are concentrated on single parents and the disabled; for the former, they average $100 per month and for the latter, $220.[10] If we add the in-kind transfer programs of Medicaid, Food Stamps, and Housing, the total pool is essentially doubled,[11] but the levels are still minimal. Given these low levels and the hostile political environment transfer programs face, a primary concern must be to improve the labor market prospects of low-income people.

How large is the problem? How many people need interventions aimed at improving their employment prospects? The answer depends on two key strategic decisions. First, we need a criteria below which we declare people "in need." Second, we have to decide for how long people should fall below the cutoff point before being of concern. There is no generally accepted rule for choosing this level. One candidate is the poverty line itself, but that line varies with family size. Another alternative is to select a point on the earnings distribution. This is the approach we take. If an individual's annual earnings fall below 50% of the median annual earnings of full-time workers (for a given period of time to be discussed shortly), we assign that person to the "in-need" pool. For example, if the median annual earnings for full-time workers is $19,000 (as it was in 1981 for males), a person is termed "in need" if his or her annual earnings falls below $9500. For men the reference group is the median annual earnings of full-time men; for women we will employ two criteria: the median annual earnings of full-time men and of full-time women.

Over what period of time must an individual fall below the cutoff before we are concerned? This is important because low income is a transitory state for many people; they may have lost their job for a short period or experienced some other sort of bad luck. By the following year they will be back on their normal income path. It would exaggerate the problem to include these people in our count. On the other hand, if people consistently fall below the cutoff for several years, we would count them as in need.

It is apparent that to estimate the size of the "in-need" pool we need longitudinal data that contain information on earnings and labor market status. The best such source is the University of Michigan's Panel Survey on Income Dynamics, which contains data on earnings for 1971 to 1981 for a representative sample of roughly 12,000 people.[12] We will analyze these data separately for men and women and, in both cases, will limit the sample to people who were between the ages of 25 and 53 in 1971, hence avoiding the special situations of young people and those near retirement age.

Table 2.10 Number of Years Individuals Fell Below the Earnings Cutoff, 1971–81

			Females		
		Heads		*Wives*	
Frequency Below Cutoff	*Males (%)*	*Male Standard (%)*	*Female Standard (%)*	*Male Standard (%)*	*Female Standard (%)*
0	70.3	25.4	41.4	21.9	30.9
1	9.0	13.7	12.6	9.6	13.6
2	7.2	4.4	8.4	7.1	10.2
3	1.6	4.2	3.7	5.6	9.4
4	3.7	5.3	6.9	7.8	7.3
5	2.0	4.4	7.0	6.6	5.9
6	1.1	6.6	6.0	7.5	4.9
7	1.1	2.8	5.2	5.6	4.4
8	0.9	6.6	3.8	5.5	4.5
9	1.5	7.0	2.8	5.9	3.5
10	0.7	7.0	1.1	7.3	3.3
11	0	0	1.4	0	2.1
N	1582	162	162	1061	1061

Source: Panel Survey on Income Dynamics. The sample is limited to individuals between the ages of 25 and 53 in 1971 who had no long-term disabilities and who had never retired. An individual falls below the cutoff only if he/she had positive earnings in the given year. The median earnings data for 1971–81 are taken from regular reports in the *Monthly Labor Review* for the period up until 1978 and from *Employment and Earnings* for subsequent periods. The data in fact refer to median weekly earnings of full-time workers, and we have calculated the annual figure by multiplying by 52. The data from which we calculate the distribution of people who fall below the cutoff are from the Michigan Panel Survey on Income Dynamics. The earnings figure with which we work includes all labor income, not simply wages and salaries.

The first column of Table 2.10 shows the number of years in which men in the survey fell below the cutoff. It is apparent that for the majority low earnings is no problem: 70.3% never experienced a year in which their earnings were below the threshold, and an additional 16.2% had only 1 or 2 years and hence clearly fall into the transitory category. Beyond this, however, we enter an ambiguous realm. There is no objective basis for choosing where to draw the line. If we classify those with 3 years or more below the cutoff as troubled, then 13.6% of the sample are of concern; if the criteria are 5 years of problems, the group falls to 8.3%. Even 8.3% represents a very substantial number of people: if we apply this percentage to 1980 labor force data, about 3.9 million men are labor market participants between the ages of 25 and 63 who have had 5 years or more of persistent low earnings.

Another approach is to ask how many people were in the low earnings group both at the beginning and the end of the period. If we subdivide the 10-year span into two 3-year segments, 1971–73 and 1979–81, and ask how many of the men in the sample fell into the low earnings category at least once in the early period and once in the late period, the answer is 7.6%, a rate that is consistent with the preceding estimates.

Estimating the number of women who fall below a similar standard is more difficult. Defining the cutoff itself is problematic, as is how to deal with the intermittent participation rates of women in the labor force. One issue is whether to use the male earnings standard or a comparable figure for full-time women to calculate the cutoff. The argument in favor of the male standard is that to do otherwise legitimates the male/female earnings gap. Set against this is the special topic of interest here; we are less concerned with the general question of sex discrimination—a problem faced by all women—than with identifying the size of the group that faces particular problems. This calculation would be confused by conflating the problem of sex discrimination with the special needs of a particular group. To provide the most conservative credible estimates, the following discussion will focus on estimates based on the female standard. However, we will also present data based on the male standard.

Even using the female standard does not resolve all ambiguities. Many women choose not to work full time, yet the earnings standard we are employing is based on full-time work. We deal with this in two ways. First, we only count toward the total figure the years in which people actually have positive earnings. The downside of this choice is that someone who is unemployed for a portion of the year and fails to earn any income is ignored. However, this bias seems less serious than counting people who are voluntarily out of the labor force as if they were unable to generate any earnings. Second, we present data separately for women who are family heads—and hence, being responsible for family support, are more likely to be concerned with full-time work—and for wives.

Table 2.10 shows that if we use the more conservative standard of requiring 5 years or more of low income to classify a person as troubled, then 26.9% of female household heads and 28.6% of wives fall beneath our standard. These are very large numbers and are still inflated. Within each group are many individuals who choose not to work full time and, therefore, their incomes fall below the cutoff as a result of choice.[13]

Persistent low earnings may be due either to inability to find steady employment or to a low wage or some combination of the two. Table 2.11 describes the annual labor income, hourly wage rates, annual hours worked, and annual hours spent unemployed for those who were above and below our cutoff point in 1981. Panel A contains the relevant data for men, Panel B for female household heads, and Panel C for other women.

For men, the two groups display nearly identical labor supply behavior. Adding together work hours with unemployment hours shows that both groups were in the labor force for essentially the same period of time. The low-income group has roughly 200 hours, or 5 weeks, more unemployment than the nonpoverty individuals. This disparity is of concern, but its impact is dwarfed by the difference in hourly wages: the wages for the nonpoverty group are nearly three times higher than for the poverty group. Put differently, if the hours worked of the two groups were equalized but they kept their same wage distribution, this would add $941 to the income of the nonpoverty group, but if their wages were equalized with the same work hours, then the income of the

Table 2.11 Characteristics of Individuals By Whether They Fell Above or Below the Income Cutoff in 1981

	Above Cutoff	*Below Cutoff*
A. Men		
Average annual earnings	$26,845	$6353
Hourly wage	$12.18	$4.40
Annual hours worked	2261	2001
Annual unemployment hours	28	242
B. Women, household heads		
Annual earnings	$14,125	$3257
Hourly wage	$7.43	$4.32
Annual hours worked	1968	1137
Annual unemployment hours	83	179
C. Women, wives		
Annual earnings	$13,789	$3329
Hourly wage	$8.19	$4.02
Annual hours worked	1796	987
Annual unemployment hours	17.9	124

Source: Panel Survey on Income Dynamics.

nonpoverty group would shoot up by $15,447. Clearly, the problem of low income for these men lies not so much in finding work but rather in the low wages, and presumably low wage growth, of the jobs that they do find.

For women the story is quite different. Among household heads who were in need in 1981 the wage level of $4.32 per hour compared poorly with the advantaged group's $7.43. A similar gap is apparent in Panel C for women who were not household heads. However, unlike the case of men, there is also a very large difference between the labor supply of the groups. For both heads and wives the gap in hours supplied (counting both hours worked and hours looking for work) was over 700 hours per year, or 20 weeks at 35 hours per week. This difference is large and makes it difficult to interpret the wage differential, since part-time workers generally earn less per hour than full-time employees. Hence, to the extent we wish to estimate how much of the persistence of low income is due to people's low earning power and how much is due to voluntary behavior, the case is more ambiguous for women than for men.

The conclusion is that roughly 8% of men in their prime working years who are active labor market participants and (even more roughly) perhaps double that same fraction of women are unable over a long period of time to earn enough in the labor market to raise them above what is a very minimal cutoff. It is worth repeating that these are estimates of the *persistence* of low earnings; we are paying no attention to 1- or 2-year spells of difficulty. Even these brief spells can create considerable hardship, but it seems reasonable to treat them as more the sphere of the welfare system than labor market policy (and, in fact, most people on welfare use it only briefly to assist in periods of transitory difficulty).

Conclusion

The main goal of this chapter was to demonstrate that there is a need for an active employment policy viewed from the perspective of labor market outcomes. The traditional objective of employment policy has been aid to the economically disadvantaged, and we showed that this objective remains valid in that substantial numbers of people persistently experience low earnings. The central thrust of the chapter was to explore the impact of unemployment, and we concluded that joblessness has considerable adverse consequences for many people. All of this might have seemed obvious but, given the growing acceptance of, or acquiescence to, high unemployment rates, it seems worthwhile to make these points as clearly as possible. It is also important to understand that the recent upturn in the economy does not alter our conclusions. In a January 1986 replication of the survey we have used, 29.1% of men and 30.3% of women who had lost their jobs failed to find new employment. Taken together, the findings in this chapter suggest that there is a "problem" to be "fixed." It remains, of course, to learn whether there are effective ways of undertaking these "repairs."

The findings in this chapter also imply that labor markets do not adjust smoothly to economic shocks. As we already argued, the finding that unemployment has persistent adverse consequences is contrary to what one might expect from a well-functioning market. In such a market new openings would emerge to absorb the unemployed. Furthermore, if the market worked well, then if substantial reallocation of labor was required the burden would fall on new entrants, not experienced workers. Evidently, however, market institutions are not well geared to absorbing the unemployed. The discussion of the role of industry and occupation strongly implied there is something about the organization of work that impedes easy mobility and adjustment. In Chapter 3 we ask why this might be and, in the process, begin to probe deeper into how labor markets work.

3

The Postwar Labor Market Model: Its Current Difficulties and Future Prospects

Chapter 2 identified two problems central to the case for an active employment policy. The first is persistence of low earnings among a significant fraction of the labor force. This is an issue that has long been at the heart of social policy and is hardly news. Chapter 2 distinguished between transitory and long-run difficulty and helped sharpen our sense of the magnitude of the difficulty.

The second issue we emphasized concerns the long-run adverse impact of unemployment. We showed that a substantial group of people who lose their job experience very sharp setbacks, with many not finding a new job and the others frequently suffering considerable earnings loss. Furthermore, these problems are not simply transitory but seem to be permanent.

The findings developed in Chapter 2, help us understand the nature of recent unemployment trends. The amount of unemployment due to job loss has increased from 1.6% in 1967 to 2.4% in 1974, 2.5% in 1978 and 3.6% in 1985. During 1974–85, none of the increase in the overall unemployment rate was due to job leaving. Furthermore, over the same 1974–85 period the duration of unemployment increased: the mean duration of a spell of unemployment grew from 9.8 weeks to 15.6 weeks, and incidence of unemployment of 27 weeks or more doubled.[1] The 1974–85 period contained severe shocks to the labor market and, evidently, as the data developed in Chapter 2 suggest, the labor market responded poorly.

The questions raised by these unemployment data and the findings of the previous chapter are more difficult and novel. Why are many individuals— most of whom are experienced workers with good skills and a longstanding commitment to work—unable to get back on track after losing their jobs? What does this tell us about how the labor market functions or, using our earlier language, how it adjusts to shifts in the pattern of demand and supply? Once we learn about the characteristic adjustment mechanisms of the labor market, what are the implications for the future? How will the market absorb changes in technology, demand, and demographics?

These questions form the core of this chapter. The topics have a heightened

36

interest, given the content of recent policy debates concerning employment policy. Although concern for poor people is not in vogue, the problems facing so-called "dislocated workers" have captured attention. These individuals, who have lost work because of technical change, changing consumer demand, or international trade, are the very people who seem unable to find new employment commensurate with their old jobs. However, most of the disucssion thus far has emphasized efforts to identify how many people fit this category and whether the numbers are getting better or worse.[2] More recently, some researchers have focused on the individual correlates of reemployment or lack thereof. However, little effort has been made to understand what it is about labor market institutions that impedes reabsorption. If we can understand this and the implications for future patterns, we will have come a long way toward understanding the role of public policy.

The Chapter's Argument

The central argument of the chapter is driven by two broad patterns. The first is what we have already spent considerable time demonstrating: experienced workers who lose their jobs have difficulty becoming reemployed at comparable conditions. This seems to imply that there is some barrier in the labor market. Set against this is the second point (demonstrated below): new entrants—young people and women joining the labor force—have not had comparable difficulty finding work. Taken together, these twin findings imply that the market is well geared to handling new workers but not influxes of experienced workers. We also saw that the sector in which a displaced worker was employed is important in predicting the problems he or she will face, and this suggested that specific institutional features of the labor market need to be considered.

These facts suggest the following stylized model of the postwar labor market. The supply side of the model includes two categories of labor that might be termed "flexible" and "inflexible" labor. Flexible labor, which historically included most youth and adult women, are workers who are willing to move easily between firms, partly because their commitment to the labor market is weak and partly because they have not yet made substantial investments in particular skills, occupations, and careers. By contrast, "inflexible" workers are adults, historically adult men although increasingly women, with substantial job experience in a given firm or occupation. These workers often receive a wage premium above the entry-level wage, a premium they receive for a variety of reasons, including their investment in firm-specific training, their seniority, and the need of firms to maintain morale by establishing a positive relationship between length of service and wages. For reasons to be discussed, these employees are much less able (and willing) to shift among employers.

On the demand side of this labor market are firms that organize their work according to the principles of internal labor markets. In an internal labor market most new hires occur at the bottom of a job ladder, at the port of entry, and workers climb up a job ladder whose upper levels are relatively closed to the outside. There are a number of reasons why a firm might find such an arrangement profitable; many of these will be discussed in detail later. However, for the present we can note that this arrangment is particularly plausible when there are plentiful supplies of entry-level labor.

In an economy with the two categories of labor just described and with firms that operate according to the principle of internal labor markets, much depends on relative numbers. The postwar period was characterized by substantial supplies of flexible labor. In effect, the firm could hire as many flexible employees as they wished at a relatively constant wage. The consequence was that labor market adjustment (i.e., expansions and contractions of particular occupations and industries) occurred at the bottom of the internal labor market. The inflexible labor was protected from market shocks because its numbers were relatively small and the burden of adjustment to demand shifts therefore could be placed on the flexible labor force. However, another consequence of this pattern is that when the inflexible labor is laid off, the labor market is likely to be less effective in reemploying it. Firms are accustomed to hiring at the bottom for low wages and, indeed, perceive advantages to this practice. Furthermore, there are few effective institutions that can retrain adults or place them into new jobs. This combination of employer norms and lack of an institutional infrastructure for overcoming them explains the difficulties adults experience when they lose their jobs.

The model just described is too crude in a number of respects. First, as we saw in Chapter 2, the difficulty of becoming reemployed with comparable wages varies according to the sector of the labor market in which one is located. Hence the model is less accurate for describing the situation of white than blue collar workers (an indication of this is that there are indeed private agencies that effectively help white collar workers find new jobs). Second, under conditions of extreme pressure the more traditional adjustment mechanisms—relative wage change and alteration hiring practices—do occur. These qualifications notwithstanding, the model does provide a useful characterization of much of the labor market and, as white collar work comes under increasing pressure from cost-conscious firms, the scope of the model may broaden.

The bulk of this chapter is devoted to providing evidence in support of this model. However, in the final portion of the chapter we examine the implications of our argument in light of likely future developments. We argue that several trends suggest that the difficulties that flow from a model of this sort may worsen in coming years. First, the economy will become more subject to demand shocks flowing form various sources. Second, the age structure of the labor force will shift. The large supplies of young people will be reduced, and the large baby boom cohort will enter middle age. This means in part that the sources of flexible labor will decline, a development that may pose some difficulties to firms. More seriously, a larger portion of the labor force will be inflexible, and issues of adjustment and job security will become more central to the public discussion.

Evidence for the Model

The Contrasting Success of Supply and Demand Adjustment

We have already seen in considerable detail that people who lose their jobs due to involuntary layoffs face poor prospects. The market does not do a good job of absorbing them. This provides some evidence supporting the model described previously. However, the pattern is even more striking, and the model receives more support, when we contrast the seemingly weak absorptive capacity for experienced labor with the success of the labor market in finding jobs for the vast numbers of new entrants who sought work in the past two decades.

The dominant supply shifts in the past 20 years have been the rapid increase in the labor force numbers of young people and women. These facts are demonstrated in Table 3.1.

The steady increase in the number of women in the labor force and, since 1960, in the representation of youth is apparent in this table. Another way of framing these magnitudes is to note that since 1960 the adult male labor force increased by roughly 8 million compared to 13 million for youth and 15 million for adult women.

Such a dramatic change in the composition of the labor force is clearly a supply shock of the first magnitude. How has the labor market adjusted? The answer is very well. Table 3.2 provides the employment-to-population ratio (the fraction of the population employed) of each group in 1960, before the major surge in youth and women participation, and in 1980. As this table clearly shows, despite the substantial increase in the numbers of each group, employment grew more than proportionately. The labor market was able to handle both the increase in the fraction of women who were looking for work and the increase in the size of the youth cohort.

The major exception to this successful absorption of new entrants is minority youth, whose unemployment rates are extraordinarily high. This is ex-

Table 3.1 Composition of the American Civilian Labor Force

Year	Youth 16–24 Number (000)	Percent of Labor Force	Males 25+ Number (000)	Percent of Labor Force	Females 25+ Number (000)	Percent of Labor Force
1950	11,523	18.6	36,684	58.9	14,003	22.5
1960	11,543	16.5	39,480	56.7	18,606	26.7
1970	17,876	21.5	41,503	50.1	23,421	28.2
1980	25,300	23.6	47.848	44.7	33,791	31.5

Source: Calculated from U.S. Department of Labor, *Handbook of Labor Statistics*, Bulletin 2217, July 1985, p. 14.

Table 3.2 Employment-to-Population Ratios

	Youth 20–24	Men 25+	Women 25+
1960	0.595	0.821	0.349
1980	0.682	0.745	0.459

Source: Calculated from U.S. Department of Labor, *Handbook of Labor Statistics*, Bulletin 2217, July 1985, pp. 10 and 40.

tremely serious and, indeed, one of the major justifications for an active employment policy. Although the interpretation of the plight of minority youth is subject to the same inconclusive debates as those described in Chapter 1 concerning low earnings, it seems clear that these 40% plus unemployment rates are good evidence of the continuing power of racial discrimination the labor market.[3] However, this problem does not throw into doubt the central argument about the absorptive power of the economy. Minority teens represent a small fraction of all new entrants, and their situation has to be understood as an example of the problem confronting all minorities in the American labor market. Put differently, were the American labor market race blind, minority teens could get their fair share of jobs with little discernible impact on the overall unemployment rate or new entrant absorption rate.

In short, the overall patterns of adjustment are consistent with the model we have suggested. Experienced workers have difficulty finding new employment, while vast numbers of new entrants have been successfully integrated into the market. Indeed, one might even argue that the data presented here understate the size and employment of the flexible labor supply, since the movement of blacks from the rural south into the northern industries and the flow of undocumented workers have been two additional sources of inexperienced or new entrant labor. We have not emphasized these latter two categories because, in general, they have moved into low-wage/high-turnover (so-called secondary labor market) jobs; our argument is not about the dynamics of the secondary labor market[4] but about sources of supply to mainline primary jobs.

The Inadequacy of the Conventional Adjustment Model

How is adjustment supposed to occur? In the textbook (and therefore overly simplified) version the key action occurs through shifting wage rates. If, for example, the relative supply of a given group (youth, for instance) increases, then each young person would find himself or herself in the position of having to agree to work for a lower wage than past comparable cohorts. A sufficient drop in the wage will induce employers to offer enough jobs to employ the newly enlarged labor supply. Demand side shifts would work in a similar way. For example, an increase in the demand for a category of service workers would lead employers to increase the wages offered, and this would induce workers to shift from other jobs, particularly those jobs where demand and, hence, wages, are falling.

There are two direct methods for testing whether wages play this role. One is to see how responsive individuals are to wage changes. For example, do people change jobs or choose careers on the basis of wage considerations? Many researchers have taken on this question, but the answer remains unclear at best. The classic local labor market study of blue collar workers by Lloyd Reynolds[5] concluded that already employed workers are frequently unaware of wage differentials between their current employment and other opportunities and will very rarely move to a new job. When people do have to search for work, they move through traditional (family or neighborhood) search channels and tend to take the first job offered. These findings have been confirmed by other interview-based studies.[6] Economists are frequently leery of believing peoples' explanations for their behavior; however, Lloyd Ulman used aggregate data to reach a similar conclusion. He showed that increases in an industry's employment levels were, at best, weakly correlated with changes in the wage rate (i.e., employment levels of specific industries expanded without the customary use of wage increases as a means of attracting labor).[7] Ulman also identified particular periods in which wages did perform their assigned function; we will return to these exceptions shortly, but the general point stands.

The preceding research suggests that wages do not perform the role assigned them as market signals. However, in specific markets, wages may, in fact, more closely meet their assigned task. For example, work by Richard Freeman suggests that students choosing careers in high-level occupations are often guided by relative wage considerations.[8] However, even here Freeman's models suggest a failure of the wage mechanism in that people misperceive the signals and fail to realize that high wages may simply denote short-term shortages instead of long-term growth in demand. The consequence is that many fields experience a boom and bust cycle. In any case, these occupations account for only a small fraction of the economy and do not seem important enough to overturn the findings of the earlier research.

Scholars schooled in the central role of prices and wages may find the foregoing evidence unconvincing in that it is often possible to generate alternative and more congenial explanations of any set of research findings, including those that point to the minimal role of wages in stimulating mobility. For example, much of the evidence cited here refers to average workers, while economic theory would suggest that we examine the behavior of those who are on the margin and whose movements account for the observable shifts.

An alternative approach, which avoids many of these objections, is to examine the wage structure itself. If the wage structure plays its assigned role, we would expect it to change over time. Data on wages should show movements that reflect shifts in demand and supply (the only acceptable excuse for lack of movement is the unlikely case of demand and supply shifts moving in tandem and offsetting each other). The remarkable fact that emerges is that the U.S. wage structure is strikingly rigid.

Wage data may be organized either by industry or occupational groups (or, of course, by both). That is, one can ask whether the relative wages found between a set of industries at one point in time is replicated later and can also ask a similar question about occupational rankings. Evidence on the stability of industry wage relationships is longstanding. For example, in 1956 Donald Cullen found a correlatiion of .86 for manufacturing industry wages between 1919 and 1939, and in 1950 Sumner Slichter found that "the wage structure changes over time, but the changes are fairly slow and the wage structure between industries over a period of twenty or thirty years exhibits only moderate change." More recently, Krueger and Sumners have employed more sophisticated econometric techniques to isolate the industry wage effect in a wage equation from the contribution of worker quality, region, and other variables. They found, using a detailed industry classification, that the industry wage structure in 1974 and 1984 had a correlation of .970, nearly perfect.[9]

If the industry wage structure is quite rigid, so too is the occupational wage structure. One question might be whether the industry effect described here is common to all occupations or limited to a few. In a recent study Dickens and Katz convincingly show that it is common to all occupations. They write "[does] an industry which paid its blue collar workers more also pay its secretaries more? . . . this is exactly what we find." Specifically, working with a sample of over 100,000 workers (drawn from the Current Population Survey), they calculated correlation coefficients between occupations and industries and found that the average coefficient was .78. In other words, if an industry (say electrical manufacturing) is high wage on average, this means that all of the occupations in that industry are extremely likely to be high wage.[10]

The results do not show necessarily that the occupational wage structure is rigid over time, since they refer to occupational correlations within industries. However, the data in Table 3.3 dispose of final doubts. The table is based on the Department of Labor's Area Wage Survey, which collects wage data on detailed occupations in a sample of firms. It is apparent that the wage structure exhibits remarkable stability over a 16-year period. Not only do the relative wages between manufacturing and nonmanufacturing and regions remain stable but, of the 24 occupationally specific comparisons, only four changed their ranking between 1967 and 1983.

We now have three kinds of evidence: the stability of the industry wage structure, the fact that the stable average industry wage also leads to a comparable industry/occupation wage pattern, and the evidence of stability in the occupational wage structure over time. Taken together, this suggests that wages do not move in the manner necessary for them to act as effective signals or adjustment mechanisms.

The failure of wages to adjust over time does seem incontrovertible given the data, but it raises several puzzles relative to the recent literature on the topic. One such difficulty is the evidence presented by Richard B. Freeman, Finis Welch, and others that the relative earnings of youth to adults has fallen and that this shift corresponds to the movement of the large baby boom cohort through the labor market. This seems on the surface to be just what the standard model would predict and contradicts the material just discussed. Freeman, for example, shows that for men, the ratio of the relative income of full-time 45 to 54-year-olds to full-time 25 to 34-year-olds rose from 1.18 in 1967 to 1.26

Table 3.3 Occupational Wage Patterns Over Time for Males (Ratio of Wages to Those of Mechanics)

	Northeast		South	
	1967	*1983*	*1967*	*1983*
Manufacturing				
Janitors	0.68	0.67	0.69	0.72
Shippers	0.71	0.66	0.72	0.63
Material handlers	0.73	0.66	0.70	0.70
Truck drivers	0.95	0.88	0.81	0.73
Maintenance	0.81	0.75	0.93	0.94
Electricians	1.03	1.04	1.21	1.23
Nonmanufacturing				
Janitors	0.60	0.54	0.47	0.36
Shippers	0.68	0.59	0.61	0.59
Material handlers	0.81	0.85	0.65	0.61
Truck drivers	0.96	0.96	0.81	0.80
Maintainence	0.83	0.84	0.76	—
Electricians	1.07	1.08	1.10	1.02

Source: Calculated from U.S. Department of Labor, *Handbook of Labor Statistics*, Bulletin 2217, Table 96.

in 1975.[11] These findings are not, however, quite as powerful as often thought, since the ratio remained flat for women. Freeman interprets this as evidence of greater substitutability between young and older women, and this is possible, but another view would be that something other than the baby boom cohort effect (e.g., the growth of the union wages in the middle 1970s) influenced the results for men.

Even if we take this analysis at its face value, the difficulty is that wages are not set by age group in the United States (they are in parts of Europe) but by occupation. Thus shifts in an age cohort's earnings must be linked to observable shifts in wage structures, and we have already seen considerable evidence that this did not occur. Hence the Freeman evidence must be interpreted in another light and not as conforming to a world in which relative wages lead firms to substitute among demographically denominated inputs. Instead, what seems to have happened is that the occupational distribution of young people has shifted. The fraction of the cohort in low-paying jobs increased and promotion rates to better paying jobs slowed. Hence average earnings level fell. The point is that the adjustment occurred through occupational quantity shifts, despite an unyielding wage structure.

The second puzzle is whether we are in the midst of a major realignment of the wage structure, a realignment due to the breakdown of traditional wage patterns in heavily unionized industries and the spread of concession bargaining. Examples of such agreements include the willingness of many unions to accept so-called two-tier pay arrangements in which the newly hired are placed on a lower pay schedule (this has been common in the airlines industry), or simple wage reductions as have occurred in steel and other basic industries. Daniel Mitchell has estimated that between 1981 and 1985 the number of industries in which at least one concession bargain occurred increased from 10 to 39.[12] The consequence of this, according to Mitchell, is that wage determination equations estimated over the preconcession period tend to overpredict actual wage settlements in the 1980s. This period of wage moderation, combined with explicit consideration of product market conditions in wage setting, raises the possibility that traditional wage relativities will be upset.

It is too early to evaluate just how much of a shift the era of concession bargaining actually represents. The union/nonunion wage differential has never been stable. During the 1970s, for example, it grew extremely wide. According to Mitchell's figures, by 1985, after several years into the concession bargaining era, the differential still remained above its mid-1970s peak. Hence the recent developments might be read as a return of traditional relationships, not a movement to new ones. This view is reinforced by the fact that there have been previous episodes of union wage moderation that were followed by renewed gains. However, the new patterns are also consistent with a broader range of changes in work place relationships—rise of sophisticated nonunion personnel practices, breakdown of traditional job classifications and work rules, growing deployment of temporary and other forms of flexible employment arrangements—which we will discuss in Chapter 4. To the extent that human resource policies in general are shifting then a new wage pattern would be consistent.

Fortunately, we need not decide for present purposes whether wage patterns are shifting in a manner that might imply more flexibility than has been typical historically. The topic here is the postwar labor market and how it has adjusted to demand and supply shocks, and it seems apparent that the wage structure has not played a role in the process. Whether it will do so in the future depends on a broader set of questions about shifting labor market institutions.

Hiring Practices in Internal Labor Markets

The evidence presented thus far concerning the difficulty of absorbing experienced workers, the ease of absorption of new entrants, and the inflexibility of the wage structure has all been supportive of the model we have presented, but it has also been indirect. What direct evidence is there that the hiring practices of firms conform to the pattern we have suggested?

Central to the argument is the concept of an internal labor market. A firm's internal labor market comprises the rules, administrative procedures, and norms that govern the hiring, training, deployment, and compensation of labor. In Chapter 4 we will spend a great deal of effort in describing and analyzing variations in these arrangments, but for now we can simply note that in the "ideal type" internal labor market, individuals enter at the bottom of a job ladder and over a long career with the firm move up, acquiring skills along the way.

There is good evidence that such lifetime or near-lifetime employment patterns are widespread. Akerloff and Main,[13] working with data from the 1960s and 1970s, compiled data on tenure with employers and reach the following conclusions:

- The attachment to a firm is relatively short, just under 4 years for white males and under 3 years for white females. Since these data cover all age ranges, they imply that the typical job held by a young worker is very short.
- This average, however, is deceptive since although people typically hold a series of short jobs, they eventually settle into a job that lasts a very long time. The average duration of a job currently in progress is over 18 years for men and 12 years for women. Working with a different source, the National Longitudinal Survey, Ackerloff and Main confirm this finding by noting that the average 45-year-old man in the sample had already been employed in the same job for 15 years.

In such a circumstance the incentives facing firms in the hiring process are different from what might be expected in a spot market (i.e., one in which attachment to particular firms was low and the employment relationship was frequently renegotiated). Given long-term relationships, the company is not very interested in recruiting individuals who are already trained in the relevant entry-level skill because the particular jobs will change during their career with the firm. Instead, a premium is placed on two characteristics: ability to learn the relevant range of skills, and ability to get along well with the prospective work group. The first trait is important because of the need to learn new skills as one moves up a job ladder. The second is necessary because the long-term attachment of the labor force to the firm makes the degree of group cohesiveness an important component of productivity.

In addition to the reduced importance of prior skills (and hence of experienced workers) in hiring, other aspects of the system also mitigate against recruiting people directly into middle jobs on the ladder. An important purpose of the internal labor market structure is to provide the appropriate set of incentives to the labor force to invest in on-the-job training and to remain loyal to the firm (and hence not leave after receiving expensive training). The company's part of the bargain is that the available jobs are in some sense the "property" of the incumbent work force, which has first claim on promotion opportunities. Obviously, this understanding would be violated if incumbents were placed in competition with outsiders. Some theorists also emphasized the role of internal labor markets in providing the employer with the opportunity to monitor and assess employee performance over a substantial period prior to promotion. This is important since day-to-day effort is hard to observe yet the firm wants an accurate sense of the person's worth prior to promotion. Again, this consideration mitigates against outside hiring into more senior positions. Finally, an important function of long-term employment is socialization into company norms. This is especially important in white collar work. Herbert Simon[14] characterized this as inculcating the implicit "premises" of the firm and hence increasing the chances of appropriate decision making. Again, long-term employment, and hence avoidance of outside hiring above the entry level, is conducive to this objective.

There is a variety of evidence, mostly drawn from interviews with firms, that the foregoing description of hiring practices is accurate. In the middle 1950s Richard Lester conducted a study of hiring practices and cited a typical employer as commenting that "We would rather hire a young man with no . . . experience and train him ourselves than to hire a man with experience from another firm and have to break him of acquired habits and really retrain him."[15]

A similar set of findings, concerning the relative unimportance of prior skill in hiring for blue collar jobs, emerged from more recent studies of the youth labor market.[16] In addition, broader based surveys of firms—union and non-union—have found that seniority is generally the decisive factor in promotion.[17] Finally, the "classic" description of blue collar internal labor markets provided by Doeringer and Piore is consistent with the view that most hiring occurs at the bottom of job ladders.[18] Many of the arguments just presented apply equally well to white collar employment, and some evidence is available for white collar jobs: in a series of interviews with large white collar employers we asked about hiring practices and found that for 90% of the firms in the sample, middle-management job ladders were closed to the outside at all but entry-level positions.[19]

Some Qualifications

The model we have developed is one in which experienced workers remain attached to firms, companies avoid hiring experienced workers and instead expand their labor force at the "ports of entry," and hence the major source of adjustment in the economy comes from employment of new entrants. The traditional equilibrating mechanism of theory—the wage structure—does not perform this role and, instead, the system "works" because the flexible new entrant labor is in plentiful and elastic supply and flows toward vacancies (sometimes guided by institutions such as schools). One consequence of this system is that when experienced workers do lose their job they have a hard time finding a comparable new one.

Although accurate in its main lines, the story is overstated when put so starkly. There are several kinds of evidence that the "classical" adjustment mechanisms work in some circumstances. First, and perhaps most simply, although we have seen that nearly 40% of laid-off workers are "losers" as we have defined the term, it follows that the remainder do land on their feet. Of course, many of these simply get recalled to their old jobs, some withdraw from the labor force, and for others a variety of idiosyncratic developments help them make the transition. Nonetheless, a nontrivial fraction do find new work that is better than the old. This implies that adjustment mechanisms are not quite as rigid as we have painted them. In particular, firms faced with labor shortages will hire experienced workers at upper levels of the job ladder, and in some craftlike occupations there is no compunction at all about opening job ladders at all levels.

It is also apparent that the wage structure is sometimes capable of adjusting. In the research cited earlier Lloyd Ulman made the point that while wages generally do not provide market signals, in some extreme episodes they do so,[20] and this remains true today. Consider the example of computer programmers, an occupation whose wages took off in the late 1970s in the face of high demand and short supply.

Despite these qualifications, the model seems to capture a substantial aspect of reality, particularly for blue collar jobs but also increasingly for a variety of midlevel white collar occupations. Although not universal, the mechanisms outlined here introduce friction into the adjustment process, and difficulties accrue for a substantial fraction of those who lose their job. The model is sufficiently general and the difficulties sufficiently widespread that serious concerns are raised for public policy. Equally important, the model gives us a way of organizing our thoughts about the likely implications of several future developments in the American labor market, and it is to this topic that we now turn.

Implications for the Future

If the American labor market works along the lines we have posited, what are the implications? One point that is apparent is that the problem of dislocated workers are appropriate topics for public policy because "normal" market processes are not well geared to address them. Hence policies aimed at finding ways to reintegrate these workers into good jobs seem to be needed. In this sense, even the analysis thus far has built a case for active employment policy.

What about implications for the future? Any particular market structure has strengths and weaknesses. The structure just described was very well adapted for the circumstances of much of the postwar period. Steadily growing demand provided the basis for job security for the experienced labor force, while the hiring patterns of firms absorbed the substantial increase in new entrant labor. Will conditions in the future be as kind to this model? Assuming (for the moment) that the institutional structure is static, what is the course of events likely to be? The argument developed next is that the postwar model will not be well adapted to future conditions. For several reasons the demand for labor will be more variable than in the past, and this will tend to spin off more potentially dislocated workers than before. At the same time, the age structure of the population will create a less flexible labor force, and this will increase the pressure for improved job security and adjustment mechanisms.

Demand Is Growing More Variable

The pattern of labor demand over time has two dimensions: its level and its variability. The level of demand is largely a matter of aggregate macroeconomic policy, domestic and foreign. Furthermore, unemployment and other difficulties that stem from inadequate aggregate demand can be remedied with the appropriate fiscal and monetary tools. These issues therefore belong to the domain of other branches of economics.

The question of dispersion, however, is another matter. For any given level of demand there still remains the issue of its location. In one extreme all firms might share proportionately in whatever rise or fall in demand the macroeconomy generated. In such a world there would be a few problems of labor market adjustment, only questions of macropolicy. By contrast, one might live in a world in which demand grew steadily, but the location of that demand constantly shifted. Under such circumstances the labor market would be under considerable pressure to reallocate labor from one location to another. It is our contention that the degree of variability in employment location is rising and that, given the labor market structure we have described, this will pose increasing difficulties.

We might ask two questions concerning this issue. First, is there any evidence based on the past record that the dispersion of employment is growing? Second, what reason and evidence do we have to support the suggestion that the dispersion will grow in the future?

Any newspaper reader is aware that many segments of American industry are under severe pressure. These pressures come from multiple sources: international competition due to wage differentials between U.S. and foreign labor, deregulation within key industries, foreign exchange fluctuations, foreign management techniques that are in many respects superior to ours, and so on. The list of the "causes" of our difficulties is endless, and every commentator has his or her favorite explanation. For now we need not worry about why firms are under pressure in the product market (this will be of concern later, to the extent that labor practices are part of the puzzle). However, we do want to ask whether the perception of increased variability is well grounded.

One natural way of answering this question is to determine whether the rate of change in employment has been more variable than in previous periods. Imagine, for example, that in the current period the average (across industries) change in employment was 5%, but that this average masked wide variation, with some industries growing at a rapid rate while others declined precipitously. If, in a previous period, most industries were closer to the average, we would conclude that the current period was one of greater structural change and hence posed more serious problems for adjustment.

To answer this question, we constructed an "index of structural change." As suggested, the index measures the dispersion of employment changes across industries. Our index is measured on a peak-to-peak basis. This is important because it avoids the pitfalls of a recent debate concerning the relative role of sectoral change versus aggregate demand in explaining the movement of unemployment over the business cycle.[21]

The values for the index are presented in Table. 3.4. It is clear that the past 13 years have been a period of above average structural change. This, in turn,

Table 3.4 Index of Structural Change

Equal Length Peak-to- Peak Periods	Index
1960–73	0.206
1973–85	0.231

Note: The index is calculated with employment data for 20 manufacturing industries plus transportation, services, retail trade, wholesale trade, government, mining, and construction. The data are taken from *Employment and Earnings* for various years. The index is the standard deviation of the following expression: sum of [(percentage change in total employment over the period)—(percentage change in employment in industry i)], with each observation weighted by the employment level of the industry. 1985 is not a peak as measured by the NBER but is a year of strongly improving employment conditions.

has put a greater burden on the very labor market adjustment mechanisms that, as we have seen, are not as strong as might be.

A second way of asking whether structural change is increasing is to examine the geographical dispersion of employment. Have employment growth rates become more dispersed across space? To answer this, we collected data on the growth rate of nonagricultural employment in each of the 10 federal census regions for 5-year intervals for 1960–85. For example, we gathered data on the growth rate of nonagricultural employment in New England between 1960–65, 1965–70, and so on up to 1985 and did the same for the remaining regions. The question we ask is whether there are greater differences in the later years in regional growth rates than in the early years. Our measure of this is the coefficient of variation of growth rates, that is, the standard deviation (a measure of spread) of growth rates divided by the mean growth rate for each period. These coefficients are presented in Table 3.5.

As is apparent, this index is consistent with the earlier one. The figures for the last three periods are all higher than for the previous two, indicating that growth has been more geographically dispersed in the later years. It seems that this second measure also supports the argument that we have developed.

Future Shock

The foregoing material suggests that in the past decade and a half the dispersion of employment increased and, with it, the pressure on the labor market. What

Table 3.5 Coefficients of Variation of Geographic Growth Rates

1960–65	.30
1965–70	.19
1970–75	.76
1975–80	.38
1980–85	.50

Source: Employment and Training Report of the President, 1981, Table D-1, and *Employment and Earnings*, May 1986. As noted in the text, these figures are the coefficients of variation of growth rates across the 10 regions.

are the next years likely to bring? Here we enter the realm of speculation. However, several developments suggest that dispersion is likely to grow more marked.

Perhaps the most important reason for believing that the dispersion of employment will widen lies in the nature, pace, and motivations for introducing new technologies. It is common to observe that we are entering a new wave of widespread innovation based on the wide distribution of computing power and other microelectronic developments. However, the debate has only recently been joined concerning the likely impact of these innovations.

Technological innovation has long been a feature in the evolution of American labor markets. From the development of interchangeable parts at the Springfield Arsenal to Ford's conception of the moving assembly line to today's diffusion of computer-based production and communication techniques, new ways of producing goods and services have steadily improved our productivity and standard of living. From a historical perspective it is difficult to argue against the proposition that new technology has been a consistent force for improvement of economic performance and the level of rewards for all segments of the labor market.

While in retrospect technology may seem a blessing, from close up the issue is more ambiguous. The typesetter whose job is threatened by computerized printing equipment, the clerk whose filing assignments are done much more rapidly by a computer, and the welder whose place may be taken by a robot all may view the matter more skeptically. For these reasons considerable effort has gone into understanding how technologies affect the work process.

In thinking through the possible impact of technology on labor market disequilibrium, we must make a series of distinctions. First, it is important to distinguish between the impact of new technologies on employment levels versus the effect on the organization of work. New ways or producing goods may reduce the required labor input but leave work organization relatively intact: robots may eliminate welders but the rest of the factory remains unchanged. Alternatively, the technology may require, or point toward, new forms of production. For example, as operatives learn to manage computer-controlled machinery, they gain the ability to monitor data and take over some of the functions of production planners. As the job boundary expands, this calls into question previous training arrangements, rules for choosing who is promoted, and even pay systems. In short, the structure of an internal labor market can be transformed. For now we will leave aside internal organizational issues and only focus on the impact of technology on employment levels. Ultimately, however, these two issues are related. If technological innovation is threatening to job security, firms will find it more difficult to achieve internal reorganization induced by the same technologies. This is a theme we will return to in Chapter 4.

The two questions that interest us are whether new technologies will actually reduce employment levels and hence cause severe labor market adjustment difficulties or, without that dramatic effect, whether technologies are likely to increase the dispersion of employment growth even if the sum or total level remains constant or increases.

There is no question that, all else constant, technology is laborsaving. That is, for a given unit of output, less labor is required under the new technology than under the old.[22] The extreme modern examples of this are the so-called Factories of the Future, such as the new General Electric plant in Lynn, Massachusetts, where robot carts will move engine parts between computer-controlled machining centers and only 100 workers will be employed in the factory.[23] However, as virtually all analysts are quick to point out, it does not follow that the laborsaving character of technology means actual employment loss. The most commonly cited countervailing effect is that new technologies produce sufficient efficiencies that the price per unit falls and this, in turn, increases product demand. The increase in product demand can maintain or even boost employment levels despite lower labor content per unit. The most widely cited interindustry study of technology found just this sort of pattern.[24] A dramatic example is the impact of mass production technology applied to automobiles. The amount of labor needed to produce a single car fell sharply, but the demand for cars skyrocketed and, of course, employment in the automobile industry increased.

The automobile example points to another reason why aggregate predictions about new technologies, especially major innovations are hazardous. The initial innovation may lead to new products and businesses—auto parts factories, service stations, and car dealerships—that could not be envisioned when the technology was initiated. At an even deeper level, the way business is conducted will be transformed as the technology stimulates broad changes (e.g., by making transport of products by trucks a viable alternative to railroads). As trucks reduced the relative cost of short hauls (which had been prohibitive given the large fixed costs of railroads), they shifted the location of manufacturing and the residences of people, and generated yet another wave of new jobs.

The foregoing examples provide ample warning against any effort to project the aggregate employment impact of which basic innovations as automobiles or microelectronics. It is clear that in some occupations there will, in fact, be substantial employment loss. For example, in a recent study we conducted combining time series and cross-sectional data on employment in 54 industries with data on computer usage in each industry (and other control variables), we showed that increases in computing power were associated with sharply reduced employment of clerks and managers.[25] However, nothing in that study precluded the possibility that these employment losses were offset by corresponding gains elsewhere; for example, in the computer industry itself.

Although we shrink from aggregate predictions, we do not want to argue that new technologies will increase the dispersion and volatility of employment change. There are two reasons why we expect this to be true. The first rests on the motivation for the introduction of new technologies, particularly in so-called mature industries. The second is that the diffusion process is in its early stages.

It is no secret that American industry is under great pressure, especially industries producing a standard product that can be provided by foreign producers operating with cheaper labor. Devising solutions to this problem has proved a cottage industry among advocates of industrial policy. Some have argued that national investment be directed away from these "sunset" industries in the direction of new, or "sunrise," firms. Others have developed a sophisticated case for a new form of product development, termed "flexible-specialization," in which firms identify products that are nonstandard, and have relatively short production runs and high skill content. Microelectronic technology, with its capacity to build flexibility into the software and hence permit rapid shifts among products, promises to ease this transition.[26]

These suggestions may capture powerful trends but, in the meantime, another, perhaps simpler, strategy is also possible. This strategy involves competing through mass production based on sophisticated capital equipment and very little labor. With labor content driven out of the product, the advantage switches to U.S. producers, who have access to capital equipment that is as sophisticated and cheap as that available abroad, and who are close to domestic markets. The upshot is a widespread effort to use technology to reduce employment in many basic industries. Furthermore, to the extent that this occurs in mature industries (i.e., industries that produce products the demand for which will not expand rapidly as income rises), this strategy is unlikely to lead to expanded employment through the impact on demand of lower prices.

The essence of this strategy was dramatically stated by a vendor of machine vision systems.

> I think it is going to provide a fantastic competitive edge. It will eliminate a lot of the advantage of low labor costs elsewhere by cutting down on the amount of labor needed and the amount of material wasted.[27]

The optimism of vendors concerning the capabilities and diffusion rates of such innovations is often overstated, but the basic strategy is clear. The drive to reduce labor content is widespread among firms that find that their products are not sufficiently distinctive that they must compete at least substantially on cost. This strategy is not limited to the so-called sunset industries. Consider the following description of IBM's effort to build plants located in the United States that produced standard products with little labor.

> [To become the low cost producer] IBM decided to design products around certain standard modules and, although it provided different configurations of thcsc standard modules to customer order it would not manufacture customized modules. . . . IBM [also] rethought its entire manufacturing measurement system with the intent of reducing its historical focus on direct labor with the intent of giving more emphasis to materials. . . .[28]

IBM's automated factories are now regarded as a key to its comptetitive edge against both new entrants and the Japanese computer manufacturers. Indeed, IBM has pushed this mass-production automation strategy so far that inside the firm the strategy is referred to as a "Model T" approach in homage to the original Ford approach to mass production. The director of the IBM

Manufacturing Technology Institute commented (in reference to the new Se-lectric typewriter line), "Rather than a black Ford we call it a vanilla product." In this particular product IBM's new production facility cut labor input by 75%.[29]

IBM shares this strategy with other high-technology firms as well as most so-called smokestack industries. Another example is Smith-Corona, the type-writer firm that in recent years has regained profitability against strong Japanese competition. The president of the firm commented, "Direct labor is now less than two hours per machine. At that rate you can afford to build it in the United States."[30] In quite a different industry, steel, the percentage increase in research and development expenditures in 1986 exceeded all other industries and was aimed at transforming "a batch-production, capital-intensive technology into a continuous, streamlined, and more versatile operation."[31] Under some of the technologies being adopted, labor costs savings are expected to exceed 60%.[32] Indeed, everywhere one turns there is evidence of mature firms whose major competitive strategy is to reduce employment levels through technical inno-vation.[33] Indeed, it is just this strategy that explains why manufacturing pro-ductivity has increased in recent years while employment levels have remained stagnant.[34]

The point therefore is that as mature industries employ new technologies to reduce labor content in the face of heightened competitive pressures, the dispersion of employment growth will increase and, with it, pressure on the labor market. We are not arguing here that aggregate employment levels will fall, but that in many sectors the pace of work-force reduction is accelerating. These may, and probably will, be offset by the growth of jobs in other sectors, but then the question becomes one of the labor market's ability to effect the matching process.

This line of argument rests on the point that specific segments of the econ-omy are likely to follow a particular competitive strategy. The second reason why new technologies will increase employment dispersion is more general and emphasizes the diffusion process itself. The argument rests on two points. First, we are in the early stages of the diffusion of various computer-based office and production technologies and, therefore, the rate of utilization throughout the economy is uneven. Second, this unevenness means that there will be a higher variance in productivity change and hence employment change.

Taking the argument in reverse order, why does the diffusion process (i.e., the shift from one form of production to another) increase pressure on labor market adjustment? A simple answer is that although the aggregate employment numbers may not fall, and may actually rise, the occupational composition of the labor force will shift, as may the physical location of employment. We have already seen that the employment of clerks and managers will fall with the expansion of computer power. Most researchers believe that with respect to aggregate numbers, this will be at least partly offset by increased employ-ment of professionals. For example, Wassily Leontiff and Faye Duchin share my projection that managerial and clerical employment will fall (they see a 40% employment drop in each occupation by 2000 compared to the base pro-jection, which assumes 1980 technology levels), but they also predict that professional employment will grow by 17%.[35] The question, of course, is whether individuals will be able to make the transition. Consider also the adjustment requirements implicit in their projection concerning the impact of robots.

> The impact of robots on the demand for the affected semi-skilled occupations and laborers is much more modest. While the reduction in demand for these catetories of workers which is directly attributable to robots is about 400,000 in 1990 and almost 2 million in 2000 under Scenario S3, the net demand is about the same as Scenario S1, apparently due to the offsetting effects of increased production of capital goods.[36]

The view that the production workers who lose employment in one setting will be able to find it in another is implicit. However, given the kinds of adjustment issues that we have documented and the probable geographic dispersion of these settings, this assumption is very problematic.

The notion that the diffusion process associated with the adoption of new technologies can cause labor market difficulties is most strongly associated with the work of Joseph A. Schumpter. Indeed, Schumpter viewed the business cycle itself as resulting from waves of innovation moving through the economy. With respect to unemployment he worte:

> Technological unemployment is the essence of our process and, linking as it does with innovation, is cyclical in nature. We have seen, in fact, in our historical survey, that periods of prolonged supernormal unemployment coincide with the periods in which the results of innovations are spreading over the system and in which reaction to them by the system is dominating the business situation . . . it further follows that, like profits, technological unemployment is ephemeral. It might nevertheless be ever present, but, as in the case of profits, every individual source of it in the industrial organism tends to exhaust itself, while new ones emerge periodically.[37]

What gives this argument practical content is the notion that diffusion is not instantaneous (indeed, most research suggests that it follows an S-shaped or logistic curve) and, hence, the uneveness of adoption will produce uneven employment growth as different firms and competing industries find themselves, and their employment, growing at different rates. At the conclusion of the diffusion process the competitive advantages of firms will be stabilized and the variance of growth rates will fall.

What evidence is there that we are in an early wave of technological change? It is clear that in a wide range of areas, from the plant floor to the office, computers in general and microelectronics in particular, are transforming how work is accomplished. But will this transformation accelerate?

The answer can only be speculative, and considerable caution is necessary. New technologies are generally created with a burst of enthusiasm and exaggerated expectations about their effectiveness and diffusion. The most widely discussed new technology, computer-based numerically controlled machine tools, even in 1980—after nearly two decades of availability—accounted for only 26% of the value of all machine tools shipped.[38] In reality, technologies do not work as expected, take longer to integrate into the production process than envisioned, and require more human intervention than vendors claim. An irony of American automobile manufacturers' obsessions with Japanese competition is their discovery (based on observation of Japanese-owned plants in the United States) that the level of technical sophistication in Japanese plants is far lower than expected. The competitive edge seems based on management and human resource practices.[39] This observation, along with the difficulty of making new systems work as advertised, has led to a pull back from plans to automate American plants fully.

Despite these cautions, the potential power of various microelectronic-based systems is such that a wide range of observers believe that their use will accelerate. For example, with respect to robots, the Congressional Office of Technology Assessment believes that the number installed will move up an exponential curve from 8,200 in 1983 to over 100,000 in the early 1990s.[40] Hunt and Hunt, whose careful study based on extensive interviews in the automobile industry generally debunked popular predictions of vast displacement, nonetheless share the view that diffusion is accelerating.[41] Other microelectronic-based technologies display the same pattern. The tremendous increase in microcomputers is too well known to recount, but they probably represent an early stage in the transformation of office work. As work stations are linked and increasingly share common data bases, a wide range of new applications become possible. One management consulting firm estimated that word processing reduced costs for producing a letter from $7 to $2 and that electronic mail will lower the cost to 30¢.[42] Similarly, annual sales of computer-assisted design equipment increased from approximately 400 units per year in 1976 to 6035 units per year in 1982, with sharp future increases projected.[43] Dataquest data show that investments in factory computers and software grew from $935 million in 1980 to $2,861 million in 1986. They project the 1990 figure to be $6,500 million.[44] The data show similar patterns for other components of computer-assisted manufacturing. Finally, the suprisingly low fraction of the value of machine tools accounted for by the numerically controlled equipment previously alluded to is expected to accelerate to 63% by 1990.[45]

In short, evidence from a variety of sources suggests that we are at the beginning, not the middle or the end, of the S-shaped diffusion curve of microelectronic-based office and production technologies. This, then, suggests an additional source of pressure on the labor market since, as we have argued, while the diffusion process itself does not necessarily reduce aggregate employment, it does generate unevenness in employment growth across firms and sectors.

Changing Supply Conditions

The foregoing argued that employment growth is likely to become more dispersed over time and that this will place pressure on the market adjustment mechanisms. The other shoe that will drop is the decreased flexibility of the labor supply. This contrasts with the conditions that shaped the postwar institutions, and therefore will pose even more problems for market adjustment.

Demographic developments will reduce the numbers of new entrants, both youths and adult women, coming into the market. Although the actual reduction in numbers will ease labor market pressure in the sense that fewer jobs will be necessary, there is a correlary that is considerably more problematic. The average age of the labor force will rise: as the baby boom generation moves through middle age, a bulge will develop in that range. Workers of this age group historically are considerably less flexible than new entrants. Labor market institutions that, as we have seen, are not well equipped to induce movement and flexibility will have to cope with a less flexible labor force combined with the more difficult demand environment that we have described.

The demographics underlying the changing supply situation in the labor market is shown in Table 3.6.

These projections show that the number of young men and young women (aged 16 to 24) will actually decline from their 1980 levels. In addition, among people aged 25 to 54 the increase in the male labor force will roughly match the increase in the female labor force. Both developments starkly contrast with the trends of the past several decades. Furthermore, although the overall labor force is projected to increase by only 22% between 1980 and 1995 for men, the group aged 35 to 54 will grow by 82%, and for females the growth rate for that age group will be 61%.

We have characterized these experienced workers as "inflexible" In part this referred to employer behavior in that the nature of internal labor markets makes firms reluctant to hire them. However, the inflexibility also has a foundation in the character of the labor force. As individuals age, they become less mobile. This is true both with respect to geographic mobility and job changing in general. Migration is a young person's game. Table 3.7 shows that the relationship between age and migration is dramatic. Migration propensities peak for the 25 to 34-year-old cohorts and thereafter decline quite sharply. In addition, the younger cohorts account for the bulk of migration: fully 65.6% of

Table 3.6 Labor Force Projections

	Numbers (000)			Percent Participation Rates		
	1980	1990	1995	1980	1990	1995
Men						
16–24	13606	11274	10573	74.4	74.7	74.5
25–54	38712	48180	51318	94.2	93.8	93.4
55–64	7242	6419	6311	72.1	65.5	64.5
65+	1893	1828	1728	19.0	14.9	13.3
Women						
16–24	11696	10813	10557	61.9	69.1	71.6
25–64	27888	40496	44852	64.0	75.6	78.7
55–64	4742	4612	4671	41.3	41.5	42.5
65+	1161	1329	1337	8.1	7.4	7.0

Source: Monthly Labor Review, November 1983, p. 5.

Table 3.7 Relationship of Interstate Migration and Age

Age Group	Males		Females	
	Percent of Civilian Labor Force Moving Between States per Year	Percent of Total Civilian Labor Force Moves Accounted for by Age Group	Percent of Civilian Labor Force Moving Between States per Year	Percent of Total Civilian Labor Force Moves Accounted for by Age Group
16–24	10.3	23.1	11.2	29.3
25–34	14.9	42.5	14.8	42.5
35–44	9.3	19.1	7.9	16.5
45–64	5.0	15.2	4.1	11.5

Source: Calculated from *Current Population Reports*, Series P-20, No. 368, December 1981. The labor force status is as of 1980. The conclusions do not change if population rather than labor force is used as the base. For males the population-based propensities of movement are 9.7%, 15.0%, 9.9%, and 5.5% for each age group; for women the figures are 10.3% 14.1%, 8.1% and 4.8%.

all interstate moves by male labor force members between 1975 and 1980 and 71.8% for women members were accounted for by the 16 to 34 age group.[46]

There is an additional reason to be wary of relying on migration to adjust the labor market: migration propensities have been declining over time, even after controlling for age. Table 3.8 provides data on this trend.

Not only migration is strongy age related; much the same is true of job changing in general. Table 3.9 shows the percentage of different age groups that voluntarily changed jobs during a 5-year period. As is apparent, the fraction remaining in the same job rises sharply with age and is very high in the middle-aged years.

A final point concerning the impact of the new demographics is that it will become more difficult to use attrition and retirement as adjustment mechanisms. Many firms currently are responding to the pressures we have described

Table 3.8 Migration Propensities Over Time

	All Ages	Ages 20–29
A. Percent of population changing residence		
1960–61	20.6	40.8
1970–71	18.7	39.7
1980–81	17.2	34.7
B. Percent of population changing state		
1950–51	3.5	
1960–61	3.2	
1980–81	2.7	

Source: Bureau of the Census, Report Series P-20, Nos. 118 and 377.

Table 3.9 Fraction of Men with No Voluntary Job Changes Over a 5-Year Period

Age	Percent
20–24	50.3
25–29	70.5
30–34	78.2
35–39	82.0
40–44	88.8
45–49	83.7
50–54	83.7
55–59	96.5

Source: Panel Survey on Income Dynamics. The data were calculated from 1971–76. A job change is considered voluntary if it results from a quit.

by offering voluntary early retirement programs to reduce the work force. In other instances, the impact of new technology has been cushioned by the fortuitous attrition resulting from a work force near retirement. These options will diminish as the bulk of the work force becomes middle aged, and the absence of these "gentle" adjustment mechanisms will create considerable difficulty.

Conclusion

The fundamental structure of the American labor market has been generally successful in the postwar period. It was well adapted to the problem confronting the labor market: how to incorporate a rapidly increasing labor force in an environment of job growth. The solution to this problem involved considerable quantity adjustment, flexibility at the bottom of the hiring queue, and a relatively rigid system of wages and mobility for the more mature labor force. This system was not without its problems, as Chapter 2 demonstrated. However, these problems were never pressing from a purely system maintenance perspective.

   However, we conclude that more serious difficulties may emerge. We are in an era of more pervasive demand shocks, and the aging of the labor force will provide less flexibility. This should not be taken as a prediction of cataclysm. Instead, it is better to think of an accelerating accumulation of difficulties. Many, indeed, most, workers will successfully adjust to the new environment. First, the majority will not be touched in the sense that their jobs will not be threatened. Second, many of those whose jobs are jeopardized will find new ones. The point is that the fraction that does experience significant difficulty will grow, and the numbers will be such that what has been a bothersome but not major phenomenon in the past will become more serious. The difficulties faced by this small but growing minority is likely, however, to have broad consequences, because workers generally will feel less secure as they confront an economy in which more of their neighbors, friends, and relatives are having trouble. This concern will be accentuated by the aging of the work force, for age brings with it insecurities. It will also be amplified by the fact that women will become increasingly less content with their marginal (or flexible) status and will also want security.

The difficulties of the small but growing minority and the associated security demands of those who retain their jobs will challenge public policy. The situation will also pose a problem to firms because, at the same time that job security becomes more salient, other considerations have accelerated efforts to introduce greater flexibility in employment practices. These efforts are related to this chapter's concerns in two ways. First, some of the techniques, such as the growing use of temporary and part-time workers, may reduce security further. Second, it is possible that in order for firms to achieve greater internal flexibility successfully, they will need to offer their workers greater job security. This is because many of the rigid work rules in place now are really mechanisms that protect jobs. These devices will not be easily abandoned without other forms of security. However, if the labor market as a whole is becoming less secure, this will be an obstacle to the reform of internal practices. This linkage between the external environment and the personnel practices of firms leads us naturally to the material in Chapter 4: the evolving nature of internal labor markets.

4

Reorganization of Work Within Firms

Chapters 2 and 3 focused on labor market outcomes for individuals. Our conclusion was mixed. For most people the market has performed well, but there are substantial numbers of individuals in difficulty. Furthermore, there are signs—the changing age structure of the labor force and the increased frequency of demand shocks—that adjustment problems may increase. Unchecked, this implies a rising unemployment rate and increased economic woes for an unlucky minority.

To understand why market adjustment is problematic we drew on the concept of internal labor markets: the hiring, promotion, and wage-setting practices of firms. In our abbreviated discussion of this topic we argued that for various reasons many firms limit hiring from the external to entry-level positions. To the extent that this pattern prevails in sectors of the economy impacted by the damand shocks outlined earlier, adjustment problems can be explained in these terms.

In this chapter organization of work within the firm assumes center stage. Just as we have sought to understand the problems of individuals, so we want to examine the problems of employers. Much of the current uncertainty and sense of flux in the labor market can be interpreted as firms seeking to reshape and redefine how their organizations work. It is our view that these developments can be fruitfully understood as changes in internal labor markets. We can gain considerable insight by learning what the key choices firms face are, what considerations lie behind their decisions, and what the difficulties are that limit their freedom of maneuver.

Insights into these questions will also help frame an approach toward an employment policy that is relevant to the needs of employers. If we can identify the fundamental dilemmas facing firms, we can think through how an employment and training system can help. Put somewhat differently, Chapters 2 and 3 developed the case for an employment policy by examining the difficulties confronting individuals. In this chapter we develop a comparable case by understanding the concerns of firms. Then we see what intersections permit creation of a policy of interest to both sides of the labor market, a policy that therefore would be more effective than past efforts.

Introduction

If the past decade and a half was difficult for many individuals in American firms it was an era of rude awakenings. The twin oil shocks of 1973 and 1979, along with the steep recessions in 1975, 1980, and 1981, created a sense that the economic ground was anything but firm. However, the unease went deeper. For the first time since the Great Depression a widespread feeling emerged that the "American way" of doing business was not adequate, that others had surpassed us in management, productivity, and quality. The loss of market share to foreign competitors and the trade deficit are daily reminders that in many markets others seem to be doing a better job than is accomplished at home.

There are almost as many explanations of this reversal as there are commentators and consultants, but prominent on virtually every list is human resource management. The content of the indictment, however, does vary according to the perspective of the prosecutor. Hardline management in blue collar industries charges that wages are too high and work rules too rigid. A softer criticism points to the minimal participation and commitment of American workers compared, for instance, to the (perhaps idealized) loyalty of Japanese employees to their companies. In the white collar world the charges range from complaints about overstaffing and superfluous administrative layers to concern that firms have stifled creativity and entrepreneurship.

Although the tone and substance of these observations vary, they share a perception that the employment practices of American firms need improvement. The consequence has been an explosion of innovation perhaps unequaled since labor relations was transformed by the union movement and legislation associated with the Great Depression. Examples include agressive concession bargaining in which firms force unions to accept substantial changes in work rules; widespread interest in and adoption of quality circles and other strategies for involving employees in shop floor decision making; large-scale layoffs from previously secure managerial positions; growing use of temporary employees, subcontracting, and other mechanisms for shifting employment outside the firm; new commitments to job security and to joint labor-management training programs aimed at making the commitments credible; and new compensation strategies including pay for knowledge, pay for performance, and other schemes aimed at distributing the benefits of productivity improvements.

The volumn of innovation has been substantial, interest and concern remain high, and it seems apparent that the human resource management system of many firms in being transformed. What is problematic is the direction and consequences of these developments. As the preceding list suggests, there is no simple way to characterize recent innovations and, in fact, many of the innovations point to opposing tendencies and strategies. Tough concession bargaining is not consistent with efforts to induce commitment and loyalty through worker participation strategies. Layoffs and the use of temporary workers are very different from making security promises and extensive training investments. All we can conclude from surveying the scene is that something is happening and that the "something" is extensive. Firms think that they have problems and are designing strategies for solving them. There is a great deal of activity, but it is not clear what lessons to draw from it. To make sense of events, we must step back and develop a framework for interpreting the "problem" and understanding the nature of various "solutions." Such a framework may help sort through the confusion and point to the real issues and consequences of the choices being made.

The Employment Systems of Firms

The most useful way to understand trends in employment practices is to place these developments in the context of the firm's internal labor market. An internal labor market is defined by the administrative procedures and rules that organize the utilization of labor.[1] A simple example concerns hiring and promotion practices. For some occupations in some firms it is possible to be hired only at the bottom of job ladders; all other jobs on that ladder are filled by promoting incumbents. In other firms the same job ladder may be open to the outside at several different points. These alternative patterns have important implications for job security (typically, in the former case, incumbents have job security and any layoffs occur in reverse order of seniority), training (the former case implies considerable on-the-job training while the latter example often implies training in outside institutions such as schools), and adaptability to change (a firm with limited commitments to incumbents can more easily alter the size and skill mix of its labor force).

Although the term "internal labor market" is sometimes used to denote a particular pattern—the seniority-based closed job ladder system that characterizes much of America's heavy industry—it is more useful to recognize that all firms have rules and procedures, but they may vary in important ways. The high turnover and dead-end clerical job is organized by a set of rules, just as are more stable occupations, but the rules and procedures differ. Similarly, white as well as blue collar jobs are embedded in an internal labor market. For example, in many firms managers work in the same kind of structured job ladders as do skilled blue collar workers, while computer programmers may move between firms with the same frequency as construction workers.

Most firms have numerous rules and procedures, and lengthy personnel textbooks and professional journals are devoted to developing and elaborating them. However, at the risk of oversimplification, it is useful for our purposes to distinguish four categories that, taken together, define the internal labor market for a set of occupations.

1. *Job Classification and Job Definition*. Under this category fall rules that determine whether jobs are defined broadly or narrowly (i.e., include many or few tasks) and whether job definitions are rigid or loose (i.e., whether a person doing job A does only those tasks or whether he or she will do other work).

2. *Deployment*. This refers to rules concerning how employees may be moved

from job to job in the organization. For example, in some settings seniority determines bidding rights, while in other settings management retains complete discretion as to how to deploy labor.

3. *Security.* Some firms operate with explicit or implict promises of lifetime job security; other companies make no promises beyond payment for the current day's work. In some settings layoffs are determined by (reverse) seniority and elaborate job bumping rules, while elsewhere management is free to release whom it chooses.

4. *Wage Rules.* The major distinction here is whether wages are attached to jobs or to individuals. In the former case all individuals in a given job classification receive a given wage; in the latter circumstance some combination of personal attributes (skill, education, performance) and seniority determines wages regardless of what set of tasks the individual is currently engaged in.

The most important point to grasp concerning these rules is that within a given firm they fit together with a coherent logic. For example, in companies in which lifetime job security is guaranteed, there are likely to be fewer and less restrictive job classifications than in firms in which hire/fire is the rule. The logic is that rigid job classifications are a form of security or protection (since such rules limit management's ability to reduce employment by combining jobs and—if jobs are cut—seniority combined with job classifications establishes control of who is at risk). In an environment in which security is provided through other mechanisms, strict classifications are less necessary. A comparable point might be made concerning the relationship between rules concerning deployment and security. In the same spirit we can also see that in circumstances in which wages are attached to specific workers, job classification will be less rigid than where wages are determined largely by job assignment.

If we interpret human resource policies as systems of internal labor markets with rules covering the four areas just described, we have a framework for understanding the innovations currently being tested. For example, the increased use of temporary workers can be viewed as an effort to transform the employment rules of the occupation in question from one involving stable internal employment with an element of job security and training to (from the firm's perspective) a hire/fire relationship with no commitment. Efforts to introduce greater job security in return for easing of job classifications can similarly be understood as attempts to transform the internal labor market for the occupation in question.

Alternative Internal Labor Market Systems

The central argument of this chapter is that it is useful to pose the problem facing firms as one of choosing among alternative models of internal labor markets. The confusion, the experiments, and our uncertainty about the direction of change all flow from a common sense that traditional models of internal labor market structure have proven unsatisfactory. However, there is no comparable consensus about the appropriate new model.

The core[2] firms in the American labor market have traditionally organized work according to the logic of one of two dominant models that we will call the *industrial* model and the *salaried* model. Our image of what work is like and how it must be changed are reflections of the strengths and weaknesses of these two paradigms. Although these two models have been dominant, there are also two additional "minor" models of internal labor markets, what might be termed craft and secondary forms of organization. We will ignore these latter two alternatives except when they are specifically relevant to the argument of this chapter.[3]

The industrial model represents the manner of organizing blue collar work that became the norm as a result of the unionization drives of the Great Depression and that was solidified in the era of postwar prosperity.[4] In this model work is organized into a series of tightly defined jobs with clear work rules and responsibilities attached to each classification. Wages are attached to jobs; therefore an individual's wage is determined by his or her classification. Management's freedom to move individuals from one job to another can vary from situation to situation, but the typical case is that both promotions and lateral shifts are limited by seniority provisions and by requirements that workers agree to the shift. Finally, there is no formal job security, and it is understood that management is free to vary the size of the labor force as it wishes. However, when layoffs do occur, they are generally organized according to reverse seniority.

Although the structure of this model emerged from the spread of unionism, it should not be construed as limited to such situations. Because of fear of unions, government pressures for uniformity,[5] and imitation, the model spread throughout the economy.[6] Hence a recent survey of nonunion firms found that seniority-based promotion and layoff systems were extremely common, even in the absence of formal contracts.[7]

This model has a strong internal logic and, as the previous discussion suggested, necessarily fits together in a coherent way. Because wages are attached to jobs, it is necessary that the jobs be carefully defined so that there is a common understanding concerning who is doing what work and is entitled to what wage. Similarly, while the system provides no overall job security (management can vary the size of the work force at will), individual security is based on a bumping system grounded in seniority; for that system to be effective, careful job classifications are necessary. Furthermore, the system was established partly because it was attractive in several ways to both management and labor. In his thoughtful study of the American automobile industry, Harry C. Katz characterizes this model as one of "job control" and notes that:

> For management the job control focus served the important function of containing the union's and worker's penetration of issues deemed to be management prerogatives. . . . furthermore job control unionism meshed well with management's adherence to scientific management, which professed the ad-

vantages of supervisory authority and a clear definition of worker's responsibilities.[8]

For workers the system has the overwhelming value of creating security in
the face of an insecure environment. Given fluctuations in product demand and
management's unchallenged right to lay off employees, the job control model
uses the organization of work as a shield. The tight definitions of jobs means
that management cannot reduce staffing by reorganizing tasks or combining
jobs; hence the volume of work is regulated (if not maintained) by the system.
The job-based bumping system also means that if layoffs occur they are implemented impartially; the only relevant criterion is seniority. This blocks favoritism and also permits workers to make plans reasonably and gauge their
degree of security. There are costs to this model, of course; notably the difficulty of altering work organization in the face of changing technology or other
pressures. This difficulty arises because of the logic of the system itself and
because, over time, that logic takes on a moral legitimacy that adds to its weight.
However, for a long time these difficulties have seemed minor compared to
the logic and stability of the industrial model. We will see shortly that this
assessment may be changing.

Most labor economics and industrial relations research has emphasized blue
collar work; consequently, it is more difficult to describe the salaried internal
labor market model. However, understanding the model is important for three
reasons: it describes the employment pattern of large numbers of workers, it
extends beyond salaried work to a number of innovative blue collar employment settings, and some of its characteristics represent the direction in which
management generally is trying to push work.

The salaried model combines a more flexible and personalistic set of administrative procedures with greater commitment to employment security. Although individuals have job descriptions, much as industrial employees have
work rules, these descriptions are not intended to have legal or customary force.
They are subject to revision by superiors, and the employees are prepared to
take on new activities as demanded. By the same token, the clearly defined
job ladders and promotion sequences that characterize industrial settings are
absent. For example, one observer reported in interviews that:

> People in the same position [in the same firm] disagreed among themselves
> about its place in the organizational career map. Twenty distribution managers
> identified seven routes to their jobs . . . and they imagined that there were
> three likely and seven rare moves from their job.[9]

The flexible career lines and job descriptions are consistent with another
aspect of this employment system, the greater role of personalistic considerations in wage setting. There is a considerably greater scope for merit considerations in pay setting, and the wages of two individuals in the same job can
vary considerably.[10] Put differently, the pay system of industrial settings, in
which the dominant consideration is job assignment, is far less prevalent in the
salaried model.

If rigid job classifications and reliance on nonpersonalistic procedures are the key to job security and worker acquiescence in the industrial system, what plays a comparable role in the salaried model? One long-time theme in the literature, first expressed by Selig Perlman, is that white collar employees view work in different terms than blue collar workers. Whereas a sense of limited opportunity and collective consciousness is central to the blue collar mind, the white collar worker is an individualist who believes that hard work will pay off and that no artificial limits prevent individual success. In this view, then, the salaried employment system works because its flexibility and fluidity are not viewed as a threat.

Surely many employees in the salaried system share this view and are therefore willing to forego the protections inherent in the industrial model. However, this cannot be the complete explanation for the important reason that the salaried system is not limited to white collar work. As we will discuss momentarily, a number of highly visible employers apply the salaried model to blue as well as white collar employment. Furthermore, many white collar workers are clearly interested in security and protection from arbitrary administrative actions.

What completes the salaried model is employment security. In the classic salaried model individuals, once they pass a probationary period, can expect lifetime employment with the firm. Unlike the industrial model, in which it is explicitly understood that the firm will adjust the size of the labor force in response to product market conditions or technological change, the implicit promise in the salaried system is that layoffs either simply will not occur or that the firm will be strenuous in its effort to avoid them. This latter point, that absolute promises are not necessary, is important because without it the scope of the salaried model would be limited. What is crucial is that employees are sufficiently convinced of the sincerity of the firm's commitment to employment stabilization that they are willing to provide the degree of flexibility that is the firm's reward in the system. We will refer to the "security pledge," but this is merely sufficient employer commitment to employment stabilization to obtain employee consent. Exactly what that level of security is will vary from situation to situation, depending on the nature of the industry, the firm's history, and other variables.

What is being "bought," then, is commitment, and the exact price will vary from situation to situation. However, the nature of the bargain is clear, as is the distinction between the salaried and the industrial model.

The salaried model clearly characterizes much white collar work (or at least it has until recent years, a caveat discussed shortly). The career patterns of most managers and many professionals who work in bureaucracies are accurately captured by the model. However, the salaried model is *not* simply another way of describing white collar work. There have also always been a few American firms that have stood outside the mainstream industrial model for their blue collar workers. In the 1920s the exception was termed "welfare capitalism" and represented an effort to develop an alternative to unions.[11] In the postwar period the alternative has taken the form of applying the salaried model in a blue collar setting. In return for flexible work rules and a willingness to accept managerial prerogatives with respect to deployment, these firms offer their workers employment security. Probably the best-known example is IBM, a firm that has never had a layoff. The personnel director at IBM captured the nature of the bargain in these words: "We believe that if people are not worried about being laid off they are flexible in making the changes we ask of them."[12] In order to make this model work, IBM employs a number of "buffers" such as temporary workers, overtime, and outsourcing of work so that when demand falls the buffers can be laid off and work brought into the regular labor force. In addition, IBM engages in extensive training and retraining and is willing to finance large-scale relocations of its labor force to new sites around the country.[13]

Other well-known firms also have applied the salaried model to blue collar work. IBM's major competitor—Digital—has followed a no-layoff rule and has extremely fluid work rules and job descriptions. Polaroid and Kodak also sought to follow the model although in recent years both have had to back away from the security pledge. Taken together, firms that operate their blue collar labor practices along these lines probably do not account for a large fraction of blue collar work. However, they are important because they tend to be visible and viewed as "progressive" companies and because they demonstrate the potentially broad applicability of the salaried model.

Choosing Among the Alternative Models

The categories and choices just outlined are only interesting if they correspond to actual decisions and dilemmas facing firms. That these decisions are important can be demonstrated by showing that there is some conflict among the goals and that trade-offs therefore are necessary.

Both the industrial and salaried systems share common features: employees spend the bulk of their careers within the firm, and training (and socialization) is provided by the company. The chief differences lie in the kinds of flexibility each model provides. The industrial model permits firms to reduce staffing levels almost at will in response to changing product market conditions. There are limitations on the willingness of firms to follow this tack, since they may have made considerable investments in on-the-job training, but ultimately the firm is free to fire employees. The price of this freedom is the narrow job classifications inherent in the system. When the job classifications correspond reasonably well to the requirements for accomplishing the task, this is a small cost. However, when the work is variable (as in much managerial employment) or when the technology changes, the cost may be high.

The salaried model provides much greater flexibility in job assignment and job definition. However, the cost is that firms cannot easily reduce staffing levels. This is indeed a costly commitment. For example, one high-technology firm that we have studied, when faced with the need to reduce staffing levels, went through an extremely lengthy and expensive process of retraining some workers, moving others to different parts of the country, and buying out yet others, all in the name of maintaining the implicit job security pledge. Perhaps even more costly was the fact that that company delayed any action for a considerable time and also had a hard time convincing its middle-level personnel of the legitimacy of any corrective action, whereas a firm that organized work along industrial lines would long before have laid off workers. And, as we have already noted, some companies have been forced to back away from their commitment to employment continuity. This is not to say, however, that such commitments were only fair weather vows. Many other firms, even in good times, maintain hire/fire policies. Enterprises that adhere to the salaried model—at some cost even under favorable product market circumstances—gain the benefits of commitment and flexibility.

The tensions between the advantages and disadvantages of the salaried and industrial models represent one of the main stories currently being played out. The other is the question of whether it is possible to move away from both models, each with their own rigidities, and instead arrange to increase the amount of work done under even more flexible arrangements. It is in these terms that we can understand the rise of part-time work, temporary help services, and other forms of external flexible labor. This represents an effort to expand what we earlier mentioned in passing, the secondary internal labor market model.[14] These low-commitment/high-turnover internal labor market patterns maximize flexibility. However, this comes at the expense of predictability, since such workers tend to have minimal loyalty to the firm and have not been socialized into its norms.

What gives special interest to these choices, between salaried and industrial systems on the one hand and between those two choices and secondary systems on the other hand, is that in recent years, perhaps for the first time since the Great Depression, there are widespread indications that internal labor market structures are changing. The forces that led to this development, the difficulties encountered by firms as they attempt to alter their employment arrangements, and the consequences for the welfare of workers are the topics of the remainder of this chapter.

The Construction and Deconstruction of the Firm

We begin by examining the pressures on the two dominant models, the industrial and salaried internal labor market systems. We will see that the industrial model is under extreme pressure from several sources. On the one hand, new technologies are altering the traditional job classification systems and are pressuring the firm toward the more flexible salaried model, with its broad job structures and implicit job security. However, there are offsetting considerations—macroeconomic uncertainty and management ideology—that make the job security promise problematic and push firms toward higher turnover and less costly systems. Employers face tension from a different source for white collar work. These jobs are already organized along the lines of the salaried model. However, the model is somewhat endangered as competitive pressures and the nature of new technologies lead to employment reductions and hence call into doubt the job security aspect of that model.

These often conflicting pressures on both blue and white collar employment help us understand what seem to be two new patterns. Some firms are introducing the salaried model into previously industrial settings and restructuring that employment, as well as already existing salaried internal labor markets in white collar employment, by what might be termed the "core-periphery model." Under this arrangement firms reduce the portion of their work force covered by the salaried model and attempt to shift some of their work load outside the protected portion of the internal labor market through various techniques such as temporary help, part-time arrangements, and so called "two-tier" arrangements within the firm. The second strategy, most applicable to blue collar work, is inconsistent with the first but has many advocates. The strategy ignores the conflicting pressures and simply tries to force work rule changes by management fiat or concession bargaining.

Although both of these strategies are widespread, we conclude the chapter by arguing that neither are likely to succeed as long-run solutions to the dilemmas that generated them in the first place. This uncertainty implies that firms will not be able to resolve the conflicting pressures easily and that human resource strategy may continue to remain in flux. This is unfortunate, however, because the salaried model has substantial public as well as private benefits. These considerations open up the possibility of policy measures that will help "solve" the dilemmas facing firms and, by being "useful" in this sense, will also have an opportunity for effectively achieving public objectives.

Pressures on the Industrial Model

Despite the advantages of the industrial model and its long-standing dominance, it is under increasing attack and most of the innovations in human resource policy in the past decade can be read as efforts to move away from and transform this system. Why should this be happening? The two fundamental reasons are that the system has a tendency to become costly and wage costs are of increasing salience to firms and, second, the system is poorly adapted to easing the introduction of technologies that challenge traditional job classifications, yet this is exactly the characteristic of many innovations.

The industrial system is vulnerable to unplanned wage increases, or what in Europe is termed "wage drift," because the wages of the different jobs are tightly linked together. This is a consequence of the system's tendency to attach wages to job titles, not to individuals. In a typical system wages are set as fixed multiples (greater or less than one) of a few key jobs, and these ratios tend to become quite rigid as with time they take on normative value to the work force.[15] In addition, similar patterns tended to develop across firms as specific competitors or firms with similar skill mixes became identified as appropriate comparison points to determine the proper level of wages.[16] The consequence is a tendency for increases in one part of the system to be replicated throughout as the external comparisons lead to comparable increases across firms and internal structures propagate the increase throughout the company.

Such a system is acceptable provided that wage drift is generalized across all potential competitors. In this case wages are "taken out of competition" either by unions or by other aspects of the industrial relations system. What has made the system unacceptably expensive is the increased opening of the U.S. economy to foreign competition, generally from nations whose wages were below ours. The wage structure obviously does not extend overseas, and hence U.S. firm are forced to become more cost conscious. The consequence is a growing refusal to accept traditional wage patterns across firms (e.g., the rubber companies have ended their traditional practice of modeling their wage settlements on those of the automobile companies) as well as general efforts to reduce wage levels through the "concession bargaining" discussed earlier.

Perhaps of greater importance than efforts to change the level of wages have been attempts to alter the mechanisms for wage setting within the firm. These efforts include traditional devices such as increased use of merit pay or even piecework and newer schemes such as "pay for knowledge" in which workers' pay is tied to their skill level, and various "gain-sharing" plans in which pay is tied to profits or productivity. All of these efforts share the characteristic of partially severing the linkage between job title and pay and instead linking pay to individuals or to organizational performance. As such, these are part of the growing effort to transform the industrial model for blue collar workers into one that looks more like the salaried model. Furthermore, one might expect that as these systems spread, they will free job classification systems from their role in the wage-setting process. This, in turn, may permit more flexible classifications.

Pressure on the wage structure of industrial internal labor market systems is important but is fundamentally self limiting because in the end the U.S. economy cannot compete on the basis of wage costs. The wage differentials between American workers and those in developing countries are so great that at best the differentials can be marginally reduced.[17] The consequence is that technological innovation becomes centrally important and represents the key pressure on the traditional industrial system. One source of pressure is the effort to reduce labor content and the tremendous power of new technologies in accomplishing this. We already saw in Chapter 3 the importance of technological change in generating pressures on employment levels, and we argued that the logic of competition will lead to accelerating diffusion of these technologies. We now ask about the impact of this diffusion on job structure and content.

Technology and Job Structures

We have already seen that the modern discussion of new technologies is ambivalent. On the one hand, technological innovation is seen as America's comparative advantage in world competition and hence as the savior of jobs. On the other hand is the fear that the "Factory of the Future" will be populated with robots, not humans, with the possible consequence of widespread joblessness. These alternative views reflect competing positions on the question of displacement: will the laborsaving character of technology cost so many jobs as to outweigh, or be outweighed by, the employment gains that result from the lower prices (and new products) that technologies generate?

There is a similar set of mixed messages regarding the impact of technologies on the quality of work. Many of the dirtiest and most dangerous jobs are also the most routine—painting and routine welding in auto factories being classic examples—and hence are obvious candidates for technological elimination. These same robots will create new, and better, jobs for programmers and technicians. From this perspective technology is beneficial, but set against this is the fear of losing traditional craft skills to machines operated by deskilled operators. This is the argument made by Braverman and his many followers.[18] One standard example is the shift from skilled machinists to operators of numerically controlled machine tools. Another is computers, monitored by semiskilled operators, that can diagnose and repair malfunctioning equipment, hence replacing skilled craft repair personnel.

A vigorous debate around technology and the quality of working life has taken on strong normative aspects as participants feel forced to reach conclusions about whether management deploys technology to deskill or upgrade workers. This has generated a set of case studies and theorizing, with the bottom line being the inconclusive finding that "it depends." This should not be surprising, since the theoretical arguments cut both ways. Deskilling may be attractive because it enhances shop-floor control but, from a cost-minimizing perspective, firms may prefer to replace large numbers of semiskilled operators with a few highly skilled workers operating sophisticated machinery. The empirical work reflects this ambiguity, with each side able to generate case studies supporting its perspective. If one were forced to generalize, the conclusion would be that technology tends to "deskill" traditional craft jobs but upgrades most other employment, including semiskilled and unskilled work.[19]

Our interest here, however, is not to settle this debate. The reason the debate is inconclusive is that the trajectory of specific job skills is part of a more general problem: how new technologies are impacting the internal labor market structures of firms. To understand the impact of new technology on any specific job or group of workers, it is necessary to step back and survey the choices the firm has made among the employment systems described earlier.

The question before us then is this: How are new technologies affecting industrial-type internal labor markets? Are the characteristics of these technologies compatible with industrial internal labor markets or are they instead forcing a rethinking of that model? Our view is that modern technologies are challenging one of the core characteristics of the industrial model—narrow job classifications—and hence are pressuring management to move blue collar work toward the internal labor market structures characteristic of the salaried model.

Modern computer-based technologies seem to be extraordinarily powerful along a number of dimensions. For example, by collecting real-time data on production, they permit far greater monitoring of employees than ever before. The phone company,[20] for example, collects contemporaneous data on the location of repairpersons, the time they have taken on the task they are currently working on, and the projected travel time to the next assignment. The assignments of each are optimized in order to minimize travel time, maximize the number of assignments completed per day, and—as a bonus—move the repairperson away from home in the morning and toward it in the afternoon. Operators are continuously monitored by the number of calls they take and the length of each call. Communications technologies also permit considerable spatial reorganization. Citibank, for example, has used satellites to establish six regional collection centers and hence, in effect, a single national bank. Numerous firms have established overseas locations for data entry work, taking advantage of cheap labor pools; keyed-in data are simply beamed to locations in the United States for processing and analysis.

As interesting and important as these applications are, our interest is in the work place, be it shop floor or office. To provide a concrete sense of the changes implied by new computer-based technologies, we will briefly describe innovations in three industries spanning the range of the situations that characterize American manufacturing: the automobile industry as the most traditional example, General Electric's appliance production as a middle range, and telecommunications as among the more flexible industries. The point is to observe the pressures that new technologies place on internal labor market structures.

The American automobile industry represents the purest form of the industrial internal labor market model. Narrow and rigid old classifications have been developed, and wages are tightly tied to these jobs. Harry C. Katz reproduced a portion of a typical assembly-line job ladder; among the job titles in his chart are "install front seats. "install rear seats," "install garnish mouldings," and "install door trim panels."[21] These are each separate jobs; workers in one job will not do another. Recall that the logic to this system is that it is tied to wage determination and, in an environment in which the firm will make no promises concerning employment levels, it provides a predictable way for workers to enforce and gain a measure of security.

Contrast this system with the assembly system being built for several new G.M. plants.

> . . . the company plans to assemble cars using hundreds of motorized unmanned carriers . . . which will guide the car through the assembly process. If a particular car has a heavy load of options, though, the vehicle may be directed to move out of the main queue to have those parts installed. . . . G.M. plans to split the line into multiple parallel branches at a variety of locations, allowing the vehicles to stop and have groups of workers perform logical blocks of work, such as the installation of all the accessories on an engine . . . the carrier cannot move out of a work station until it is released by the group. . . . "We couldn't have done it a few years ago (said a G.M. official) . . . we need computers that can keep track of hundreds of carriers and decide on a minute-by-minute basis what station to assign them to based on variations in the model mix" . . . the carriers will make it easier . . . to assign different models of cars to the same plant.[22]

It is apparent from this model that what drives the change is a desire for greater flexibility in production systems (i.e., the ability to shift easily between models and variations within models) and what makes this possible is computer power. What is also apparent is that under this system tight job control is more costly than it was under a rigid assembly-line system. An observer of one prototype system structured along the lines just described concluded:

> There were numerous examples in this particular plant where hourly and salaried personnel required a greater breadth of knowledge of to carry out jobs as a result of modernization . . . electricians needed to learn how to use a number of different types of programmable devices, including robots, programmable logic controllers, programmable weld timers, and communications equipment that is used to link these devices to computers. Production workers on parts of the assembly line had to learn inspection techniques that were previously not a part of their tasks.[23]

One can, of course, imagine that a new industrial internal labor market/ job control system might emerge around this new production technology as workers gain seniority rights within teams, establish division of labor within teams, and develop bumping rights across teams. However, such a development would tend to rob the technology of much of its potential power and hence would be resisted by the firm. The key question, then, is how to avoid successfully a re-rigidification and what alternatives the automobile industry can offer its workers. In the automobile industry, and others like it with a long tradition of job control industrial internal labor markets, making this transition is very problematic. This is precisely the importance of the innovations that have accompanied some of the Japanese and joint Japanese-American automobile plants in the United States as well as the (not yet existing) Saturn Project.

In traditional American firms there are often over 100 job classifications. By contrast, in the words of researchers who have examined the new plants, "All Japanese (and Japanese-American) companies now operating in the U.S. emphasize a single broad job classification for production workers."[24] This job classification leads to an extensive job rotation system in the plants (i.e., flexible deployment) and substantially more extensive training than in comparable American plants.[25] How do these innovations influence productivity? It is very difficult to control carefully for all factors affecting the productivity of a plant, but the level of technology in these plants does not strike experienced observers as more advanced than American plants and, in the case of the G.M.-Toyota joint venture, the former G.M. plant itself is being used and the labor force is made up entirely of former employees from the old plant. Yet productivity in that venture, as well as in the purely Japanese plants, exceeds U.S. levels. At the G.M.-Toyota joint venture absenteeism is 3 to 4% compared to the former level of 25%, and labor productivity is estimated at 50% higher.[26]

In an effort to expand this system, G.M. has signed an agreement with the United Automobile Workers to establish at its new Saturn plant a production system with work teams, three to five job classifications, and a substantially diminished role for seniority. In return (as our discussion of the salaried model would lead us to expect), G.M. has agreed that "Saturn will not lay off Saturn members [regular employees] except in situations arising from unforeseen or catastrophic events or severe economic conditions."

The logic of the automobile production system described resembles the model developed by Michael Piore and Charles Sable, which they term "flexible specialization."[27] By this they mean use of computer-based technologies to create a more flexible production process that can economically produce shorter runs and hence respond to variations in demand. By achieving this flexibility, firms can offset the wage advantages of developing and midrange countries. In fact, many observers would dispute Piore and Sabel by arguing that the production system we described remains mass production, since most of the product variation comes from mixing together standardized parts that, in turn, are produced in long production runs. However, it is worth noting that Piore and Sable argue that flexible specialization will require more skilled labor, and they draw on the metaphor of craft production (i.e., a worker who has a broad concept of the production process and is able to respond effectively to unexpected or changing conditions). From our perspective it is better to think of such a labor force as embedded in a salaried internal labor market, since this makes it clear what kinds of arrangements are necessary to obtain the necessary flexibility in skills and deployment. What is useful about the typologies of internal labor markets developed here is that they focus attention not on polyvalent skill per se but on the conditions necessary to attain and deploy polyvalent skill in different settings.

At the heart of the Piore-Sable model is the view that changes in product markets explain the rise in flexible specialization. New technologies may make the model more widespread but are not central, since the technologies can be used in mass or flexible-specialization models and since flexible specialization can exist without new technologies.

> The implication of the ethnographic studies is that computers adapt to *any* environment. . . . Had the mass markets of the 1950's and 1960's endured in the 1970's, computer technology would have mirrored the rigidity of mass production. . . . There is another weakness in the technological determinist case . . . there are many instances of the flexible use of technologies which do not depend on computers. . . .[28]

The reason the G.E. case is important, then, is that it concerns a very rigid product design explicitly intended for mass production. Despite this focus on a standardized product with long runs, the G.E. case, driven by new technologies, also required a restructuring of internal labor market patterns away from the industrial model.

At the core of the G.E. example[29] was a decision in the early 1980s to invest in a new model dishwasher and a modern manufacturing facility (actually a facility within an existing plant) with which to produce it. What makes this different than the automobile case was that the product and the process was based on extreme standardization. The facility went from seven final products to one, with the production of so-called niche products removed from the plant and sent elsewhere. Within the product itself the number of parts was reduced from 5600 to 850. This plant, then, was designed as a dedicated plant aimed at the mass production of a standardized product. However, at the center of the production process was a computer-based manufacturing system, with many of the same characteristics (flexible carriers, computers tracking and providing real-time data on production flows and inventory, robots performing many functions) as that described in the automobile example, as well as more advanced aspects (the dishwashers are never touched by human hands during production).

Labor relations at the facility had been poor, with the company withdrawing several major technical investments—including a new foundry and a robot installation—due to resistance and sabotage. Yet in order for the new production procedure to be effective, the traditional job classification system had to change. Jobs on the new assembly line had to be broadened to include a diverse range of activities. These included tasks—maintenance of equipment, monitoring of the line, setup, repair of dishwashers with defects, data entry, and cleanup— that had previously been spread among a series of tightly defined jobs whose boundaries were enforced by union contract and custom. The new complexity of the work is illustrated by the comment of the plant manager: "We learned that training programs for this type of plant can't be off and on; they must be continuous and permanent features of the overall operation."[30]

The firm's solution was a combination of improved communication with the union, quality of work life groups, and the creation of a new and higher paid job classification. In addition, employment had been declining steadily in the plant as a whole and in the dishwasher production unit. The firm therefore explicitly linked future employment levels to the success of the new technology, and statements by the union made clear that their acceptance of the program was related to this link. In the end the program was successful, as productivity, output, quality, and employment all exceeded the expectations of the planners.

The automobile industry requires a wrenching organizational change, exemplified by Saturn Project, to transform effectively the industrial internal labor market system. The G.E. case represents a less extreme version of the same dilemma, one in which a new plant within a plant and a reverse of traditional union-management relations was necessary. The phone company case is perhaps at the other extreme. Here we can witness an equally revolutionary technological transformation with far-reaching implications for job content as well as employment levels. Yet the change was accomplished smoothly and with little difficulty because it was done in the context of a job security environment, with the union accepting broad and flexible job grades.

The example we work with here involves a new computer-based telephone repair system that was introduced in one of the regional phone systems.[31] Prior to the installation of this system, a residential customer calling to report a problem would be connected to a local (i.e., near the customer's home) office staffed by a clerk, who would take the call and record the customer's complaint. The complaint would then be passed to a screener (a high level clerical job), who would pull a card describing the customer's equipment and make an initial evaluation of the nature of the problem. The screener would then pass on the complaint, either to a tester in the central office or one in the local office, depending on the nature of the difficulty. The tester (a high-level craft job) would evaluate the problem and, if possible, fix it. If a field repair was necessary the complaint would be passed to a dispatch clerk, who would determine which crafts-level field repairperson to pass it to.

In the new system the residential call goes to a central office, which may be in another state. The call is taken by a clerk, who keys in the caller's phone number and, within 5 seconds, receives an on-screen description of the equipment in the customer's home, a diagnois of the problem, and an estimated repair time ("commitment time"). The message is then passed through computer to another central facility where, in most cases, it is routed to a field repairperson or is automatically fixed in the central office. In difficult cases a screener works with the repairperson in diagnosing the problem. The routing to the field repairperson currently involves a dispatch clerk, who works with a computer program that determines the nearest repairperson and makes the assignment. This dispatch clerk job is an atavism and is on the way out.

The key changes in the system involve centralization (one office for an entire state can handle all complaints and two or three can handle the repairs), the complete elimination of the skilled office testers, a job that had been on the top of the craft ladder, and a sharp reduction of the number of clerical workers required to receive complaints and screen problems. Only the field repair job remains intact, in content and number. From the customer's viewpoint the repairs are either effectively instantaneous or highly predictable in their timing and more rapid.

In a sense these changes were more far reaching than those described in the previous cases because more than expansion of job duties through flexible classifications was involved. In the phone case not only were employment levels reduced throughout the function, but several jobs were completely eliminated. Furthermore, the remaining jobs were very different in content, particularly in relationship to computers. Finally, the conditions of employment changed. Jobs that had been dispersed were centralized with consequences both for residence of workers and also for the employees' sense of connection with the customers. Furthermore, the jobs became increasingly paced by computer, with the frequency of calls and assignments machine paced and with considerable monitoring of individual productivity.

Despite all of these changes, the system was smoothly implemented from a human resources perspective. In part this was due to fortunate demographics: the work force was older and a number of people retired in the course of implementation. However, two additional elements were important. The first was the company's commitment to employment security. There were no layoffs, and all who wished them were offered positions (in the same wage grade) elsewhere. Second, the existing job classification system permitted considerable flexibility. Although there were many job titles, there were relatively few pay grades in the system. Each grade could contain as many titles as management desired. Hence the firm had considerable freedom in creating new titles and moving people from one title to another, provided that they stayed within the same pay grade.

To put these matters differently, the internal labor market system in place in the phone company was closer to a salaried than to an industrial model. Hence, what might otherwise have been a wrenching change, probably resisted and undermined, instead was accepted smoothly. As some regional phone companies now seek to reorganize work without employment security, our analysis suggests that the transition will be much more difficult.

Stepping back from the specifics of each case, several general conclusions stand out. First, as we asserted earlier, a dominant characteristic of the current generation of technologies is to alter traditional job classifications substantially. It is not possible to say with certainty whether the impact is in the direction of broader (more skilled) or more narrow (less skilled work); the automobile and G.E. examples suggest upgrading, while the phone company example points to deskilling. However, it is clear that considerable work reorganization is necessary. In fact, in many cases the reorganization is so substantial that it undermines traditional distinctions between blue and white collar jobs, a trend that is notable in cases in which shop-floor workers take on data entry, monitoring, and planning functions.

The second general conclusion is that changes of this magnitude seem to require systemwide adjustments. This is just what we would expect, given our view that the elements of the internal labor market fit together. Of particular interest is that the firm needs to address how the role of the rigid classification in providing security can be accomplished in other ways. We can also understand from the perspective of systemwide changes why the new pay plans— pay for knowledge, gain sharing, and so on—have become more popular. They can be interpreted as the sorts of shifts in the compensation system, from job-based to individual-based, which we would expect given the other transformations of industrial internal labor markets.

Pressures on the Salaried Model in White Collar Employment

Generally, one would expect that white collar employment would be under less pressure than blue collar industrial internal labor market systems because it is already organized along the lines of the salaried internal labor market model. Firms therefore should experience much less difficulty introducing new technologies, redefining jobs, and reallocating labor among various tasks. As an added buffer, white collar employment has long been regarded as overhead and hence as a fixed cost, while blue collar occupations were seen as a variable cost. However, as the number of blue collar workers fall and the perception emerges that firms are excessively staffed with overhead employment, employers are increasingly drawn to white collar labor as variable labor. Furthermore, this trend is exacerbated by the somewhat surprising fact that for some white collar occupations the amount of dislocation—job loss—induced by new technologies may be substantially higher than in blue collar work.

These shifts in the security of white collar employment are important because the resulting layoffs or induced retirements have the potential of undermining the premises of the salaried internal labor market system. Put differently, the problem in white collar work is not how to achieve a transition from an industrial to a salaried model but, instead, how to maintain the salaried model in the face of substantial employment reductions.

There are two fundamental reasons why new technologies place disproportionate pressure on certain categories of white collar work. On the shop floor there are a series of white collar workers—production planners, schedulers, inventory control staff, and even first-level supervisors—whose jobs are threatened by the reorganization implied by the new technologies. The functions of these workers now are accomplished either by the technology itself, or—perhaps more interestingly—are put into the hands of blue collar operatives who are now much more active in manipulating information and in planning. In fact, as both blue and white collar employees increasingly work with information, the boundary between them tends to vanish. A particularly dramatic illustration of the occurred recently in Sweden, a nation with strong separate blue and white collar unions, when the chairman of Volvo proposed that in a new plant the two unions be combined because the distinction between the categories of work was losing meaning. As an observer recently noted:

> Direct labor accounts for only 10 to 25 percent of the cost of manufacturing, and working engaged in such tasks make up only two-thirds of the total manufacturing workforce. The major challenge now, and the major opportunity for impoved productivity, is in organizing, scheduling and managing the total manufacturing enterprise, from product design to fabrication, distribution, and field service. . . . For this reason the most important contribution to the productivity of the factory offered by data processing technology is its capacity to link design, management and manufacturing into a network of commonly available information. The social outcome of linkage may be to alter far more white collar jobs than blue collar ones.[32]

In addition to changes on the shop floor the other, and numerically more significant, development is in the office. Here the impact is potentially very large. A major function of managers and clerks is information processing: digesting large amounts of data and presenting them in more accessible form to higher levels of management. With new technologies top executives are better able to access these data directly, and the need for numerous intermediate layers of management is reduced. In addition, information technology makes planning itself more efficient and less labor intensive. Finally, at a less grand level, the data entry and retrieval work of clerks can bc accomplished more effectively by computers and, as the clerical work force is reduced, the number of managers who supervise that work force can be limited. For these reasons we can expect potentially large displacement effects.

A recent study we conducted found just such impacts. Working with time series data on employment, wage rates, output, and use of computers in 40 industries, we studied the impact of increases in the use of computers on the employment of clerks and managers.[33] Our finding was that a 10% increase in computing power (the details of how this is measured are provided in the reference) reduced clerical employment by 1.8% and managerial employment by 1.2%. Given the very large increase in computing power of the period, this represents a substantial employment effect. In looking at the time paths of the displacement, we discovered evidence supporting the hypothesis that some employment came back as firms used computers to expand management functions. Nonetheless, the net effect was substantial employment loss due to the expanded use of computers.

These results are the only generalizable (i.e., noncase study) direct evidence currently available on how new technologies impact certain categories of white collar work. However, the case study literature also suggests a similar conclusion. The nature of this literature is best summarized by the Leontiff-Duchin review. They predict that by 1990 the employment of managers will be 13.8% below what it would be without the expansion they project of information technology, and the employment of clerks will be 32.3% below baseline levels. By 2000 they project enormous declines of 41% and 45% respectively.[34]

There is considerable surface evidence that white collar work has become more insecure. In the past few years a series of substantial white collar layoffs in large companies—Kodak, Ford, New York Life, AT&T, CBS, and so on—have made the "squeeze on middle management" a prominent topic in the business press. Indeed, *Business Week* reported recently that 89 of the largest 100 firms have established programs aimed at reducing management levels.[35] As we have suggested, the problem that this poses is how to maintain commitment and consent of the labor force, a commitment that is part of the salaried model, at the same time that a key element of that model is being called into question. This tension is the most difficult issue facing human resource management in white collar employment.

The Firm's Dilemma

We have argued that in the case of blue collar work currently organized along industrial lines there is a set of incentives for firms to shift to salaried internal labor market structures. Thus far we have made it seem as if this choice was clear. In fact, there are several complications, notably the opposition of many managers to employment systems that provide explicit job security and an uncertain macroeconomic environment that may make job security too expensive.

A serious difficulty confronting any advocate of transforming the industrial internal labor market into a salaried system is the costs that firms perceive to be associated with commitments to employment security. One such cost lies in perceptions about what such a system would do to worker incentives and management power. Most Americans actually enjoy considerable job security. We have already seen that job durations for a substantial fraction (although still a minority) of the currently employed are very long—usually greater than 20 years—and there is also good evidence that firms resist layoffs (or hoard labor) over the business cycle.[36] We have argued that absolute promises of job security, or the sort provided by IBM and the handful of "model" firms such as Lincoln Electric that have adopted job security, is not a necessary component of the salaried model. What is important is that job security be an important "value" of the firm and that the labor force perceive this and be convinced of it through a series of actions intended to stabilize employment and eliminate or reduce layoffs. However, even the more modest security pledges implied by the salaried model pose problems when implemented on a large scale. The reason why job security is often unacceptable to firms is illustrated by the explanation provided by a Polaroid manager for the *abolition* of its security pledge and the subsequent layoff of thousands of employees: "A lot of people thought working at Polaroid was like having a government job. That just couldn't go on."[37]

Put less vividly, the cost of explicit job security—even when product market conditions permit it—is perceived to be the loss of initiative by the worker and the loss of control by the firm. Whether this is true is, in present circumstances, almost beside the point, so widely shared is this perception. In this regard it is worth noting that the Japanese system, which is often celebrated for its "life-time employment," did not simply emerge either from an alternative cost benefit calculus by firms or from an alternative cultural tradition. Employers initially opposed security pledges, and the current system emerged from a very heated period of labor unrest.[38]

A second cost that makes managers leery of the salaried model follows from uncertainty about the level of demand in the economy. One source of uncertainty is at the product level. Here some observers are arguing that the trajectory of technical change is reducing economies of scale and hence permitting easier entry, that consumer tastes have become volatile, and that marketing practices increase volitility.[39] Although the popular press is full of claims that tend to support the general notion of increased variety and uncertainty in the product market, rigorous tests of these arguments are hard to find. The best evidence seems to be drawn from studies of product life cycles. If life cycles (defined as points on a curve that plot growth rates in sales) are shortening, there is reason to believe that firms will find themselves needing to retool more often. In fact, the only study with time series data along these lines, an examination of trends of sales of home appliances over a 60-year period, finds clear evidence of a reduction in life-cycle length and that this reduction has accelerated in recent years (1965–79). The research determined how long it took sales growth rates to reach a plateau, found that "maturity" occurs much more rapidly than in the past, and concluded that: "Today's marketing managers face Product Life Cycle's approaching the kind that have historically characterized the clothing or fashion industries."[40]

A second source of uncertainty lies at the macrolevel of economic performance. If demand fluctuates, it becomes difficult to implement any sort of security pledge. Although the economy has experienced a lengthy expansion, the continuing problems of trade imbalances, budget deficits, and currency fluctuations must force business to conclude that the aggregate economy has grown more uncertain over the past decade and a half.

What these facts do is to raise a flag to firms concerning their ability to forecast and maintain employment levels. The rules of industrial internal labor markets are more accommodating to layoffs than those of salaried models, and if aggregate demand, and hence employment demand, is likely to exhibit large and unpredictable swings, firms may respond by exercising caution in making implict or explict employment promises.

In the case of white collar employment the difficulties and qualifications are less severe but still nagging. Although many white collar occupations do not face the kind of reductions described for managers and clerks (e.g., the employment of professionals is expected to surge in the next two decades), it remains true that many firms are seeking to reduce management employment levels and bureaucratic layers. The salaried model is already in place in these settings, so the key issue is whether it can survive the pressure that employment reductions will place on it. If the promises that employees assume exist are violated as white collar work becomes more insecure, firms may face, at the minimum, loss of commitment and goodwill by their employees—a substantial loss given the inability of firms to monitor employee performance continuously—and, at the maximum, a growing interest in white collar unionism. Indeed, there is some evidence from opinion polls that negative ratings by managers and clerical workers toward their employers have increased more rapidly in recent years than those of hourly employees. One such survey found that "managers and professionals show signs of the same degree of discontent that used to be more typical of clerical and hourly employees. Middle managers feel expendible."[41] Other polls find similar patterns.

The concern of firms to maintain the flexiblity of salaried internal labor markets in the face of the need to reduce employment helps explain the popularity of early retirement or "incentive retirement" schemes. Under these arrangements employment is reduced by offering sweetened pensions and other financial incentives in return for early retirement. The question, of course, is why these firms do not save the expense by laying off the workers just as they have customarily done in the case of blue collar employees working under industrial internal labor markets. The answer is that such bold actions would risk losing the commitment of the workers who remain at the firm and hence undermine the advantages of the salaried model.

An example of how these expectations are expressed is found in the reactions of an Exxon employee to that company's recently announced plan for substantial reduction in white collar employment levels:

> Employees have come to expect a certain concern from the company. Now, there's a feeling that something as drastic as this wasn't necessary and that it's being rushed through. There's a feeling that established systems are being ignored and a lot of cronyism as to who stays is going on. It's very un-Exxon.[42]

The sense of betrayal and the fear of favoritism are precisely the concerns that led to industrial workers in the 1920s seeking to alter the so-called "drive" system of foreman control and replace it with a system of unionism of the sort we have characterized as the industrial model.[43]

Some Resolutions of the Dilemma

What is the nature of a solution to these conflicting pressures? As we have already observed, the current period is marked by numerous efforts at experimentation in employee relations and human resource management, and it is far from clear how matters will be resolved. An illustration of this confusion is provided by the recent negotiations in the steel industry. In the past the industry had negotiated a uniform national contract with the United Steel Workers. However, competitive pressure undermined this uniformity and, in 1986, the union was forced to negotiate separately with each firm. The diversity of the offers illustrates the lack of clarity concerning the direction of industrial internal labor markets.

National Steel, the sixth largest steelmaker, offered its workers a no-layoff pledge over the life of the contract, profit sharing, and increased worker responsibility on the shop floor. In return it asked for revision of the job classification system and elimination of some restrictions on the deployment of workers to the various jobs. In short, the company attempted to move from an industrial to a salaried model. Set against this was the Bethlehem Steel position, which envisioned little revision of the basic industrial system but simply worker pay concessions. The other firms were arrayed between these two extremes.[44]

This diversity and confusion is mirrored throughout the economy, and it is not possible to claim that a single pattern is emerging. Instead, it seems that the organization of both blue and white collar work can go in one of several directions. Perhaps the two most common efforts both represent efforts to finesse the issue. In the first strategy, which is most relevant to blue collar work, firms simply attempt to force a series of work-place changes without offering any compensating modification in internal labor market rules. In the second case, which applies to both white and blue collar employment, firms establish or maintain the salaried model but only for a limited segment of their labor force. We discuss each of these options and, in both cases, our tentative conclusion is that the strategies are self-limiting and unlikely to succeed on a broad scale over time.

Concession Bargaining or Employer Militancy

One entirely plausible strategy is for firms to avoid the costs of the salaried model—the explicit or implicit job security component—by simply forcing work rule changes within the context of the industrial model. This, of course, is a central aspect of concession bargaining in which modifications of work practices are often as important to the firm as reductions in wage levels. Outside collective bargaining management would seem to have even a freer hand in unilaterally imposing changes in work rules, and there have been numerous recent examples in which they have done just that.

How viable is this strategy? We can first note that it cannot be universally applicable, since even its short-run success rests on a balance of power decisively in favor of management. Despite the weakened position of unions, this cannot always be assumed, as several recent union successes illustrate.[45]

Although it cannot be applied universally, it is apparent that the aggressive management strategy is increasingly possible, at least in the short run. The question remains whether is represents a stable, long-run solution.

Unilateral imposition of work rule changes in effect violates the bargain implicit in the industrial model in which management retains the power to hire and fire at will while workers partially protect the volume of employment and individual outcomes through the work rules. The issue is the range of possible responses to a one-sided shift in these terms. The obvious response is to withhold effort on the shop floor and hence reduce productivity. This threat, if carried out aggressively on a broad basis, has the potential of raising the cost of the work rule changes and hence rendering the new system more costly than its potential gains.

Although this argument makes sense in principle, the question is whether there is any evidence of its validity. It has long been a fundamental assumption in the industrial relations literature that shop-floor peace and mutually acceptable human resources practices are an essential prerequisite for productivity but, in fact, there is very little hard evidence on this point. One might argue instead that after an initial period of difficulty, the labor force will simply come to accept the new situation and work as before.

Although the research on this point is extremely thin, three recent studies provide some evidence that productivity is related to shop-floor consent. The first two studies are based on automobile industry data. Using time series data on the entire automobile industry, Norsworthy and Zabala[46] estimated cost functions using the standard price and input variables and then added variables measuring grievance rates, strike behavior, and quit behavior. They found strong evidence that increases in grievance rates were associated with drops in productivity; their results for strikes and quits were similar, albeit somewhat weaker. They also constructed a "worker behavior" index and found that a 10% improvement in that index was associated with a 5% increase in productivity.

Time series results of this sort are always slightly suspect because they are highly aggregative, and much else may be going on in the data. However, the second study provides complementary microlevel confirmation. Harry Katz, Thomas Kochan, and Kenneth Gobeille collected data on a set of industrial relations variables and outcome variables in 18 G.M. plants.[47] The four industrial relations variables were grievance rates, absenteeism rates, discipline rates, and the results of a survey on shop-floor "climate." These variables were correlated against two measures of output: a quality index for cars produced in each plant and an index of labor input per car that controlled for capital in place and the model being built.

The results of these correlations were striking. Of the eight pairs of correlations (each of the four industrial relations variables against each of the two outcome variables), the correlations were in the expected direction and statistically significant in seven cases. That is, increases in grievance rates, discipline rates, and absenteeism rates reduced quality and output, while improvements in climate increased output and quality.

Katz, Kochan, and Gobeille also examined a specific program, quality of work life, and here their results were much more equivocal. Nonetheless, it is clear from this research that at least in the automobile industry poor shop-floor relations entails a cost.

The third research project along these lines, conducted by Thomas Weisskopf, Samuel Bowles, and David Gordon, is helpful in generalizing these findings.[48] They were interested in demonstrating the general point that shop-floor relations affects output, and they proceeded by estimating a regression model explaining year-to-year changes in productivity for the U.S. economy. Their argument is that the puzzle of the U.S. productivity decline can be explained by explicit consideration of work-place relations. They included a number of variables aimed at capturing both the cost (to workers) of uncooperative behavior and the quality of jobs as provided by employers. The most unproblematic of these variables is the industrial accident rate, which they interpret as a measure of working conditions. When this rate is used as an explanatory variable in equations estimating the determinants of year-to-year changes in productivity, the results consistently showed a negative relationship. That is, in years in which the accident rate is high, the change in productivity is low. A skeptic, of course, would question the explanatory mechanism and claim that it is not surprising that if accidents are high productivity is low, but Weisskopf, Bowles, and Gordon also report finding (in unreported regressions) that the accident rate measure is a powerful variable in an equation explaining year-to-year levels of reported worker satisfaction.

The three studies reported provide some reason for believing that the management militancy or concession bargaining approach will be limited in its results. None, however, is fully convincing on this point because while they demonstrate costs it is still possible that the benefits (from management's perspective) are higher. Furthermore, it is hard to know whether an initial period of unrest will tail off into acceptance. There are, however, other reasons to believe that the strategy is limited. The kinds of pressures on the industrial model that we have described will be on-going, not one-shot affairs. Put differently, an effective firm will want a work force that is willing to accept continually new technologies and new assignments. It is more plausible to believe that the management militancy strategy can gain acquiescence once than it is to believe that it will work again and again.

These arguments suggest that in the long run firms will find it necessary to reach an accommodation. If they want to alter the industrial model, they will have to offer a version of the salaried model. Although persuasive, however, the point is speculative and it may be, the foregoing evidence notwithstanding, that a more draconian policy is possible. We will have to remain open minded on this question (at least from a positive if not a normative viewpoint), and part of the confusion in the current human resources scene results from the fact that a number of companies are following this strategy. At the same time, others are rejecting it. A very common alternative is the core-periphery model to which we will now turn.

The Core-Periphery Model

Unlike the concession bargaining or employer militancy approach, the core-periphery model offers at least half a loaf and also cuts across both blue and white collar employment. The model can be characterized as an effort by firms to combine features of the salaried and the secondary models. This implies the creation of a relatively small-core labor force organized along the lines of the salaried model and a peripheral labor force consisting of temporaries, part-timers, and other employees who are simply not provided with the protections afforded the core workers.

The logic of the core-periphery model is straightforward. By establishing a labor force that is smaller than that actually required for normal production levels, the firm is able to offer that labor force relative security. In return, these employees are willing to work under the salaried model and to provide both flexibilty and commitment to the firm. The peripheral labor force provides the firm with a buffer against either macroeconomic—cyclical—downturns or labor force reductions necessitated by technical change.

Several problems are raised by this model. In particular, it is not clear whether the peripheral labor force will be sufficiently skilled or committed to perform the same tasks as the core group; if they are not, the firm may be unable to create buffers in the key positions. In addition, it is unclear whether the model is stable. Over time the peripheral labor force may seek employment arrangements more comparable to those of the core group. For the moment we will ignore these caveats and examine the evidence that this model is spreading.

Returning first to the automobile industry—the prototypical traditional industrial internal labor market—several innovations suggest a shift in the direction we have described. As part of the 1982 contract, Ford and G.M. agreed to experiment in several plants with a job security pledge. In return—just as our discussion suggests—they asked for the elimination of restrictive work rules (i.e., flexible job classification and deployment) and authorization to hire 10% of the work force as temporary employees with no security rights. This deal was made and is currently in force at the Ford Rawsonville plant in Michigan. A similar agreement was signed between the I.U.E. and G.M. for the Packard Electric plant in Ohio. The joint G.M.-Toyota venture, New United Motors Manufacturing Inc., which produces cars in the former G.M. Freemont, California, facility, has provisions in its contract permitting the use of temporary workers with no permanent job rights. The foregoing are examples of core-periphery arrangements in existing automobile plants. The Saturn contract, for a future plant, establishes a category of employee termed "associate member," and the contract states that "up to 20% of the work force may consist of associate members. While every attempt will be made to avoid layoff of associate members, they will not be covered by the Job Security Provision." In effect, the firm is establishing a class of employees outside the protected core, and this group will bear the brunt of insecurity.

Similar arrangements are found in some of the recent so-called "two-tier" agreements generated in recent rounds of concession bargaining. Under two-tier plans newly hired workers receive lower wages than incumbents. Plans of this sort are becoming more common; according to the Bureau of National Affairs, 11% of 1985 labor agreements included two-tier plans, up from 5% in 1983.[49] Although these plans vary—some call for the second-tier workers to catch up eventually with incumbents, while others leave them at a permanent disadvantage—for our purposes what is interesting are provisions that create less job security in the second tier. An example is the American Airlines contract in which the incumbents received lifetime job security while the second tier did not. In addition, that contract permitted increased use of part-time and temporary workers who received no protection at all under the agreement.[50]

Although the previous examples are drawn from collective bargaining situations, the core-periphery model is hardly limited to that setting. We have already described how IBM protects its core work force with a number of buffers. In white collar work extensive anecdotal evidence as well as field research suggest that firms are increasingly employing temporary staff, outside consultants, contract workers, and the like. These employees work at all skill levels. For example, in interviews with 12 large white collar employers in Boston, we found that 8 had recently established in-house temporary work pools, in effect internalizing the profits of outside agencies while maintaining the same flexibility by creating a work force outside normal personnel rules. The interviews also demonstrated that the use of such temporaries is not limited to clerical workers but includes occupations such as engineers, computer programmers, and draftspersons.[51] This same point was made forcefully by Mangum, Mayhill, and Nelson in their report of interviews with 74 San Francisco employers:

> Those interviews showed that if the "Kelly Girl" image of the Temporary Help Service Industry as primarily a clerical phenomenon was ever accurate, it is no longer. Electronics firms used temporary drafters and assemblers . . . mechanical engineers, technical writers, and programmers were also hired through Temporary Help Service Firms. Chemical firms . . . hired temporary computer programmers and chemical engineers. In finance and insurance . . . there were switchboard operators, data-entry operators, and accountants evident as well. . . . Trucking firms deployed temporary workers as both drivers and warehouse help . . . at hospitals the . . . demand was primarily for nurses, but some technician occupations were also required.[52]

An especially striking example of the use of the core-periphery model is found in the high-technology Silicon Valley of California. Estimates of the number of temporary workers in the labor force range from 10 to 30%[53] and, in addition, heavy use is made of undocumented or illegal workers. According to one estimate, 25% of the labor force is illegal.[54] *Business Week* characterized the situation in particularly graphic terms: "Blue Collar Workers in Silicon

Valley seem almost akin to migrant workers travelling from one semi-conductor 'field' to the next as crops flourish or fail."[55]

These examples all suggest that the core-periphery model represents a real phenomenon and describes an important category of employment arrangements. However, it would be helpful to have more than simply anecdotal evidence on the extent of this pattern. Unfortunately, there is no easy way to provide a measure of the prevalence of core-periphery systems in a national cross section, much less over time.

Data on the increase in temporary help agency employment are strongly suggestive. Figures supplied by The National Association of Temporary Services, Inc., suggest that between 1971 and 1981 gross revenue increased from $612 million to $5.2 billion. Data supplied by the same organization for the 1980s, using a different measure, shows payroll increasing from $3 billion in 1980 to $6 billion in 1985.[56] In fact, a recent independent study suggested that between 1982 and 1984 the temporary help industry grew faster than all other industries, with employment greater than 50,000.[57] Working with a different source—the Bureau of the Census's County Business Patterns—Mangum, *et al.* report a 50% growth in the number of temporary help firms between 1977 and 1979.[58] These agencies provide temporary help for a wide range of skills, with a recent survey finding that the employment of clericals accounted for just under 60% of such jobs, professionals 20%, and other occupations the remainder.[59] According to the best available estimate, in 1983 a total of 2.5 million persons worked for these agencies at some point during the year.[60] A broader concept of "contingent work" led to an estimate of 18 million total employment, up from 8 million in 1980.[61]

The use of formal temporary help agencies is, in fact, an understatement of the extent of this practice. As we have already noted, it is common for companies to establish in-house temporary pools, internalizing the advantages and avoiding fees. The best available survey (a national probability sample of 1200 firms in six industries: health, business service, finance and insurance, retail, transportation, and manufacturing) found that 25 to 35% of firms over 250 employees had established such internal pools.[62]

Limitations and Alternatives to the Core-Periphery Model

It is apparent that the core-periphery model holds a number of attractions to firms. It enables them to achieve substantial internal flexiblity with a highly trained and committed labor force while, at the same time, maintaining the ability to adjust employment levels at will. Given these advantages, one would expect it to expand and it is almost certainly doing so. Nonetheless, there are good reasons to doubt that in the United States employment systems will evolve toward the extreme version of the core-periphery model that characterizes the Japanese system.[63]

One limitation on the model comes from the supply side. The core-periphery model can only work on a large scale if a sufficiently large labor force is available for the unstable and inferior conditions associated with employment under secondary subsystems (i.e., in the periphery). Peripheral work arrangements take various forms, ranging from permanent part-time employment within firms to temporary workers to contracted work. Each of these has a slightly different character and draws on a different labor force. Hence the total peripheral labor force might include women looking for part-time work, undocumented workers working on production lines, young people just entering the labor force, and skilled workers who, for "life-style" reasons, want to maintain flexiblity in their work attachment. It is obviously difficult to generalize about the supply trends for such disparate groups. On balance, however, the trends seem to be in the direction of a more slowly growing supply than has characterized the past two decades.

No one would dispute that women historically have formed the largest group of peripheral workers. Two facts suggest that growth of this pool will slow. First, although female participation rates will continue to rise, they will surely do so at a diminished rate. In 1960 the gap between the male and female participation rates was nearly 50 points; in 1983 it stood at just over 20 points. Although the gap will continue to close, there are limits; even in Sweden, the nation with the most generous family support policy in the West, the participation rate gap between men and women remains 10 points.[64]

Even more significant is the changing character of the female labor supply. Women are less interested in peripheral work and are more committed to full-time labor force participation under more stable and rewarding conditions. A strong signal of this is that although part-time employment by women increased sharply during the 1960s and most of the 1970s, it leveled off in the early 1980s. Between 1982 and 1985 full-time employment of women over the age of 20 increased by 11.9%, while part-time employment for the same age group increased by only 4.4%.[65] In the more sophisticated econometric work that controls for the business cycle, Bernard Ichniowski and Anne Preston found no significant time trend for voluntary part-time work for 1973–85.[66]

We have already seen that another potential source of peripheral workers, young people, is drying up; this is especially significant, since available surveys suggest that temporary workers are overwhelmingly young.[67] This leaves basically two options for a sharply increased supply. One group might be the middle-aged people who are interested in working as contractors or temporaries in order, among other reasons, to maintain their independence or be able to work at home. Although much is made of this group in the business press, it is difficult to believe that they represent a substantial number of people. Indeed, the hard evidence suggests that as people age, they become more interested in security, not less. The second possible source are older workers, but this would require a reversal of the trend toward declining participation rates of older workers.[68]

In response to these arguments one might argue that in the long run, firms have shown great ingenuity in overcoming labor supply constraints. While more difficult and costly, firms might only offer peripheral jobs and attempt to induce (and coerce) an adequate labor supply. Even if such a strategy were possible, there are, from the company's perspective, reasons to limit the size of the peripherial labor force. That labor force is, by definition, not committed to the firm and has not been socialized in its norms. Commitment and socialization are, as we have seen, very valuable, and it is highly doubtful that a prudent firm will be willing to entrust a substantial fraction of its work load to such a labor force. Furthermore, as we will see in a moment, one cannot simply assume that firms can shape the labor supply to their own needs.

Another way of highlighting the limitations of the core-periphery model is to ask whether firms that have followed it have indeed been able to maintain employment security in the face of fluctuations in aggregate demand. We will take up this question in more detail in Chapter 7, but for now we can note that there is substantial reason for doubt. For every IBM or Eli Lilly that has maintained its commitment to employment security, there is a Polaroid, Kodak, or Data General that has backed away. Furthermore, the firms that have maintained the policy have often done so through disguised layoffs (e.g., early retirements that are generated under somewhat coercive circumstances).

None of the foregoing is intended to argue that the use of peripheral labor is not likely to expand somewhat. Indeed, there may be alternative ways of accomplishing the same functional outcomes (e.g., by establishing the sort of mother firm-supplier arrangements that typify Japanese manufacturing). However, short of such a major reorganization of the production system, which itself entails difficulties, the use of peripheral labor, while significant, seems unlikely to expand sufficiently to represent an adequate solution to the earlier dilemmas we posed.

An Additional Constraint on Managerial Options

In the foregoing material we argued that both the employer militancy and the core-periphery strategies are not likely to serve as stable, long-run solutions to the pressures on the industrial or salaried models. Our arguments were, in effect, that each "solution" is self limiting in its own terms: the employer militancy approach will lead to reduced productivity and conflict, especially in the context of the need for continual flexiblity, while the core-periphery model requires a larger flexible labor force and more employer risk-taking than is likely to be forthcoming. There is another reason why firms will be leery, and this is that they may well set the stage for a new round of aggressive and successful union organizing.

Although unions are clearly on the defensive, it does not follow that companies may organize work with impunity. A strong historical lesson can be drawn from the 1920s and 1930s. Throughout most of the 1920s, union weakness was widespread and companies reacted by either simply ignoring worker interests or by attempting to create a new form of internal labor market organization—the so-called American Plan—which in many respects resembled what we are calling the salaried model.[69] With the onset of the Depression the American Plan was abandoned, and the only strategy that endured was employer militancy. As the subsequent surge of unionization demonstrated, employer militancy is a tenuous approach that may well undermine itself. Employer strength and union weakness at one point does not imply that the balance of power cannot change in the next period.

This lesson might seem most applicable to blue collar settings in which the potential for renewed union strength or new organizing drives seems strongest. However, in white collar work the human resources staff of firms certainly remain concerned about the potential for new organizing efforts, particularly among groups that have been marginalized by the employment system. For example, in the Boston white collar inteviews cited earlier, the firms that had not set up internal temporary help pools were those who felt most threatened by union organizing campaigns. Indeed, prominent among recent organizing efforts are those by clerical workers and hospital workers that have been aimed at the peripheral work force. The lesson, then, is that for both blue and white collar work it may not be possible for firms to maintain successfully the temporizing strategies implied by employer militancy or core-periphery approaches.

The Firm's Dilemma Once Again and the Role of Public Policy

Blue collar and white collar work are under different pressures, but the central nature of the dilemma is the same in both cases. White collar employment has historically been structured along salaried lines, but pressures on cost (the drive to reduce overhead staff) and technological displacement are increasing insecurity. The problem facing firms is how to achieve these employment reductions while maintaining the salaried model for those who remain. For blue collar employment the salaried model remains a goal. The issue is how to transform industrial systems in that direction. More generally, both blue and white collar work firms face conflicting objectives, and the current institutional structure does not offer them support for finding a solution.

Blue collar employers have the option of attempting to force through the necessary flexiblity by what we term the employer militancy strategy. Although there are opportunities for short-run success, it is our best judgment that this strategy is unlikely to be successful in the long run. Other blue collar employers and many white collar firms are experimenting with a second strategy, the core-periperhy model. This seems to hold out greater promise but, for the reasons noted, it seems self limiting.

It therefore seems that many firms will find it difficult to alter their internal labor markets successfully or to maintain what they have achieved. In addition to the objective constraints, there is also the matter of managerial ideology. The key bargain of the salaried model, placing a high value on employment security and being willing to endure costs in order to maintain that value, is difficult for many managers to accept. What, then, is the likely course of events? The best guess would be a modest expansion of core-periphery arrangements combined with continued confusion concerning the shape of industrial and salaried models elsewhere. In some instances assaults on industrial models will succeed and through concession bargaining, relocation of economic production, or substantial technological change combined with layoffs, a new pattern will emerge. In other instances firms will succeed in achieving a transition from an industrial to a salaried system. More often than not a stalemate will result, and little change will ensue.

Why should this be a matter of public concern? At the center of our answer is the view that economic and perhaps political performance would be improved with more widespread adoption of the salaried model. From the firm's perspective the salaried model offers precisely those characteristics, flexibility and commitment, that optimize the productivity of new technologies and enable adequate responses to a more volatile competitive environment. From the worker's perspective the job security commitment, if credible, is highly valuable and, in all likelihood, a more than adequate substitute for relaxed work rules. An easy way to see this is to observe the long queues for employment at the few firms that currently organize blue collar work along these lines. From a societal perspective the higher productivity associated with the salaried model is valuable, but possibly of equal value is the greater economic equity. The salaried model entails greater employment security and, in contrast to the employer militancy strategy, broader acceptance of work-place jurisprudence and employee rights.

If the salaried model is superior, why the difficulty in achieving it? It is apparent that the reason for its attractiveness is a mixture of efficiency and equity considerations. The equity issues are unlikely to excite private action or risk taking. Even the efficiency rational may not be enough if the risk of action is seen to be too high. To put the matter differently, we may be in a trap similar to that identified by Kenneth Arrow in his analysis of discrimination.[70] A combination of ignorance, uncertainty, and risk prevent firms from taking actions that, if taken, would ultimately improve their performance.

The case for public action is therefore that the salaried model is "better" in the equity sense and that once adopted it would improve private performance, but to accomplish the adoption requires a mixture of public incentives and risk sharing. Public policy would therefore take two forms. The first would be a set of incentives that lower the costs and ease the diffusion of the salaried model. The second would be an employment policy that helps provide the degree of job security necessary to close the salaried model. Put differently, if job security cannot currently be provided by the firm on its own, perhaps it can be provided publicly and linked to shifts in internal labor market structures. Could societal or "external" job security be a substitute for firm-based policies? Can we conceive of a public employment policy which is linked to internal labor markets in a way that addresses the dilemmas facing firms? To answer this question, we need to understand the history and structure of U.S. employment policy, a topic that Chapter 5 takes up. We will then turn, in Chapter 6, to an extensive discussion of Sweden and Germany, two nations where, in fact, public employment policy is linked to the operation of internal labor markets in many of the ways that seem relevant to our discussion.

5

The Record of American Employment Policy

Chapters 1 to 4 assessed the performance of the American labor market and reached a judgment about some appropriate areas for an active employment policy. We approached this from two vantage points: the individual and the firm. Although the labor market performs well in several ways, there are still significant problems facing individuals. These fall into two categories: persistent low income and difficulty in adjusting to layoffs and unemployment. Although there is some overlap between these categories, in general, each refers to distinct groups. We also saw reason to believe that these difficulties may increase. In particular, as the labor force ages, it will become less mobile and flexible and therefore have greater difficulty adjusting to demand shocks caused by product market developments or new technologies. Furthermore, the aging of the labor force is likely to bring job security to the fore as a serious issue.

When we inquired about the organization of the labor market from the firm's perspective, job security also emerged as a central issue. We saw that the structure of internal labor markets is a choice variable and is subject to a set of conflicting objectives and constraints. It seems optimal today for firms to shift in the direction of what we termed the salaried model, but there are a number of obstacles to this transition. Chief among these is the difficulty of providing sufficient job security to serve as an exchange for changes in the industrial job control model, in the blue collar case, or for technologically induced slimmed-down staffing in the white collar setting. Many firms currently avoid the hard choices by taking advantage of their power in the labor market to force employees to give up job control without compensating them with security. However, there is considerable doubt that this solution will prove viable in the long run as the current economic and political climate changes. Here again we suggest that there is a potential role for public policy.

What are the possibilities and limits of employment policy? The argument as developed thus far would lead us to search for an employment policy that could effectively help ease labor market adjustment, provide a measure of employment security and, in doing this, be useful to firms as they attempt to transform their internal labor markets. However, most U.S. employment pol-

92

icies have not been aimed at broad-based labor market issues but, instead, have been limited to the problems of poor people. Furthermore, the evaluation evidence of these programs leads to the inescapable conclusion that they have not worked well. One of the key reasons for the failure of these policies has been their narrow focus on the bottom segment of the labor market. This has left the programs' "graduates" stigmatized as they sought work, and has led firms to view these programs as irrelevant to their needs. Hence what might seem at first glance a reasonable allocation of scarce resources has led, by its very logic, to failure. The ultimate argument of Chapters 6 and 7 is that the difficulties facing firms and the work-force issues of adjustment and security may open up new interest, possibilities, and constituencies for an active employment policy. Were that to happen, one of the key challenges would be to find a way to link programs addressed to poor people with those aimed at better established workers and firms. This would provide a way to serve the traditional clientele of these programs in a manner that avoids stigmatization and failure. At the same time, by addressing a broader range of concerns, employment policy as a whole might move closer to being a central element of economic policy.

In this chapter we describe and assess the record of U.S. employment policy. The results are not encouraging, despite all the work and commitment that those involved in the programs have provided. This suggests that the problem is structural, that the programs have failed to link with real economic needs. In order to explore what such linkages might look like, in Chapter 6 we examine the structure of European employment policy, notably those of Germany and Sweden. The point here is not to identify programs to borrow, but to demonstrate that under some circumstances employment policy can be linked to the larger economy. Chapter 7 sketches a possible set of policy considerations for the United States.

The Structure and Performance of American Employment Policy

Even though labor market programs are small by comparison with some European countries, we do have an array of tools—a large vocational education establishment, vocationally oriented community colleges, a labor exchange (the Employment Service), and various job training programs—that we might deploy. There have also been recent suggestions for new initiatives, for example, Individual Training Accounts (a technique for providing vouchers to individuals for retraining over their working life), and programs that link the receipt of welfare payments with acceptance of job training. However, before we begin suggesting new ideas, it seems important to get a sense of the scope and performance of past efforts.

The first task in analyzing American employment policy is figuring out what we mean by the term. Most commentators probably think first of the array of remedial job training programs that were launched early in the 1960s, reached their (financial) high point in the 1970s with the Comprehensive Employment and Training Act (CETA), and currently are delivered by the Job Training

Partnership Act (JTPA). In fact, however, very similar training is also provided in the public schools by vocational education programs and at the postsecondary level by community colleges. In addition, the government attempts to speed job matching through the Employment Service.

Once we begin adding programs to the list, the harder question is not what to include but what to exclude. After all, in addition to the activities just listed the government also establishes minimum wages, requires that federal contracters pay "prevailing wages" in construction activities (the Davis-Bacon Act), sets the rules for union activity, and in numerous other ways influences the functioning of the labor market. Although a fully general treatment of all public policy aimed at the labor market would be an admirable achievement, we will not attempt it here. Instead, we will return to the themes of the prior chapters and define employment policies as those programs aimed at addressing the problems of employment dislocation, job security, and low earnings. These interventions are to be distinguished from legislation, which sets the framework or rules for the functioning of the labor market as a whole. Hence we will consider programs aimed at teaching skills so inner-city youth, community college students, and dislocated workers as well as efforts to establish an efficient labor exchange. However, we will take as given the legislation that frames the American industrial relations system or the Fair Labor Standards Act, which establishes compensation rules for the entire economy. Of course, we recognize that this distinction between interventions and rule setting carries a degree of naiveté: advocates of one or another set of rules regard them as tactics for influencing the well-being of specific groups. It may also be that rule setting and not activist intervention is ultimately a more effective way to affect the functioning of the labor market. We will return to these questions but, for now, will use the distinction as a handhold on what would otherwise be an unmanageable topic.

With these distinctions in mind it is possible to identify three categories of American employment policy: remedial or ameliorative programs, skills training for the masses, and the labor market exchange. We will describe each of these and provide a summary of what the social science evaluation literature has to say about their effectiveness.

The Remedial System

A significant and, in the minds of many observers, major element of American employment policy are the programs aimed at helping people at the bottom of the labor queue. These programs are typically income targeted and the "clients" must be "economically disadvantaged," that is, have a family income below some specified level.[1] The programs offer a range of services such as remedial education, classroom-based skills training, assistance in job search skills, and so on. In addition, programs may have tools for providing incentives (subsidies) to private firms to hire program participants.

The modern history of these efforts begins with the passage of the Manpower Development and Training Act (MDTA) in 1962. That legislation was enacted in a period of increasing concern that technological change was rendering old skills obsolete and causing structural unemployment. This view was at the heart of a debate about whether simple stimulation of aggregate demand would suffice to reduce unemployment. The MDTA embodied the view that more than macropolicy was needed and thus was intended to retrain workers with strong labor force attachment but whose skills were devalued by the structural change thought to be transforming the economy. Ironically enough, therefore, the legislation was aimed at what today would be termed dislocated workers. However, by the mid-1960s most observers concluded that skilled labor had found jobs in the upturn fueled by the Kennedy tax cuts and the Vietnam War. It seemed instead that the real problem lay with the urban poor (of course, the structuralists can point with satisfaction to the current debate about dislocated workers. This debate has many of the earmarks of that earlier discussion).

MDTA programs were redirected toward economically marginal groups and, with the War on Poverty, numerous job training efforts were launched. Many (but not all) of these were consolidated with the passage of the Comprehensive Employment and Training Act (CETA) in 1972. Later in the decade programs under the CETA ageis also came to include public job creation (or Public Service Employment [PSE]). The PSE effort discredited the entire CETA structure because of charges of corruption and make-work. This, of course, was unfair, since PSE was intended largely for countercyclical purposes and was conceptually very separate from the older remedial training programs. In any case, both CETA and PSE were abolished and in their place came the Job Training Partnership Act (JTPA), a program that retains the essential characteristics of the CETA remedial training programs (with the exception that clients cannot receive stipends while in the program) but in which administrative power is shifted from the federal government and mayors to governors and the private sector.

As noted earlier, another component of labor market programs for poor people are subsidies to employers. The largest of these is the Targeted Jobs Tax Credit, which provides income tax credits for new hires who fall within the eligibility requirements. Various other subsidy programs are available, although on a smaller scale.

How well have these programs worked? After nearly three decades, what can we say about their effectiveness? In answering these questions, we should be very clear about the goal of the programs: raising the earned income of the participants. Although other objectives (e.g., reduced crime) are often proclaimed, increased earnings has always been the single most important objective against which success is measured.

There is a vast literature evaluating these programs, a literature that varies in its coverage and sophistication. Early programs were evaluated with simple pre- and postprogram data, and the question was simply whether clients were better off before than after the program. This technique cannot control for the possibly special characteristics of applicants (e.g., they may be more ambitious than similarly situated people who do not enroll) nor for the possibility that programs may select—cream—those most likely to succeed. Fueled by a growing interest in social science experiments, some programs were established as demonstrations with clients randomly assigned to the program or to a control group. In other instances advances in statistical technology, when combined with newly available longitudinal data, opened the way to control partially for unmeasured differences between clients and the target population as a whole.

The problem of adequate controls is not the only difficulty plaguing evaluations. Another troublesome issue is whether the programs included in the evaluation are representative of the best programs in the field. In fact, they almost certainly are not. At one extreme, many of the demonstrations suffered from start-up problems and implementation difficulties. At the other extreme, evaluations based on national samples included many mediocre efforts along with good programs and hence are not generalizable to what the best might accomplish. These caveats are necessary and support the claims of many hard-working field staff that their programs accomplish more than might be suggested by the evaluation research. Nonetheless, the policy question is what might be expected from a national effort, an effort that must include good as well as bad programs and poorly implemented efforts as well as effective execution. Policy must be based on average effects and, for this purpose, the evaluation literature is useful.

The results of all these evaluations are not, of course, identical. However, taken as a whole, a clear message does come through. Employment and training programs raise annual earned income by $500 to $1500 per year.[2] This gain is (given typical program costs) large enough to justify the programs on a cost benefit basis and, for someone whose annual income might be at the poverty line, the extra funds are important. However, I would argue, these results suggest strongly that the programs are not a success and, in fact, fail to achieve their central goal. A person entering a program most likely has experienced a sporadic work history and employment in a low-wage, dead-end job. Program participation (on average[3]) does not change these facts. The modest earnings gains are generally due to longer hours, not higher wages, and in any case do not suggest that in any fundamental way the person's life circumstances have changed. The participants in these programs remain at the bottom of the income distribution, and there is no evidence that they have been placed on a new trajectory with respect to lifetime earnings.

The discussion has focused on training programs, but a similar conclusion emerges concerning the various subsidies that have been offered to firms to induce them to hire the disadvantaged. The largest of these programs, the Targeted Jobs Tax Credit (TJTC, passed in 1978), provided employers with a tax credit of 50% of the first $6000 in wages for the first year of employment and 25% tax credit for the first $6000 in wages during the second year of employment. There were some initial problems with employers claimings credits retroactively on workers they had already hired (and claiming credits for students in co-operative education programs), but these were eliminated by amendments in 1981. The program does not seem to have penetrated very deeply into the labor market, since employer surveys show that only 2.8% of firms (accounting for 15% of employment) report that they make any effort to select TJTC-eligible applicants to hire.[4] Despite this, however, a substantial number of individuals are touched by the program, with 563,000 people having received certificates in fiscal year 1984. Although the program was not intended as a youth effort, two-thirds of the certifications are youth, with the next most significant group, welfare receipients, accounting for 12%. What this suggests is that the program is mainly subsidizing the employment of youth in low-skill positions, not moving adults into "good" jobs. Evaluations of employer behavior suggest that 75% to 90% of jobs filled by TJTC-subsidized workers would have been filled anyway, either by TJTC eligibles or by other workers.[5] Put differently, only between 10% and 25% of TJTC jobs are "new" in that the program created them. We will discuss below a separate issue concerning TJTC: eligible applicants who inform a firm in advance that they are TJTC eligible are *less likely* to be hired than identical individuals who do not announce their eligibility. Finally, there seems to be no impact of TJTC on reducing quits or layoffs or on increasing the promotion rate of eligible employees compared to comparable workers not eligible for TJTC.[6]

The bottom line with respect to both the training programs and the TJTC and therefore decidedly mixed. Some readers may, however, feel that the standard against which the previous paragraphs judge programs may seem unduly harsh. There is some justice to this complaint. After all, the programs do raise earnings somewhat and they may provide other benefits, such as increased literacy and higher self-esteem. These results are valuable. Furthermore, many people would reasonably argue that given the limited resources expended, little more could be expected. For example, in New York City in 1986 for adult JTPA training programs, an average of $2984 was spent per participent, and the typical youth program expended less than half that amount while, by contrast, the public schools spent on average $4587 per pupil.[7] Put differently, most trainees spend less than half a year in employment programs, and there is no reason we should expect that much can be achieved in such a short period.

While this point is reasonable—and it is certaintly the case that better results would flow from increased resources—it does not follow that expanded programs would produce results that were different in kind, or by an order of magnitude, from past efforts. Several pieces of evidence point in this direction. First, the training programs that do expend substantially more resources deliver similar results. The most carefully evaluated program that expended substantial resources is the Job Corp; a year-long residential job training and remedial education program for youth that spent (in 1980) over $6800 per trainee. The program received one of the most careful evaluations in the literature, and it was found to be fully justified in cost/benefit terms once reduced crime and welfare payments were considered. Nonetheless, the average earnings gain was only $600 per year and was essentially double that if only program completers are considered.[8] These gains are consistent with our argument. Another expensive program for which we have good evaluation results is Supported Work. This program provided work experience and some remediation to four groups—

youth, drug addicts, individuals involved in the criminal justice system, and welfare mothers; the only group for which there were positive results were welfare mothers, and the results were within the range we have described.[9]

The evaluations cited are persuasive but still limited in that only a few programs models are included. One might still argue that it would be possible in principle to get much better results had a different treatment or set of treatments been tried or evaluated. However, other kinds of evidence also support our conclusion. For example, the results of the TJTC program—which followed a different strategy by providing substantial subsidies to firms—supports our point. Finally, no amount of resources can overcome the difficulties caused by the stigmatization inherent in income-stratified programs, a point elaborated on shortly.

It is important to emphasize that we are not arguing that nothing has been accomplished by these programs, nor are we saying that additional expenditures on them are wasted. To the contrary, there have been measurable gains, and expanded programs would lead to greater benefits. Nonetheless, the central point remains valid. The ultimate purpose of these programs is to alter the existing situation in which there is a group of people who are limited to a class of jobs with earnings near the poverty line and without reasonable chances for lifetime earnings growth. There is little credible evidence that the employment and training programs transform this state of affairs.

Seen in this light, we must conclude that employment and training programs are marginal to the operation of the labor market. Whatever process generates the low earnings of the system's clients is only glancingly affected by the existence of the programs. The system is also marginal in other ways. The changing federal legislation has so frequently shifted the respective roles of federal, state, and city governments that consistent governance has been difficult. However, it is at the point of program delivery that the true nature of the programs are apparent. Regardless of the particular federal legislation in place and regardless of the overall administrative structure, the actual service deliverers have always been a collection of community action groups and social service agencies, national community-based organizations, and city agencies. The chief characteristic of many of these "program operators" has been their instability and lack of a consistent internal stucture. In sharp contrast to the most analagous institution—the school system—these agencies come in and out of existence, there are no accepted certification or training requirements for staff, curriculum varies over space and time and changes without warning, and career lines for staff are virtually nonexistent.[10] Indeed, some estimates for the CETA period are that turnover rates of professional staff were between 25 and 50% per year![11] In short, the system is a haphazard collection of agencies of widely differing quality, some good but others very poor, but the main point is that there is no expectation that it will be different. In effect, the unevenness is designed into the structure.

Why the system has these characteristics is a matter of some conjecture. One line of argument would point to the constantly changing funding base and administrative structure at the federal level. From another viewpoint the system can be interpreted as an inner-city patronage operation that succeeds in its latent function of channeling resources to community groups. Regardless of which explanation one accepts, it is clear that the system is not seriously intended (except by its many hardworking staff) to deliver consistently high-quality services to its clientele.

Equally indicative of its marginal character, and more damning of the possibility of success, is the tenuous relationship of the employment and training system to the private economy. As we have seen, American business takes training seriously and expends considerable resources to accomplish it. Given this, one might expect that firms would eagerly turn to a public system that was prepared to underwrite some of the costs. Yet this has not proved true. Employment and training programs have found it very difficult to involve companies and have not found firms to be an eager customer for the trainees. As an example, in a recent survey of firms concerning training programs, the Bureau of National Affairs found that only 9% had any involvement at all with the Job Training Partnership Act.[12] When companies do make contact with these programs, there is usually the aura of public service and charity. These are perfectly legitimate motives but do not suggest that the business community expects the employment and training system to be of significant assistance in meeting human resource needs.

The Labor Exchange

In 1887 a German analyist of unemployment wrote, "The improvement of the care of the unemployed demands a comprehensive organization of employment offices," and within the next decade 150 offices were established in Germany. Similar offices were opened throughout Europe, and the first in the United States was opened in 1907.[13] The logic was simple and compelling: at any given time vacancies in firms coexist with unemployment. Programs to speed the matching process hold out promise for reducing unemployment. In fact, a well-developed rationale for the link between employment exchange, training, and a national manpower policy was developed by William Beveridge in the first decade of this century. In his classic *Unemployment: A Problem of Industry,* Beveridge argued that since unemployment is an unavoidable aspect of modern economies, a central employment exchange would assure that the best potential workers were matched with whatever vacancies were available, the remaining unemployed would be retrained, and those who still could not find work would receive unemployment insurance.[14]

As implied by Beveridge almost a century ago, it follows that the employment exchange should be at the center of a well-designed employment and training system. At once in touch with both firms and workers, with information available for advice, and with the power of referral to jobs or training, the employment exchange could manage the flow of people through the labor market.

Despite this promise, the U.S. Employment Service has long been regarded as unable to fill any but menial jobs. It is hard to exaggerate the consistency with which employers complain that the Service fails to screen workers and, whenever they list a vacancy, sends them large numbers of unqualified applicants. For their part, job applicants claim that good jobs are rarely listed with the Service and, when listed, are not filled with Service referrals. Statistical evaluations confirm these impressions. The Stanford Research Institute tracked the experience of U.S. Employment Service applicants who did and did not receive referrals in 1980 and 1981. If the Service was effective we would naturally expect to see higher subsequent earnings for job seekers who did receive referrals compared to those who did not. In fact, for men there was no statistically significant difference in earnings in the 6-month follow-up period for the two groups, while for women the results were much like those discussed earlier for training programs: the payoff was statistically significant but only on the order of $300 for 6 months (or a $600 difference in annual earnings).[15]

As was true for training programs, there is no reason why the public employment exchange should fail. Just as firms conduct their own training, so they also employ private employment exchanges to recruit, screen, and refer applicants. Companies pay a fee for this service and, on first glance, a public subsidy should be welcome. Some observers of the U.S. Employment Service explain its failure by pointing to the burden placed on the system by other administrative tasks that have been delegated to it[16] but, in fact, the Service has been ineffective for many decades.[17] Instead, we must conclude that the Service suffers from the same fundamental ill that plagues the training system: the system was not conceived and designed to provide genuine service to the private economy. Instead, it has been largely tied to the transfer system. For many years it was a mechanism to enforce the job search requirement for the receipt of unemployment insurance benefits: recipients had to satisfy officers of the Service that they were looking for work and, in practice, that meant ritualistically calling Service referrals. This gave the system its basic character from which is has not recovered; in recent years it has also been used to enforce work requirements for the receipt of welfare payments.

Skill Training for the Masses

Most adults who receive publicly subsidized vocational training and placement do so through different systems than those described previously. They use vocational education programs at the high school level and community colleges at the postsecondary level. To give a sense of magnitude, at the high point of the CETA system 3.6 million adults were served compared to 5.5 million youth who received occupational training in high school, and 4 million youth and adults who attended 2-year colleges.[18] With the declining scope of the CETA/ JTPA system, the balance has shifted even more in favor of vocational education and community colleges.

The place of vocational education in public education has been a long-standing and troublesome issue.[19] The turn of the century witnessed struggles between elements of the business community that wanted to establish create separate vocational and academic school systems and the labor movement, which viewed this as an effort to create permanent class demarcations. The notion of separate systems was defeated but within the public school system extensive vocational educational programs arose and, along with these, an effective political lobby with representatives in every school district arguing for expansion. Even Franklin D. Roosevelt found this lobby a difficult opponent when it came to educational legislation.[20] At the heart of the difficulty has been the troubling question of the role of public education. Is it the school's responsibility to prepare people for work or to provide a general education with broad applicablity to family, citizenship, personal development, and work arenas? If we do give the schools a vocational mission, is it best to train youth in specific skills for identifiable jobs or to provide a broader set of general vocational skills? Answers to these questions have changed with the ebb and flow of the economy and intellectual fashion.

Vocational education has certaintly proven itself a large, stable, and durable system with a clear administrative structure and reliable funding. Along these dimensions it stands in sharp contrast to the federal training system just described yet, surprising as this may be, the results are no different. Although the situation is perhaps better than in 1964, when 85% of students in vocational education courses studied agriculture or home economics,[21] recent evaluations leave little room for optimism.[22] The message from this literature is that youth who attend vocational programs earn no more—after controlling for differences between these students and others—than those who do not and, even more surprising, there is no relationship between the occupations students prepare for and what they eventually do. That is, a student who studies machining has a no higher probablity of working as a machinist after graduation than does another student in a general education track in the same high school.

The case of community colleges is a bit more complicated.[23] These institutions, which offer 2-year degree programs after high school, have experienced explosive growth in the past two decades, and their character has changed considerably. Between 1960 and 1980 enrollment grew from 650,000 to 4 million. To put matters even more sharply, whereas in 1960 they accounted for 16% of all higher education enrollments, by 1983 that figure had risen to 38% and, more startling, they claimed 54% of all freshmen first-time higher education enrollments.[24] Along with this growth came a substantial change in the mission of the community colleges: they shifted from institutions intended to help students transfer to 4-year colleges to essentially vocational training centers. While in 1965 13% of all community college enrollment was in vocational programs, in 1984 the figure was 66%.[25] These vocational courses are of two kinds. The majority are school-designed and school-based programs aimed at general preparation for a broad class of occupations. Thus, for example, a given community college may offer a program leading to an A.A. degree with a speciality in office skills, health aides, or electronic technicians. Second, community colleges are increasingly willing to contract with specific companies for training. For example, a local firm wishing to upgrade its technical sales staff might work with a local community college to develop a company-specific course open only to employees or to people applying for jobs with the firm.

According to a 1983 survey, 69% of community colleges that responded had at least once such contract, with the median number of contracts being over eight.[26] These courses represent a small fraction of total teaching in community colleges, but they symbolize the direction of the institutions and, in many cases, can set the tone of the school.

It seems clear from this description that community colleges have become a substantial element of the American employment and training system. Recent surveys of the educational enrollment intentions of adults confirm the importance of these institutions.[27] The question, of course, is whether they are any more effective than the other element of that system. On the face of it there is good reason to expect that they might be. They deal with an older group of students than do the vocational schools, and this in itself should generate better results, since the enrollees are likely to be more mature and motivated. In addition, community colleges are more flexible and entrepreneurial than is the school system. (Each college tends to be administratively independent, at least with respect to curriculum, from the central state system, and there are fewer of the bureaucratic impediments that prevent the public schools from changing.) In fact, community college administrators think of themselves as entrepreneurs, and this would suggest that the vocational material in the regular curriculum will be more responsive to market needs. Finally, the contract or customized courses arranged with companies are clearly likely to have an immediate payoff.

Given the growing importance of these institutions and the reasonable expections of success, the amount and nature of the evaluation evidence is frustrating. There have been few evaluations, and those that exist tend to be focused on the wrong question for our purposes (i.e., instead of asking whether attendence in community colleges pays off relative to entering the job market, they ask how the benefits of a community college degree compare to that of a college degree). In addition, it seems reasonable to think of community colleges as containing two broad tracks: highly specific vocational programs and more general degree programs. Evaluations should, but do not, distinguish between these.

The best evaluation we know of, by Wellford Wilms and Stephen Hansell,[28] followed a sample of entering students in six occupational fields in four cities. They found that for the three fields that they termed "high level" (accounting, computer programming, and electronic technician), there was no relationship between years of attendance or graduation and the field of the subsequent job or after-graduation earnings. For low-level occupations (secretary, dental assistant, and cosmotologist), a substantial fraction of the students did find work in their field of training, and the earnings of graduates exceeded that of dropouts. Hence, the results of this study are ambiguous, and there is no explanation of why the results differed across occupations. In addition, the study suffers from failing to compare enrollees to a control group of nonenrollees. The reasonable conclusion from this study is that the impact is highly variable and uncertain, but this is a conclusion that we can only tentatively hold. Therefore, our bottom line on community colleges has to be agnostic, and it is not even

clear what our prior beliefs suggest. On one hand, the large and growing enrollments suggest that there should be some payoff. On the other hand, the
consistent failure of other vocational training programs is cause for scepticism.

Finally, it is important to mention reemployment programs for dislocated
workers. These efforts have been funded from a variety of sources, such as
the Trade Adjustment Reassistance Act (which, in fact, delivered mostly transfer payments and little training), several Labor Department demonstration programs and, most important,—Title III of the Job Training Partnership Act.
Under Title III states are funded to assist people who are victims of plant closings and large-scale layoffs. Job loss is the eligibility criteria and, in contrast
to all other JTPA and comparable efforts, income eligibility requirements are
not imposed. As a result, the typical participant is far more likely to be a
middle-aged white male with a high school degree than is the case in other
programs.[29] The program is relatively small; the fiscal year 1984 budget was
$223 million.

The few evaluations of these efforts take one of two forms. Most are largely
narrative, with some pre- and postprogram data, and are most useful for developing a sense of "best practices" as judged by experienced observers. A
very limited number contain believable control or comparison groups and hence
can be credibly used to judge program impact in the sense that we used the
term in the earlier discussion of training programs. The lessons from the "best
practice" literature is that early notification of layoffs or closings improves the
chances of effective interventions, on-site worker assistance centers are frequently better than programs that are distant from the work place, counseling
and placement assistance are as important if not more so than training, and co-
operative efforts between labor and management work best.[30] The more statistically rigorous evaluations do show some positive impacts. For example, a
study of a program in Buffalo found that the program increased average weekly
earnings after layoff by $115 for participants versus nonparticipants.[31] Findings
this strong are not uniform (e.g., one of the initial efforts along these lines,
the Downriver Demonstration Project, did poorly), but there is good reason to
think that many programs have positive impacts.

These dislocated worker programs are generally too small and too oriented
toward an immediate crisis (as compared to ongoing efforts) to serve as models
for a full-fledged employment policy. However, as we will see in Chapter 7,
they represent an important opening toward such an effort.

Some Cross-Cutting Themes

What conclusions can we draw from this review of the three components of
the American employment and training system? One observation that imme-
diately comes to mind is that the term "system" is hardly descriptive, if by
that we mean a set of elements that fit together rationally. To begin with, none
of the three major components we have identified—training for the disadvan-

taged, training for the masses, or the employment exchange—have a consistent or regular relationship with each other. Their reporting responsibilities at the federal level are different (although the Employment Service and JTPA systems are both in the Labor Department they have different lines of responsibility, vocational education is in the Department of Education, and there is no substantial federal responsibility for community colleges) and at the state and local level there is generally little effective coordination.[32] This confusion has been noted by observers for 30 years[33] and seems impervious to reform.

A second characteristic is the economic stratification inherent in the system. Working-class youth and adults participate in the vocational education and community college system, while poor people participate in federal employment and training programs. The lines are somewhat fluid in the sense that some youth from families with low incomes attend vocational educational programs while some aspects of the federal training system—public service employment in the past and training for dislocated workers now—are directed at the working class. However, the latter do not enroll poor people. In fact, there has been considerable debate within the federal training system over just how far it should go in being income linked. Stanley Ruttenberg, who served as Manpower Administrator under President Johnson, has written that "During my tenure . . . it seemed as if people concerned with manpower programs and policy were divided into two distinct camps, poverty and non-poverty, . . . inhabiting separate worlds and loath to admit the other's existence."[34] Perhaps more dramatically, a high official of the AFL-CIO commented in the late 1970s that:

> Without in any way minimizing the serious problems of welfare recipients and "economically disadvantaged" people, we are concerned that exclusive emphasis on [their needs] will cut out opportunities for the "regular" unemployed . . . we don't want to see all the achievements of past manpower legislation wiped out by a transformation of CETA into a welfare jobs program.[35]

This tension persists, but the resolution is fundamentally a stratified employment and training system. Poor people constitute the overwhelming majority of participants in federal training programs and are a small percent of participants in vocational education and community college programs. This fact points to another characteristic of the federal system: its uncertain identity as something between an element of labor market policy and a part of the larger transfer (welfare) system. On its face the system is a labor market program aimed at providing skills and finding jobs for its clients. Yet we have seen that the private economy hardly takes it seriously. Set against this is the fact that the system has consistently been used as an adjunct of the welfare system. In part this occurred when stipends for training were sufficiently attractive that people enrolled in training simply to receive the cash. Under these circumstances the training programs were literally welfare and transfer programs. (This is not to say that the majority of enrollees signed up for this reason, but the problem was sufficiently widespread that the character of the programs were affected.) Although this is no longer possible for adults, it continues, in effect, in the summer youth jobs program that is too often a transfer and hot weather "fire insurance" effort.

The connection of employment and training to the welfare system extends beyond direct transfer. With growing public concern about the legitimacy of welfare, participation in training is often made a requirement for the receipt of transfer payments. This trend began in the 1960s with the Work Incentive Program (WIN) and continues under that rubric today and in various "workfare" programs passed at the state level. A good example is the recent initiative announced in New York State.[36] All welfare recipients (except those with very young children) will be required either to take an existing private sector job (and there will not be many of these), enroll in a job training program, or work off their welfare grant in public employment. Commendable as this may be from the perspective of the welfare system and even in terms of the mission of many job training programs (which, after all, are intended to help people escape poverty), this effort and the many others like it across the country reinforce the view that job training and welfare are parts of the same overall system for dealing with a particular segment of the population. Under these circumstances it is hard to argue with the view that training is really an element of the welfare system and, as such, we should not be surprised that the employer community views the system with suspicion.

Just how serious the stigmatization created by income stratification and association of training with welfare is was demonstrated by a recent experiment in which two randomly selected groups were sent to look for work. The first group identified themselves as clients of the employment and training system and offered employers a Targeted Jobs Tax Credit voucher good for partial subsidy of their wages. The second group made no such representation and carried with them no subsidy. The groups were alike in all other respects and remarkably, the hiring rate of the second group was substantially above that of the first. The connection with the employment and training system was so negative that it outweighed a wage subsidy![37]

We are forced to conclude that the employment and training system taken as a whole is disorganized, stratified, and confused about its mission. Nonetheless, it is difficult to blame the poor results on these characteristics. The pattern of failure is so consistent across the different elements of the system, each element having a different structure and a different history, that is is hard to believe that purely administrative considerations can explain the problem. If the federal training system has a constantly shifting delivery system and uncertain funding base, the same cannot be said of the employment service. If a system aimed at serving only poor people might be expected to fail, why should the failure extend to vocational education? Why cannot the Employment Service provide the "simple" service of matching job searchers with vacancies? The answers to these questions must take us beyond organization charts and raise the question of what theory of the labor market and program strategy underlies these programs. It is to this that we will now turn.

The Theoretical Foundations of the American Employment and Training System

Over the past two decades as the employment and training system expanded there has been considerable debate concerning what, perhaps grandiloquently, can be termed the theory of employment policy. The debate focused on under what circumstances and with what strategy these programs can be effective. Implict in such a discussion must be a view about how the labor market works and, hence, the discussion about employment policy has been intertwined with parallel arguments concerning labor market structure.

The initial, and probably still dominant, view of employment policy is drawn from the human capital theory of earnings determination. From this perspective—which is essentially an extension of standard microeconomic theory—earnings (and employment probabilities) are determined by productivity which, in turn, is influenced by ability, education, and training. In this view low incomes are the consequence of inadequate human capital, and the appropriate goal of a training system is to add to the skills of clients. Most programs have followed this prescription and, in this sense, can be thought of as supply-side programs (i.e., they seek to alter the distribution of outcomes by focusing on the supply characteristics of workers).

The empirical, if not theoretical, argument against this strategy is that it does not work very well as the evaluations reviewed suggest. Even programs that are reasonably well funded seem to produce disappointing results. In fact, this observation concerning the problems of supply-side or human capital training programs was first made in a series of ethnographic studies of trainees who went through these programs.[38] All that the programs seemed to accomplish was to recycle people through a similar set of low-wage, dead-end jobs. An alternative interpretation of earning generation—dual labor market theory—emerged from this observation but, for our purposes, the key point is that an argument developed for emphasizing the demand side of the labor market, either by direct job creation or by attempting to alter the hiring practices of firms. In the former category fell, on a large scale, Public Service Employment and, on a small scale, various efforts to generate new career lines in areas such as the paralegal and paramedical. The latter category—influencing the hiring practices of firms—includes various wage subsidy efforts as well as affirmative action programs.

For a brief period the advocates of a demand-side strategy succeeded in making their case equally respectable as the supply-side/human capital view, but their time in the limelight was not long. Politically, demand-side programs were destroyed by the discredit that befell Public Service Employment. In addition, mainstream economics struck back with a different argument. In the words of George Johnson, "the competitive labor market model (held) that the relevant wage structure is free to adjust and that the high unemployment rates of low-skill workers are caused by high turnover rates rather than by rigid relative wages."[39] In this view, then, any attempt to interfere with a well-functioning labor market is doomed to failure: if the government, for example, creates jobs, this will lead to a wage increase in the private economy (because the labor supply is reduced by the new government jobs), and the higher wages will reduce private employment by the same amount as the government increased public employment. Hence, there is no real gain: only displacement and reallocation will occur.

This view is not entirely persuasive: it is hard to believe that the 40% minority youth unemployment rate is consistent with an efficient labor market equilibrium. Furthermore, we have seen that the relative wage structure is actually rigid. However, advocates of an active employment policy lack a well-grounded alternative view of how the labor market functions and therefore of how employment policy might work. The conclusion we are forced to reach is that there is no convincing theory of employment policy.

One reason there is no such theory is that economists do not agree on how the labor market works, and this naturally makes it difficult to decide on how to intervene. A more practical, and more damning, explanation is that nothing seems to work very well. Or, to be more precise, some programs seem appropriate under some circumstances (e.g., basic skills training for the illiterate or counseling for dislocated workers), but we lack a framework for fitting together the pieces. Our argument is not that, for example, human capital training programs are never appropriate. Instead, I believe that they make sense if they are embedded in a larger set of institutional training structures, an employment and training system, which transcends many of the problems we have identified in this chapter. The reason specific interventions or program models are often disappointing is not because they are poorly conceived in their own terms, but because they are forced to stand alone and are isolated from the labor market.

To overcome these problems, we must broaden our perspective. First, we must understand in a more careful way the relationship between government labor market policy and the labor market policy of firms. We have seen that in the United States there is little relationship between the two, that in effect employment policy is irrelevant to the private economy. This fact lies at the heart of both the limited effectiveness and the weak theoretical foundations of employment policy. At the same time, in the two previous chapters we saw that firms today face a complicated set of problems that involve linkages between employment security issues and internal labor market flexibility. Employment security is indeed a theme that an employment policy might address, and if it did so successfully such a policy might be of greater interest to the private economy. In order to see whether such a linkage between public employment policy and private internal labor markets is possible, we turn our attention in Chapter 6 to the experiences of Sweden and Germany.

6

Comparative Employment Policy

The record of American employment policy, as we have just observed, has not been very good. This suggests that we need to find a new foundation for policy, an approach that divorces employment policy from its traditional and stigmatizing connection to transfer and welfare programs. To accomplish this, we need to identify a role that will better integrate employment policy into the main concerns of the private economy. If such an approach can be devised, employment policy would perform broad functions and, as part of its overall activity, the traditional constituency—poor people—could be served in a system that does not label them and hence is not self-defeating.

We saw earlier that attaining flexible internal labor markets is the central issue in human resource strategy facing firms and that at its core is job security. An effective employment policy would be one that assisted in solving this problem, presumably by helping to deliver the job security component of the internal bargain. We want therefore to understand what role employment policy can play in providing the job security necessary to achieve flexible work structures. It follows that in playing this role the policy will need to address dislocation and adjustment, the key issues that Chapters 1 to 5 identified as problematic in American labor markets.

One approach to accomplishing this might be to describe a program, or set of programs, and argue for their adoption. If we choose programs already functioning in other nations, we might point to their success and claim that we should import them with whatever modifications seem required by American conditions. If we wanted to be bolder we might design our own package of interventions and demonstrate how they could meet the key deficiencies in our economic performance. Both options are appealing. It is not difficult to find attractive program models in other nations, particularly in countries with a longer history than ours of activist government labor market intervention. Even more seductive is designing one's own program: it can be shaped to meet the particular problems of concern to us, and arguments about how it will work can be both persuasive and impossible to disconfirm in advance.

The difficulty with either prescriptive style is that they focus on particular programs without adequate appreciation of the larger system in which they are embedded. In one sense this is merely a bit of practical advice: before transporting a particular program model from one country to another or before coming up with a new twist of one's own it is wise to understand how existing institutions and behavior patterns are likely to redirect and mutate the innovation. For example, in Germany unemployment insurance can be received for reduced hours, and this "short-work" system helps firms prevent layoffs and smooth employment levels over the business cycle. This seems like a sensible idea, but its impact here is likely to be substantially less than in Germany. German firms are under strong legal compulsion to avoid layoffs, since they must clear their plans with the plant's Works Council, an employee organization. By contrast, in the United States there is no such compulsion and, in fact, temporary layoffs, when combined with seniority-based recall rights and unemployment insurance, are not always viewed unfavorably.

There is, however, a deeper reason for caution. To evaluate any given innovation sensibly, we need a general theory of what employment policy is and how it works. To generate such a theory, we must understand how employment policy fits into other building blocks of the labor market. Our fundamental argument is that there are alternative national systems for meeting a common set of functional requirements for the labor market. A theory of employment policy in the deepest sense would describe those functional prerequisites, explore alternative patterns for meeting them, and delineate the implications and consequences of the alternative systems.

The best way to accomplish this is to examine employment policy in a comparative perspective. If we can identify nations with alternative approaches, we can more effectively understand what is distinctive about the American system and what the realistic alternatives are. In this chapter, then, we will describe in some detail the systems in Sweden and West Germany. These countries were not chosen simply because they have employment policies that are more extensive than ours, since, if that was the only difference, the sole lesson would be to spend more money. Instead, in both countries the employment and training system is integrated into the private economy. In particular it helps support an internal labor market structure much like the one toward which many American firms would wish to move.

Our aim is to identify the key components of an employment policy system and to understand what difference alternative systems make. Because we are interested in "the big picture," we will pay less attention to the details of particular programs than we otherwise might. Furthermore, our emphasis on the stylized facts partially rescues us from the major embarrassment involved in extolling European employment policy models. In recent years European manpower programs have moved somewhat away from what might be termed their pure model and have emphasized measures that amount to stockpiling unemployed workers or, in American jargon, public service employment. This, of course, is in response to the very high unemployment rates engendered by the rocky economy of the late 1970s (the possibility that high European unemployment rates are partially due to the programs themselves has been emphasized by critics, and this will be discussed shortly). Put differently, the description that will be provided of the German and Swedish models accurately depicts present-day characteristics, but the systems worked more smoothly earlier. This is, of course, related to the common observation that the European programs were conceived for an era of labor shortage and high growth. However, this is not inappropriate from the American perspective since, as we saw in Chapter 3, U.S. labor supplies are tightening up and the issues we face have more to do with retraining and readjustment than with absorbing surplus labor. In any case, the point of the comparison is not to assess whether we want to adopt particular programs but to open our eyes to alternative patterns of interaction between public employment policy and the private economy. With this as our goal the current difficulties in Europe are relatively unimportant compared to the opportunity to use past Swedish and German experiences to help us think through more sharply the nature and possible transformation of the American system.

Characteristics of National Systems

There is considerable variation in how different nations address the concerns that underlie employment policy. For example, in Japan—the nation often described as the exemplar of an activist industrial policy—public employment policy is essentially inconsequential. After World War II Japan faced a shortage of skilled labor. It had this in common with much of Europe. Yet whereas many European nations developed extensive vocational training in the context of public education and created a large postschool training system (all of this will be described in more detail), the Japanese solution involved very little public provision of training, either in schools or in job training programs. In 1976 Japan spent 0.04% of its Gross Domestic Product on government-provided adult job training programs, whereas Sweden, at the other extreme spent 0.72% of GDP on such efforts and the United States expended 0.26%.[1] The picture is not much different with respect to vocational education in the schools; in 1971 Japan spent 3% of GDP on public education compared with 5.2% in Sweden and 5.1% in the United States. Furthermore, Japanese public education has a very antivocational orientation,[2] and one observer concluded that "Japanese public vocational training seems to have played a surprisingly small part in the process of rapid industrialization, and in the structural change in industries."[3]

The point is not to argue that training is unimportant in Japan. Quite the contrary, Japanese firms place great weight on investing in on-the-job training in the context of their internal labor markets. The lesson is that a common labor market problem—a shortage of skilled labor—can be solved in different ways. European nations—notably Sweden and Germany—created large public or quasipublic employment and training systems. Japan eschewed this course and instead relied on a far more developed internal training pattern than is common elsewhere.

This example brings us to our main point: there are alternative "systems" for solving common problems. Before it is sensible to talk about any particular employment and training policy, we need a framework within which to place the policy. Under one particular framework or "national system," innovations such as Individual Training Accounts may work well while in another "national system" it would be irrelevant.

In each nation the national employment and training system (broadly conceived) tries to accomplish three broad tasks: manage the entry of new workers into the labor market; assure that an adequate amount of mobility occurs among firms, industries, and geographical areas; and assist those experiencing severe labor market difficulties. For brevity we will refer to these as the issues of entry, mobility, and amelioration, and we discuss each one.

It is also important to note that an additional functional task concerns providing adults with further training beyond that required at the entry stage. This is typically accomplished by firms (through internal labor markets), public agencies (e.g., the community colleges described in Chapter 5), and private agencies (e.g., proprietary schools in fields as diverse as hairdressing and electronics). There is national variation in how effectively these instruments perform; for example, the conventional wisdom concerning England is that sharp craft demarcation lines within firms so limit mobility (i.e., an individual who learned a new skill could not gain a job in that field because of union restrictions) that there is little incentive for or effective provision of further training.[4] By contrast, the Japanese system of lifetime employment and wages attached to individuals and not to jobs is said to ease the way for considerable training and retraining within the enterprise.[5] For further training in general—whether through internal labor markets, schools, or for-profit firms—several significant issues arise. Among the most important are the appropriate balance between public and private further training, and how to integrate these efforts into employment policy. For now, however, we will concentrate on the elements of explicit employment policy.

Entry

Managing the entry of young people into the labor force has proved a major problem for most industrial countries. High youth unemployment rates and the plethora of conferences, books, and programs constitute ample evidence of this assertion. In the United States this difficulty is termed the "school to work transition." However, instead of focusing on failures and high unemployment, the key point is that all economies have a system for providing youth with a basic set of skills, socializing them into the norms of the work world, and allocating them to jobs.

The sharpest contrast between national systems in how this process is managed is between West Germany (and other German-speaking nations) and the United States. In West Germany the so-called "dual" system involves roughly 70% of a cohort in a formalized apprenticeship in which time is divided between public schooling and work-place training. At age 15 youth in two of the three educational tracks[6] search for apprenticeship slots. They then spend 3 years as apprentices, during which time they work 4 days a week and spend 1 day in formal public school instruction on the "theoretical principals" of their chosen craft. The content of their on-the-job instruction is carried out according to a curriculum that is carefully defined by a government agency, the Federal Institute of Vocational Training (BiBB). Apprenticeships are available in approximately 450 fields that have been certified by the BiBB. The responsibility for assuring that the apprenticeships in a local area meet appropriate quality standards falls to a business organization, the Chamber of Industry and Commerce (or, in the case of small firms, the Chamber of Handwork). These organizations, which have full-time staffs assigned to these tasks, also administer an examination at the conclusion of the apprenticeship. Upon passing these formal written and oral tests (which are uniform nationally) the person is granted the status of skilled worker.[7]

The foregoing is an accurate but lifeless description of the system. A better sense of it can be gained from the following observations:

1. Much is made of the system's capacity for skill building, but there is a substantial mismatch between the occupations and firms in which apprenticeships occur and those in which young people eventually find permanent jobs. Small artisan firms accounted for 40% of dual system training places in 1980, yet they employed only 17% of the population.[8] Furthermore, a good deal of training occurs in occupations for which there is little demand, and over half of all apprentices leave the firm in which they received training within a year after receiving the dual qualification.[9]

Defenders of the system acknowledge these facts but argue that the attention to detail, work discipline, and the like that are learned in any given apprenticeship makes the worker valuable in other fields. Thus the common story, repeated with conviction by a wide range of observers in Germany, that apprentice bakers and hairdressers (two fields in which there is considerable overtraining) make excellent automobile workers and are coveted by major manufacturers. What all of this suggests, of course, is that a major function of the system is socialization, not skill building.

2. These mismatches also suggest that a second latent function of the system is the provision of low-wage labor to firms. Defenders of the system hotly contest this and point to the staff and materials that firms provide for training. However, attempts to determine net costs to firms are dubious,[10] and it is difficult to believe that in many fields apprentices are not up to full production standards well before their 3-year term (and period of low wages) has ended. This impression is strengthened by the contrast between practices of large and small firms. Large firms establish training centers separate from the production process and hence do in fact devote substantial (and measurable) resources to training. However, they only take on the number of apprentices they intend to keep as regular employees (and this has nothing to do with the Employment Protection legislation, which makes layoffs difficult, since apprentices are not covered). In contrast, in small firms apprentices are integrated into the regular production process, and these firms apprentice far more young people than they will eventually hire on a regular basis.

3. The system is strongly business dominated. A government agency mon-

itors the system, and the one day of theoretical education is provided by state (Lander) schools but, as a practical matter, firms manage and shape the process. Companies have complete freedom concerning how many slots to offer and whom to "hire" into these slots. Given the centrality of the dual system to the German educational system, this provides the business community with considerable leverage. Even more striking is the role played by the aforementioned Chambers of Industry and Commerce of Handwork. These are not equivalents to the boosterism-oriented Chambers of Commerce in the United States. Instead, they are business organizations that have been granted governmental powers. They perform a wide range of functions beyond those related to the dual system (e.g., assuring there is "fair competition" among firms within a market area and registering firm names) and in the dual system they hold the balance of power. They supervise the training process in individual firms, and they administer the final examinations. Far more than the distant BiBB in Berlin, in each community these chambers represent state power in monitoring and controlling the system.

The extent of business domination can also be measured by union efforts to challenge it. As was true in the United States during debates over vocational education, unions resist company-specific training and press for more general training on the grounds that the former shifts power to firms while the latter empowers workers by enabling greater mobility. Hence there is frequent union rhetoric concerning curriculum in the dual system and a few reforms (e.g., creation of interfirm training centers in which apprentices in small firms gain some exposure to modern technologies). However, the structure of the system has proved impervious to attempts to introduce more government control or to shift to a less firm-specific training model. For example, the business community fiercely fought a recent proposal to enact a tax (or "levy") for training that would be forgiven if firms provided training slots. This was seen as an attempt to alter the basic character of the dual system by reducing the firm's traditional complete discretion over how many slots to provide and whom to accept for training.

4. The preceding observations portray one side of the system and do so in perhaps a somewhat cynical or economistic light. What they fail to convey is the deep national commitment and attachment to the dual system. The overwhelming majority of working Germans received their education through the dual system and, at a level beyond simple economic calculation, Germans believe in its overridding value. Whether one talks to businesspeople, unionists, workers, academics, or government officials, a common theme is apparent: the dual system provides a high quality of training and a "community of skill" that is invaluable both to the economy and to the individuals who participate. Regardless of specific criticisms (and it is not hard to find people to voice these), it is generally accepted that the dual system offers the best way to manage the entry of young people into work. This belief is so deep that a major aspect of Chancellor Kohl's first campaign was his promise that the government would assure sufficient apprenticeship places to meet the needs of the large baby-

boom cohorts coming through the system. In this sense youth employment is a political issue of major national proportions.

The comparison between the German and American approaches to the entry stage is stark. In Germany 70% of a cohort graduate from the dual system (or from a full-time vocational school) with a recognized qualification, 20% continue to universities or further education, and 10% at most fall between the cracks. There is a standard and widely followed path. By contrast, the process in the United States is chaotic. About 15% of a cohort do not graduate from high school or receive a GED, and of the high school graduates about 60% go to college, with half of these dropping at before graduating. Particularly among non-college students, there is at best a tenuous connection between what they learn in school and what jobs they subsequently hold. The process by which these youth find their adult job is lengthy and depends heavily on informal contacts, neighborhood and family connections, and luck.[11] Many of the youth who do go to college drop out prior to graduation and, in any case, the college "track" contains a wide variety of institutions and programs with considerably different degrees of vocational orientation and impact. There is, in short, no "standard" entry path or system for guiding entry.

We will return later to assess the costs and benefits of alternative approachs but, for now, the key point is that there is considerable ambiguity in assessing the consequences of the different national systems. Most employment and training professionals and advocates of active labor market policy are drawn to the logic of the German approach. Furthermore, there seem to be obvious benefits: Germans simply do not suffer from the high youth unemployment rates that are endemic in the United States and other nations that share an unstructured entry system. However, there is very good reason to doubt that youth unemployment has any long-term adverse consequences for the overwhelming majority of youth (minority unemployment is another issue).[12] Perhaps even more to the point, there is no evidence of the sort found in national labor market data that, say, 10 years after the point of entry the American cohort is misallocated compared to the German cohort. Both systems accomplish the common goal of moving youth from school to work. The German system is ordered, logical, and essentially universal. The American system is chaotic and idiosyncratic. However, both work and, while there are consequences of one versus another style, we will have to search more deeply to discern them.

In Sweden the vocational education system is also relatively successful: roughly 55% of a cohort graduate from it and (unlike in the United States) there seems to be a correlation between the work done in the vocational track and the kind and quality of jobs subsequently held.[13] The entry process is orderly compared to the United States, with most youth either leaving the vocational track and entering what we might term "primary" employment or else continuing into further education. The U.S. pattern of a period of drift and low-wage jobs following school[14] does not typify either Sweden or Germany, although in Sweden youth unemployment is higher than in Germany.[15] Finally, it is worth noting that Sweden is considering a reform of vocational education in directions that will bring it closer to the German model.[16]

Mobility

The wide availability of further training that individuals can acquire on their own initiative suggests that the mobility characteristics of the systems are also likely to differ. In the United States there is virtually no public policy concerned with mobility,[17] whereas mobility has historically been the major preoccupation of Swedish labor market policy. The conventional explanation for this emphasis is that the Swedish industrial relations system is designed to reduce wage differentials. The Swedish labor force is highly unionized (roughly 90% of the blue collar labor force belongs to unions), and wages are set through central bargaining. Swedish unions have sought to compress wage differentials and the consequence is that the economic returns to mobility are slight. The policy response has been twofold: the labor market agency, AMS, is empowered to offer a variety of financial incentives to encourage movement from low- to high-employment geographic areas. More significantly, the Employment Service (also administered by AMS) plays a central role in filling job vacancies. Employers are legally required to list all openings with the employment service (although they can also recruit through newspapers or word of mouth), and private for-profit employment agencies are banned. This provides the authorities with a tool that they can manipulate to encourage desired mobility patterns. Swedish officials speak of "operating on the labor market," a turn of phrase and a habit of mind very foreign to American thinking.

Amelioration

The final general function of labor market policy is remedial: all national systems contain some provision for compensating workers for the insecurity inherent in the labor market and, perhaps, for altering the distribution of outcomes. Each nation provides unemployment insurance for a subset of employees who lose their jobs in economic downturns, and each nation offers training programs to enable some of those in difficulty to gain new or better jobs. However, although these categories of programs are universally present, their character is quite different, depending on definitions of eligibility and more specific goals.

Each nation limits unemployment insurance to "core" workers, that is, employees who have been attached to the labor force for a certain period of time. The consequence is that new entrants and part-time or part-year workers tend to be excluded and, not surprisingly, considerably less than the total number of unemployed workers receive unemployment insurance. However both Germany and Sweden have second-tier unemployment insurance programs that are less generous and, under some circumstances, may be means tested, but that provide a minimum level of support.[18] This is in addition to what, in U.S. language, would be termed welfare or family support programs. In the United States there is no public alternative or second-level support system other than welfare, which is both means and asset tested and hence not generally available to people who are unemployed and not receiving unemployment insurance (although there are private arrangements: severance pay, supplementary unemployment benefits, etc.).

Each country's unemployment insurance is aimed at temporary support for attached members of the labor force and is designed to reflect and be consistent with the basic industrial relations rules of the system. Thus, in Sweden, with a high unionization rate, individuals belong to union-based "unemployment insurance societies," and union membership is typically (although not always) required for receiving unemployment insurance.[19] In Germany the employment protection laws make layoffs and permanent separations very difficult, and hence the unemployment insurance system permits a combination of part-time work and part-time benefits. This allows employers to reduce their employment rolls without resorting to layoffs. In the United States union rules generally discourage work sharing and also vest laid-off workers with recall rights; hence full layoffs are required to trigger unemployment insurance benefits.[20]

The major difference in the remedial function of the systems occurs in the area of training and retraining. European programs are aimed at a broad range of workers, and "core" or "attached" workers are the largest beneficiary of programs. For example, to receive government training stipends (and hence in order to be able to afford to enroll in a program), an unemployed German must meet eligibility requirements that (like those for unemployment insurance in the United States) require a certain number of weeks of prior work. This requirement is set sufficiently high so that most women and many men who are loosely attached to the labor force are not eligible.

The Swedish amelioration system is quite extensive and, indeed, is so central to the labor market that the notion of amelioration is a misnomer. The labor market policies were first proposed by two Landsorganisationen i Sverige (LO) economists, Gosta Rehn and Rudolf Meidner. Their strategy was based on the argument that a small exporting nation cannot afford to employ macroeconomic policy to underwrite security because that nation's rate of inflation cannot exceed the world rate. Hence a more selective set of labor market policies is required. As originally envisioned, those policies included a strong employment service with the capacity to match applicants with vacancies, financial incentives to encourage geographic mobility, and training programs. Taken together, these programs were seen as structural, aimed at minimizing unemployment and maximizing fluidity in the face of wage policies which might be thought of as reducing the incentives for mobility and in the face of a general willingness to permit high wages and fiscal slack to generate unemployment. Put differently, in sharp contrast to U.S. programs, which aim at a particular marginalized segment of the labor force, the Swedish model placed labor market policy at the center of macrostrategy.

This last point is worth emphasizing: more than other nation Sweden takes labor market policy seriously. Even today when, as we will see, these programs are under attack, opponents as well as supporters continue to believe that labor market policy of one form or another is a key component of a successful national economic package. Data on funding and enrollment levels clarify just how important these programs are. As is apparent from Table 6.1, both with

Table 6.1 Composition of Swedish Labor Market Policy

| Year | AMS Budget | Percent of GNP | Fraction of AMS Budget Devoted To | | | |
			Labor Exchange	Training	Job Creation	Unemployment Insurance
1970	2,089	1.3	0.12	0.26	0.31	0.12
1971	3,461	2.0	0.08	0.20	0.46	0.13
1972	3,943	2.1	0.08	0.19	0.50	0.11
1973	3,877	1.8	0.09	0.22	0.40	0.13
1974	3,826	1.5	0.10	0.22	0.29	0.17
1975	4,703	1.6	0.11	0.21	0.32	0.14
1976	7,632	2.4	0.08	0.24	0.42	0.10
1977	10,511	3.0	0.07	0.25	0.43	0.12
1978	11,255	2.8	0.07	0.30	0.34	0.15
1979	11,919	2.7	0.07	0.28	0.27	0.15
1980	11,763	2.4	0.08	0.26	0.24	0.18
1981	13,524	2.5	0.08	0.24	0.23	0.24
1982	17,128	2.9	0.06	0.21	0.28	0.26
1983	21,246	3.2	0.06	0.18	0.30	0.28

Source: Author's calculations from EFA, "Labor Market Policy Under Reconsideration," Arbetsmarknadsdepartementet, 1984. The AMS budget (which is thousands of SEK in current prices) excludes expenditures on sheltered workshops and regional development assistance, items that were transferred out of that department in recent years. The labor market exchange is based on the budget item entitled "labor market services." The training figure excludes in-plant training. This item is added together with job creation, orders to industry and stockpiling support to sum to the column labeled job creation. The unemployment insurance column represents only the government contribution. Other items in the AMS budget include mobility assistance, measures for refugees, defense activities, and administration.

respect to percentage of the labor force involved and percentage of GNP devoted to these efforts, the Swedish model is extraordinary in its size and degree of penetration into the labor market.

The core of the Swedish model is the combination of an active job exchange function and vocational training. Swedish law prohibits for-profit placement services and also requires firms to list all of their vacancies with the employment service. Hence the local employment offices are in a powerful position and might be expected to play a central allocational role in the labor market. In addition to the placement functions the exchanges also refer clients to training or rehabilitation programs and administer the various employment subsidy programs that are aimed at lowering the marginal cost of additional employment within firms.[21] Also, the employment offices administer the work search test for unemployment insurance. The vocational training is provided by AMU centers. This training is generally at the *gymnasium* (high school) vocational level, although the AMU also will contract with firms to offer more advanced training.

As Table 6.1 indicates, over time the fraction of resources (but not the amount) devoted to these core activities has shrunk relative to alternative strategies. In particular, direct job creation and unemployment insurance have become more important. This change in the mix of programs is central to the current debate over the direction of labor market policy and, in turn, has implications for what lessons we can draw for the United States. Hence we will simply note this development and defer discussion to the conclusion of this chapter.

Returning to the central point, it should be clear from this description that in contrast to the United States, the Swedish system is aimed at a broad segment of the labor force. This can be seen in a number of ways. Unlike Germany, the Swedish system poses fewer obstacles in the way of program participation, and there is no reason to believe that poor people (although there are few of these in Sweden) are excluded. In fact, 20% of people trained in the AMU are immigrants, and another 20% are handicapped.[22] These are people who, in Swedish usage, would be termed "weak" labor market participants. However, it is clear that the system as a whole is aimed at the reemployment of core workers who are displaced by adjustments due to Sweden's solidarity wage policy or international trade. Indeed, this was the rationale developed by Rehn-Meidner for an active labor market policy, and the current reforms of the system are intended to strengthen this focus and reduce the emphasis on "weak" participants.

By sharp contrast, programs in the United States are limited to people at the very bottom of the income distribution. The fact that U.S. programs are sharply targeted by income level while the German and Swedish programs are aimed higher in the distribution points to radically different goals of the two systems. The two European systems are aimed at facilitating the functioning of the labor market by retraining and placing skilled workers, whereas U.S. programs are marginal to the labor market. Instead (depending on one's perspective), they are either aimed at redistribution for those at the very bottom or are a disguised income transfer and political patronage system for poor communities. The American system—under the best interpretation—is aimed at redistribution and making amends to a limited number of people, while Swedish and German programs are aimed at a much wider segment of labor force and have goals that extend to influencing the operation of the labor market itself.

Defining National Systems

We have seen that there is considerable national variety in how governments intervene (or refrain from intervening) to meet the key functional requirements for an effective labor market. Along some dimensions the European nations have more extensive government activity (or perhaps better put: cooperative public-private activity) than we do, although this is not uniformly true. The other major point of the previous section is that the functional prerequisites of a labor market *are* accomplished one way or another. The absence of formal government provisions to achieve them simply means that the society has developed other mechanisms. It remains to be seen which approach is the more productive.

The issue before us now is what are the key ways in which one "national system" for labor market policy may differ from another. How might we begin to pull together the various pieces? One central issue is the interaction of public and private activities. In the United States government-sponsored employment stands apart from the human resource policies of firms and, as we have argued, are largely irrelevant to them. By contrast, in Sweden and Germany the line between the public and the private is much less distinct. This is illustrated by the case of the dual apprenticeship training, an extension of public education is monitored and partially financed by the government but largely executed by the private sector.

Of special concern to us throughout this book has been the structuring of internal labor markets. It is natural therefore to ask what the relationship is between public employment policy in Sweden and Germany and what might be termed private employment policy (i.e., the nature of internal labor markets in those nations). It develops that public employment policy does interact in significant ways with internal labor markets and that it does so in a manner that is striking from the American vantage point. Both Sweden and Germany have a set of institutions, partly embodied in law and partly in strong unions, that would lead Americans to expect that their internal labor markets would be rigid and ungainly. In fact, the internal labor markets of these two countries closely approximate what we have termed the salaried model, that is, they are flexible, and this flexibility is based partly on employment security. The interesting, and key, point is that public employment policy plays a central role in accomplishing this, and it is in understanding this that we have the most to learn from these nations.

The German and Swedish Environment

The key to understanding the nature of German internal labor markets lies in examining the structure of worker representation and the web of legal regulations at the work place.[23] There are a small number of national industrial unions that represent all employees in an industry, regardless of occupation. These broad organizations have a heterogeneous membership, so the special interests of particular occupations (e.g., skilled craft workers) tend to be compromised. These unions bargain with national industry federations over wages. However, work-place issues—working conditions, promotion procedures, job security issues—are the province of another institution, the works councils (*Betriebsrat*). Under the Works Constitution Act these are elected by all employees, union and nonunion, in work places with over 20 employees. The employer must recognize these councils as representative of the work force.

The law provides that the works councils be consulted with and be provided information on a range of manpower topics including the number and procedures for layoffs, promotion criteria, changes in working conditions, the use of overtime and of "short time," and the introduction of new technologies. Although management in principle need only consult, in practice on at least some of these topics the consent of the works council is necessary. The nature of the works council agreement varies according to topic. For example, on the key issue of layoffs if, through negotiations, management is unable to reach agreement with the works council (which takes for form of a "social agreement" [*Sozialplan*]), the council can submit the plan to an arbitration committee (*Einigungsstelle*) whose binding decision must take the social situation of the employees into account along with purely economic considerations of the firm. In addition, individual workers may take legal action in an industrial court in order to obtain severance pay. The consequence is not to render layoffs impossible but to raise their cost substantially. Similarly, the works council must give its assent to overtime. If it does not do so, a request for overtime goes before a neutral "conciliation committee." By the time this committee has rendered its decision, the need for overtime may well have passed and hence in practice the consent of the works council is key. On the other hand, with respect to short work the firm can get permission quickly from the local employment office. In addition, anecdotal evidence and the reports of other observers also suggest that the works councils get involved in establishing promotion criteria and frequently even in decisions concerning individual promotions. Finally, the works council as a matter of practice can often link issues. For example, in return for its willingness to grant overtime, it might require (informally) a larger Christmas bonus.[24]

Swedish internal labor markets are conditioned by three central institutional facts, all of which are ultimately related to the same phenomenon: the strength of the union movement. Over 90% of blue collar and 75% of white collar employees belong to Swedish unions. The blue collar unions are part of a national federation, the Landsorganisationen i Sverige, or LO, and the largest white collar federation is the Tjanstemannens Centralorganisation, or TCO. The unions bargain with the employers' federation, the Svenska Arbetsgivareforeningen, or SAF, over central wage agreements. These agreements are the predominant determinant of plant level wages, although there is room for local adjustments. A portion of these local adjustments represents mechanical application of formula increases relative to the national wage, and hence are in effect determined by national bargaining, but another portion represents so-called "wage drift," which might be interpreted as market forces.[25]

There are two notable characteristics of Swedish wage setting. The first is the considerable restraint exercised by Swedish unions; the second is the solidaristic policy toward relative wages. With the exception of a wage explosion in the mid-1970s, Swedish unions have not exercised their substantial market power to raise wages beyond the rate of increase in productivity.[26] This restraint has been made possible in part by Swedish labor market policy, a point we will return to, and partly by the general recognition that a small exporting nation cannot afford an inflation rate exceeding that of its competitors. Until recently SAF and the unions shared a common econometric model that was employed to calculate the "room" available for wage increases, and a bargain was struck along these lines. The government stood outside the negotiations as a third party ready to intervene to enforce wage restraint.

Perhaps even more remarkable than the general wage restraint is the solidaristic wage policy followed in the bargaining. Since the mid-1950s Swedish unions have systematically sought to eliminate interindustry wage differentials and to narrow interoccupational wage differentials. The consequence of this policy is that the distribution of earnings by industry, occupation, sex, and any other dimension is remarkably even by international standards.[27]

Several important consequences flow from the solidaristic wage policy. The policy might be expected to increase unemployment by driving marginal firms out of business. Although the extent to which this has actually happened is a matter of some dispute, the widespread belief that this occurred set the stage for labor market policy. The converse effect is that the policy restrains wages in high-profit industries (e.g., automobiles), hence increasing the international competitiveness of those firms. With respect to internal labor markets there are two key results. The first is that the logic of the policy reduces the need for the narrow job classifications that characterize American firms. Because wage differentials are so narrow, those that exist can be maintained by a limited number of classifications and broad job definitions. This, as we will see, substantially increases the internal flexibility of Swedish firms. Set against this is the possibility, discussed in some detail next, that the narrow differentials remove incentives for mobility and acquisition of training.

Swedish labor contracts do not generally contain the extensive prescription of work rules and job classifications found in American contracts. However, in the 1970s legislation was passed that is potentially more prescriptive concerning internal labor market rules. The two key laws are the Law on Codetermination (1977) and the Employment Security Legislation (1974).

The important characteristics of these laws, for our purposes, is that the codetermination legislation requires that firms inform and consult with unions on all matters concerning job design, work organization, technological innovation, and promotion procedures. The employment security legislation requires that firms provide lengthy notification prior to layoffs and that layoffs proceed in the order dictated by (reverse) seniority.

As is apparent, the Swedish and German arrangements share a good deal in common. In both countries unions are stronger than in the United States, although the Swedish unions are far more powerful than their German counterparts. Both nations have passed national legislation that establishes workplace-based councils and restrict employer freedom to lay off employees. At the same time, there are important differences between the two countries, in particular that the German restrictions concerning employer freedom in establishing work rules and in laying off employees are considerably more stringent. In addition, social policy is much more tied to a specific work site in Germany than in Sweden. We will explore these differences and their implications shortly, but now we turn to describing the nature of the internal labor market in both nations.

The Character of Internal Labor Markets

The legal and institutional patterns just described might lead an American observer to expect that the German and Swedish internal labor markets are rigid, rule bound, and inefficient. In fact, just the opposite is true: all available evidence suggests that these internal labor markets are flexible and fluid. The key points are that there seem to be far fewer job classifications than elsewhere, promotion based more on merit and qualification than on seniority, and the labor force is more able and more willing to be assigned to a broad range of tasks.

The emphasis on formal credentials, which flows from the dual system's focus on vocational education, has imbued the German industrial relations system with a respect for merit. In most circumstances the operational problem with merit-based promotion schemes is fear that management will employ discretion arbitrarily and, in effect, play favorites. This is mitigated in Germany by the attention paid to formal credentials (and, of course, by the works council participation in the process). This observation has been confirmed by a series of cross-national comparisons between German internal labor markets and those in Britain and France. Thus Sorge and Warner examined a range of chemical and metalworking industries in Britain and Germany and found that at each level in the firm there was much stronger correlation between formal qualification (apprenticeship, further training, technical school degree, etc.) and status in Germany than in Britain.[28]

A similar conclusion was reached in a comparison of matched firms in France and Germany, and the researchers noted that an additional consequence of the emphasis on merit and formal credentials is that far fewer supervisory staff are necessary in Germany than in France.[29] This latter point indicates the great flexibility inherent in the German internal labor market. Yet another comparison of Britain and Germany, this time focusing on similar firms that introduced comparable numerically controlled machine tool technology, found that:

> In Britain there was a split at the beginning life between technician and worker apprenticeships, between programming and planning as opposed to machining occupations. Training for these operated in parallel, whereas in Germany the latter set of skills was an essential prerequisite for the former. This difference appeared likely to persist and in Britain to sustain the more polarized qualification structure; whilst in Germany C.N.C. was more usually used to reduce training differentials between technical staff and shop floor personnel, to increase the tradesman's status, to encourage even greater flexibility in production, and to reduce the "decision making overload" on top management.[30]

A similar point was developed in the earlier British/German comparison: "the boundary between production work and supervision is more blurred in Germany: working chargehands are more liable to take over duties performed by the British foreman."[31] A case study of several German automobile firms confirmed these descriptions and concluded that "Management may, by and large, apply standards of qualifications and performance when filling vacancies from within. Seniority and professional demarcation lines do exist . . . but they exist informally and seldom overrule standards of skill and performance."[32]

Finally, a management researcher wrote of his observations of German firms:

There is, in fact, no phrase in German for a demarcation dispute and the idea has to be elaborately paraphrased. One manifestation of this is the less rigid division between Production and Maintainence as functions and activities . . . another practical implication is that the German production manager has much more freedom to move workers around to satisfy immediate manning needs . . . to cover manpower gaps . . . and to deal with changes deriving from changed output priorities, re-scheduling of jobs and additional assignments. . . . German managers attach positive importance to the individual worker's readiness and ability to be so redeployed. There is a standard term for this redeployment capability, *Einsatzbreite,* which is used both formally and informally in evaluating individual workers for merit raises and possible promotion.[33]

To summarize, despite what seems to be extensive legal limitations, the German internal labor market is a supple instrument. Workers are able and willing to perform a variety of both production and supervisory tasks, and promotion is based far more on performance than is typical in the United States.[34] In effect, the key bargain that has been struck is that management has agreed to maintain a relatively "closed" internal labor market that provides security for the incumbent work force. In return, the workers (through the works councils) agree to assist and permit management in managing internal labor allocation in a manner that emphasizes flexible deployment, willingness to accept broad jobs, and willingness to learn new skills. The nature of this bargain has been well described by Werner Sengenberger:

A secure, skilled, polyvalent, and motivated labor force . . . facilitates full use of productive potential of capital equipment and increases the adaptive and innovative capacity of the economy, and thus does not conflict with flexible requirements.[35]

It is difficult to know with any precision what percentage of German firms conform to the model described. It is obvious folly to assume that the description universally accurate even in manufacturing, much less in the service sector and white collar firms. What can be said with confidence, however, is that the description represents the modal form of internal labor market organization in Germany and captures what is distinctive about the German style of organizing work. In this sense the description is as accurate as is the use of the *nenko,* or lifetime employment model, to characterize Japan or the seniority-based tight job classification ladders that characterize U.S. industrial internal labor markets. In all cases we know there are exceptions, but we also know that a key feature of the national system is embodied in the stylized description.

Turning to Sweden, we see that the structure of the legislation and bargaining system seems to push internal labor markets in two directions. On one hand, the solidaristic wage structure and absence of bargaining over working conditions permit considerable flexibility. As noted earlier, union contracts do not contain the elaborate job classifications or work rules that typify comparable U.S. agreements. On the other hand, the codetermination and employment security legislation seem to restrict management's hand. In fact, the bottom line is that Swedish internal labor markets are remarkably flexible and the scope for management discretion is very large.

This flexibility is apparent in a number of ways.[36] First, as noted, there are few job classifications, and those that exist are very broad. Thus, for example, at Volvo, the largest Swedish industrial firm, blue collar workers effectively are classified into one of six groups (in U.S. automobile firms there may be over 100 job classifications) while at the largest high-technology firm, Ericsson, there is a four-level job classification system for blue collar workers. Second, there are few restrictions placed on management concerning redeployment of the labor force. Prior to moving a worker from one job to another, the codetermination legislation requires consultation with the work group representative but, if anything, this improves efficiency, since the representative provides management with information on the relative abilities and skills of different workers. As a practical matter, with this information in hand and with the consultation requirement fulfilled, management is free to promote whom it wishes and to reassign job responsibilities as it sees fit. In particular, seniority plays a very limited role. Indeed, no manager we interviewed felt seriously constrained from promoting the person who was regarded as best qualified for or from redeploying labor as dictated by production requirements. All of this is in sharp contrast with the U.S. system of posting, bidding, and seniority.

What price is paid for this flexibility? We will shortly see that the greatest cost is carried by the government in the form of labor market policy, but firms do not entirely escape. Firms seem to accept without serious complaint the codetermination requirements but vary in their views of the solidarity wage policy and the employment security laws. For companies that are contracting the security laws require not only advance notice (which, despite the fuss raised by suggestions along these lines in the United States, is not an issue) but (reverse) seniority-based layoffs. This can be a problem for firms that believe that their most skilled workers are found in the lower seniority groups. The most common solution (negotiated on a case-by-case basis with the unions) is early retirement through government-subsidized disability pensions. The complaint about the wage policy rests on the belief that it makes recruitment of skilled workers more difficult. There is little evidence, however, that this is true (evidence is provided in the appendix to this chapter), and employer complaints along these lines have a certain ritualistic air. The major exception to this generalization seems to be engineers, but boom and bust characterizes this profession in the United States as well as Sweden.[37]

In short, taken as a whole, the logical structure of the Swedish system is that extremely flexible internal labor markets (few and broad job classifications, limited use of seniority, and few restrictions on labor force deployment) are combined with powerful unions and government legislation that provides those unions with tools that, should they wish to, can be exercised to restrain firm behavior. There is a balance of power in which firms, as it were, are given conditional rights to manage the internal labor market with great discretion but are also put on notice that the privilege can be withdrawn if abused. Put another way, the unions deliver considerable flexibility to the firms but ask for security in return. This is, of course, precisely the character of the salaried internal labor market model described in Chapter 4.

The Contribution of Employment Policy to Internal Flexibility

The question confronting us now is how, if at all, German and Swedish employment policy contributes to maintaining or strengthening the internal labor market patterns we have described.

Turning first to Germany, one fundamental contribution is that the structure and universality of the dual system create a climate in which all parties feel comfortable with merit-based personnel systems. As noted earlier, such systems face considerable difficulty in the United States because of deep worker suspicion about management motives and capacity to implement them fairly.[38] By contrast, the ubiquity of vocational (versus general education) credentials as a method both for gaining entry into the firm and for achieving promotion permits widespread use of merit as a key internal criteria.

A second contribution of the dual system is that it creates workers who are "overqualified" for their initial entry jobs and perhaps even for many of the positions along the promotion trajectory normally associated with the entry job. This, of course, has its potential costs, but the monetary calculation is eased by the low wages paid apprentices while they are in the dual system. Another potential cost—creation of a "craft consciousness" in which workers protect the boundaries of their occupation by rigid rules governing who does what work—seems diffused by the broad-based character of German unions. The benefits to this "overqualification" is that new technology can be more easily introduced and incorporated into production and, hence, more flexible internal deployment patterns are facilitated. Paul Widoff observed this in his comparison of two automobile firms: the firm with the largest number of foreign workers (who had not completed the dual degree) had the most difficulty adopting robot technologies. By contrast, the firm with "dual" degree holders in the same jobs as the foreign workers of the first firm was more successful in smoothly introducing robots and redesigning jobs to complement the new technology.[39] Note that there are limits to this argument, since the mismatch between occupations (e.g., the oversupply of hairdressers and bakers) restricts the accomplishments of the dual system. Nonetheless, on balance the system does make for a more flexibly skilled work force.

The key role played by the dual system in creating the vocational-education climate necessary to legitimize operation of German internal labor markets helps explain why the business community in Germany is so careful to maintain their central role in managing the system. Far more than is true in the United States, the business community takes the vocational system seriously and is active in protecting its interests.

In addition to the general systemwide contributions made by the dual system, there is a series of specific programs that creates the institutional framework within which the German-style internal labor market can function.

The maintenance of a stable core internal labor force within the firm in the face of restrictions on layoffs requires that the company have other adjustment mechanisms that enable it to reduce its labor force in response to downturns in product demand or to more long-run developments. Two government employment programs—short-time work and early retirement subsidies—meet these needs. We discussed short-time work earlier: in Germany the unemployment insurance system is organized to permit part-time layoffs (or "short-time work") combined with receipt of unemployment insurance. Hence firms need not formally lay off employees in order to reduce payrolls. This particular approach obviously makes sense in the context of the German internal labor market rules and can be seen as a clear example of public employment policy supporting those internal patterns.

Another key use of the unemployment insurance system has been to support the early retirement of employees as a way of easing internal personnel adjustment.[40] Under the so-called "59" arrangement, workers who are 59 or older, who have paid a certain amount into the unemployment insurance system (and hence are "core" workers), and who have been unemployed a substantial fraction of the previous 1-1/2 years can receive a "prepension" and hence retire early. This prepension is financed jointly by the pension system and the unemployment insurance system and hence is a considerable public subsidy to firm-based early retirement programs. Of perhaps equal significance are new arrangements under which all firms that offer early retirement to employees 58 years or older can receive a refund of 35% of pension costs from the unemployment insurance system. To receive this subsidy, the firm must declare its commitment to hiring an equal number of unemployed youth or adults, but promises of this sort tend to have less reality than the up-front subsidy to labor force reduction.

In a number of other ways German employment policy has emphasized supply side reductions as a central strategy for easing personnel adjustment. Legal limitations on the residence and employment of so-called guest workers—usually unskilled immigrants from other nations—are a well-known example. Perhaps less noted but equally important is the general inhospitality of the German labor market to female employment.[41] Finally, eligibility for the retraining programs sponsored by the Federal Employment Institute tends to be limited to full-time, committed "core" employees and, thus, these programs provide no incentives (or the sort found in the United States) for individuals to maintain a marginal attachment to the labor force in order to receive certain training and benefits.[42]

Returning to the Swedish case, the system has been described as flowing from a balance of power and a bargain that has been struck by labor and management. The government plays an important role in maintaining the bargain, and this is where employment policy becomes important. Unions expect security in return for flexibility, but a striking feature of the Swedish labor market is that security is not taken to mean lifetime employment or a no-layoff policy. The layoff rate in Sweden is lower than that of the United States, but the difference mainly lies in the absence of temporary layoffs in the Swedish economy, and this difference existed prior to the employment security legislation (data on U.S. and Swedish layoff rates are provided in the appendix to the chapter). Swedish industry has been permitted to rationalize, and substantial shrinkages have occurred (without serious labor strife) in many firms.[43] In addition, the solidarity wage policy is intended to force marginal firms, who cannot match the going wage rates, out of business. Security in Sweden flows from the public labor market and social policies.

We have described these policies in detail and will not repeat ourselves here. The point to emphasize, however, is that a worker who loses a job can expect a considerable investment in public resources aimed at finding new employment. To provide a sense of the magnitudes, in 1985 over 20% of unemployed 25–54-year-olds participated in a government-sponsored job training program, and this figure does not include individuals who use the employment service. It is apparent that the magnitudes of participation in Swedish programs are remarkably high. In addition, the employment exchange is also quite active. The best available evidence suggests that about 20% of all job openings in the economy are filled by the employment service offices.[44] This is a figure well above comparable "penetration rates" of equivalent institutions in other OECD nations. Since the exchanges generally specialize in blue collar work, this implies that for these occupations the penetration rate is probably around 40 to 50%. Again, this also implies that this aspect of the active labor market policy is important is easing the difficulties of finding new work.

In addition, a worker is generally protected from substantial income loss both by the unemployment insurance system and by the welfare state programs in general (people involved in labor market programs are considered employed and hence are eligible for employment-conditioned benefits). Taken as a whole, the level of security provided by labor market policy is substantial, and this is an important component of the security-flexibility agreement.

Much like the German system, the Swedes have also used retirement policy to compensate for potential rigidities in the internal labor market. In the Swedish case this takes the form of a sharp increase in early retirements due to disability, an increase that is directly related to labor market developments instead of health-related issues.[45] Under current regulations a worker with a disability claim may retire at age 58 and 3 months, receive unemployment insurance until age 60, and then receive a disability pension. Hence, in effect, early retirement is supported by the unemployment insurance system. There is a growing use of this practice, particularly in instances in which firms reduce employment, and the number of disability pensions has increased from 212,000 in 1980 to 314,000 in 1982.[46] Related to this, and the general easing of pension eligibility, is the sharp decline in the labor force participation rates of older people.[47]

Returning to our central point, the important issue to understand about the Swedish system is that it is based on a complex set of bargains. The strong Swedish union movement has granted management substantial discretion over the internal labor market (i.e., over the definitions of job classifications and rules concerning internal mobility). This is a concession that American unions have not been willing to make. The reason is that Swedes have paid for this concession by guaranteeing a level of personal income security (through the welfare state) and occupational security through labor market policy. The historical role of labor market programs has been to assure that workers who lose their jobs are effectively assisted in finding a new place in the labor market. The solidaristic wage policy assures that the personal economic cost of such mobility is not great (since the wages of the new job will not be greatly below that of the old). The society has struck a bargain in which flexibility and rationalization are traded for security. Labor market policy historically has been at the core of that bargain.

Structure and Performance

The argument thus far can be summarized as follows: in Sweden and in Germany the extensive employment and training system is well integrated into the core of the economy. The reason is that the two systems perform useful functions: in various ways they provide the premises necessary to secure flexible internal labor market systems. In both nations the key bargain is the security-flexibility deal that has been struck and, in both cases, there is, on the one hand, national legislation that provides the framework for the bargain (the code-termination and employment security laws) and, on the other hand, a specific series of policies that offsets some of the rigidities that such legislation might engender. The central lesson of this material is that under some circumstances active employment policy can be important not simply to the clients but to the broader economy and hence can achieve a centrality that is sorely lacking in the United States. Furthermore, the particular way in which the policies contribute—assisting internal labor market flexibility—is, in light of the discussion in earlier chapters, of special relevance to the United States.

Having gone this far, an American skeptic would have good reason to ask two questions. First, how much if any of these programs are applicable to the United States? Second, do the programs have substantial costs that might outweigh the benefits we have described?

Part of the answer to the first challenge is that it misses the point. We are not attempting to identify particular programs for transport west across the Atlantic. Instead, we are using Sweden and Germany to illustrate that employment and training can play a broader role than that assigned to it in the United States and that the role relates to concerns important here. With this point made, it remains to devise solutions that are appropriate to the American context.

Although this response is correct, it is a bit abstract and unsatisfying. It would be good to know whether any of the institutions or institutional patterns are relevant to the American situation. One helpful way of addressing this is to draw more sharply than we have thus far the contrast between the Swedish and the German systems.

The German system is the more "foreign" and difficult to envision in U.S. terms. In part this is due to the dual system, which is a highly ordered and bureaucratic form of schooling and labor market entry. A system in which at age 15 most youth are tracked into academic or vocational systems, those in the latter have to choose among 400 occupations that are defined by regulation, and job acquisition depends on passage of exams based on the apprenticeship strikes most Americans as hopelessly bureaucratic and authoritarian.

The second aspect of the German system, and the point at which it is most distinguishable from the Swedish model, is that job security (and other benefits) are much more linked to the firm in Germany, whereas in Sweden they are provided externally. In Germany layoffs are quite difficult; the firm must negotiate with the works council and, if the works council insists, develop a "social plan" that can be appealed to a court. In Sweden the union must be informed and advance notification is required, but the procedure is considerably simpler. In Germany the security is provided by the difficulty of accomplishing a layoff. In Sweden a greater role is played by the external (to the firm) set of training and placement programs. Another aspect of the same difference is that various fringe benefits in Germany are firm specific, whereas in Sweden they are provided by the state and are contingent on employment somewhere but not in any particular firm. All of this taken together, and combined with the obvious difficulty of envisioning in the United States job security legislation with the stringency of Germany, would seem to make the Swedish model of "externalized" security and employment programs more relevant. When we come in Chapter 7 to thinking through the possible shape of U.S. policy, the Swedish model of "external" security will be of greatest interest.

Costs and Benefits of Alternative Systems

The second difficult question is whether active employment policy entails costs that may outweigh the gains of increased internal labor market flexibility as well as the other benefits such a policy might entail.

In recent years the debate about the efficacy of alternative systems has taken on a very sharp tone. Whereas the success of European countries in the 1960s in maintaining an unemployment rate lower than that of the United States led American analysts to glance enviously across the Atlantic, relative economic performance has been reversed in the 1970s and 1980s. European unemployment rates have risen, while those in the United States have fallen, and American success in job creation has not been matched in Europe. These macrostatistics have led many observers to conclude that European labor markets are inflexible and that much of that inflexibility can be laid at the door of European employment policy. In the academic literature the criticism is that the European pattern of centralized collective bargaining and employment security has led to rigidly high real wages.[48] In Europe this view has led to extensive debate among policy analysts,[49] while in America it has been given vigorous voice by opponents of government intervention.

It is not difficult to develop an abstract case on either side of this debate. There are a number of ways in which, *in principle,* one might expect to observe impacts of different national systems. On the positive side, one approach may be more successful at avoiding (through public training or mobility incentives) skill shortages with subsequent production bottlenecks and wage run-ups; successful programs oriented toward the economically disadvantaged may create a more equal national income distribution, with political and social benefits; or systems that encourage job security might make the labor force more amenable to accepting technological change and job redesign. On the negative side, extensive systems may simply waste resources by attempting to accomplish what the market can do better and hence only achieve displacement; they might (inevitably?) misjudge the future and train for unneeded skills; and the security they provide may weaken economic incentives, leading to a less mobile and flexible labor force.

It is apparent that the question must be addressed empirically although, as we will see, this brings with it its own set of frustrations. We might also note that most advocates of transplanting European-style employment programs have not carefully examined the evidence concerning the possible costs of these programs (nor have they defined the benefits as we have, i.e., gaining internal labor market flexibility).

As we have seen, in the last decade and a half American employment and training programs have been the subject of extensive evaluations. The most sophisticated of these assign participants randomly to programs and control groups and then observe subsequent differences in wages, unemployment, or other outcomes for the two samples. This approach, as well as some alternative methodologies, provides a good basis for determining the impact of programs on individuals, and a natural approach might seem to be to compare these kinds of evaluations across countries. However, to follow this path would be to miss the point about differences among national systems. The U.S. evaluations described previously are driven by comparisons of the performance of different individuals functioning in a similar environment; the difference among national employment systems represents alternative approaches to structuring that environment. We are less interested in whether a clerical training program performs better in America than in Germany than in whether, taken as a whole, the German public policy toward accomplishing the functional requirements of a labor market leads to a more or less effective labor market. Comparing the rates of returns to similar programs across nations cannot answer this question because that methodology is based on comparing program participants with nonparticipants; yet, if the argument develped here is correct, different national employment policy systems influence the outcomes of nonparticipants (if that term has meaning in this context) as well as of participants.[50]

Another approach is to examine economywide measures and, while useful, appropriate care must be taken with this strategy. Specifically, macroindicators such as the unemployment rate or job creation are problematical because they are influenced far more by macroeconomic policy than by employment policy. In particular, after both the first and second oil shocks, the United States macropolicy deviated from that of European nations.[51] All the major nations pursued a contractionary policy shortly after the first oil shock but, in 1975, American policymakers reversed themselves and ran a stimulative macropolicy while

Europe remained contractionary. Again, after the second oil shock the common strategy was to induce a recession, but large fiscal deficits instead stimulated the U.S. economy. At the same time European nations continued their restrictive policies to the point that they were actually increasing budget surpluses.[52] It is not surprising, therefore, that the United States and Europe would have different records of job creation, but differences in labor market policy are hardly at the root of the divergence. Finally, it is worth noting that a careful econometric examination of U.S./Canadian unemployment rate differentials (Canada, like Europe, experienced growing unemployment while U.S. rates declined) found no labor market variable capable of explaining the divergence.[53]

A second more sophisticated macroeconomic criticism of the programs is the view that labor market policy, and other social policies, provide such an effective safety net that they prevent wages from falling in periods when macroeconomic events imply that they should. The evidence, however, seems to point in the opposite direction. Lloyd Ulman and his associates have described in considerable detail how the central bargaining structures of Sweden and Germany—during the years in which the welfare state model was at its strongest—moderated wage demands relative to other nations.[54] In addition, the strongest advocates of the argument that high European real wages lie behind slow employment creation, Michael Bruno and Jeffrey Sachs, also conclude that the Swedish and German models helped maintain wage moderation relative to other OECD countries.[55]

A more appropriate test of these structures than macroeconomic evidence is data on the performance of external and internal labor markets. For example, we might want to know whether one system or another is more adept at preventing skill shortages; thus, for occupations that are common across nations, we would like data on vacancies and wage developments. We might ask whether one system is more capable than another in encouraging mobility, and hence data on turnover and migration would be useful. These data, taken together with convincing measures of policies and interventions, could, in principle, permit estimation of program impacts on the labor market as a whole. At a less quantitative, but no less important, level we would like to know whether one system eases technological innovation more effectively than do other approaches and whether employees under one system are more broadly skilled and more able and willing to undertake a broad range of tasks than they are elsewhere. Finally, with all of these microlevel estimates of benefits in hand, we would like cost data and we would then be in a position to undertake the appropriate evaluations.

Data of the sort described here, however, are simply not available on a systematic basis. Even in the United States, which (until recently) excelled in generating labor market data, it would be virtually impossible to conduct such research. Quality data on local labor markets combined with convincing measures of program interventions are few and far between. Comparable data across nations are just not there. This is not to say that no information can be had, just that a complete and systematic analysis is impossible. Instead, we will work with scattered data and see what clues we can gather concerning the impact of alternative labor market systems.

In the appendix to this chapter we review evidence on the impact of Swedish employment policy on job changing by individuals, the capacity of firms to reduce employment levels in response to market conditions, and other indicators of labor market performance. We conclude that there is little or no evidence that the policies have an adverse impact along these dimensions. We also, in the appendix, report on recent critiques of the organization of labor market policies in Sweden and how Swedish authorities are attempting to respond. In the end our basic conclusion about the efficacy of active labor market policy in underwriting internal labor market flexibility stands the test of microdata.

Toward an Employment Policy

In comparing the European and American approachs to employment policy two central, and related, differences stand out. The American system does not attempt to interact with key labor market institutions. Instead, it is aimed at influencing the behavior of individuals, largely by augmenting their "human capital" or stock of skills. Furthermore, the American system tends to be highly stratified, with separate institutions for the "economically disadvantaged" and for more mainstream populations. By contrast, European systems are much more tightly integrated into the day-to-day functions of the labor market and the industrial relations system, and they serve a broader cross section of the population.

The consequence of this philosophy is that American programs aim to provide individuals with information and skills but are not integrated in any substantial way into the human resource calculations or industrial relations strategies of firms. In the jargon of the economics profession, employment policy operates largely on the supply of individual characteristics in the external labor market. Even those efforts (Public Service Employment, New Careers, etc.) that were demand-side (or job creation) efforts emphasized government jobs, not a significant interaction with the private market economy.

Set against this orientation is an alternative view in which employment policy is designed in such a way as to interact with the private calculations of the key labor market actors. Put somewhat differently, in both Sweden and Germany employment policy is *useful* to firms. Specifically, employment policy helps firms create and maintain flexible internal labor markets, internal labor markets much like the salaried model in Chapter 4. The notion of "usefulness" explains the ineffectiveness of American employment policy and the comparative importance of European policy.

Observers of social policy have discerned a parallel distinction in other programs between America and Europe. In his insightful analysis of occupational health and safety regulation in the United States and Sweden, Steven Kelman notes that we would expect that in the United States, a nation in which business has substantial political power, an accommodating relationship would exist between government regulators and firms, whereas in Sweden, a nation with a social democratic government and politically powerful unions, the relationship should be more adversarial. In fact, the situation is exactly the opposite.

> American inspections are designed more as formal searchs for violations of regulations; Swedish inspections are designed more as informal, personal missions to give advice and information, establish friendship ties between inspected and inspector, and promote local labor-management cooperation.[56]

This difference pervades the health and safety regulatory system and seems to signal a basic difference in the relationship between government and the private sector in the two nations. Despite the differences in distribution of political power and in political philosophy, actual government programs in Sweden are designed and administered to be useful to the private economy. By contrast, American programs are either adversarial or (in the case of employment policy) irrelevant.

Briefly, we have concluded that American employment programs are marginalized and fundamentally ineffective, whereas German and Swedish systems are useful and hence central to the operation of the internal labor markets and industrial relations systems in their respective countries.

This argument might suggest that America should adopt a European model. There are, however, several difficulties with such a facile conclusion. First, there may be a price to be paid for the centrality or usefulness of the European systems and it is a price that the American constituency for employment and training policy may not—and should not—accept. The German, and to a lesser extent the Swedish, systems are oriented towards the core labor force, whereas in the United States a significant component of the training system is aimed at those at the bottom of the labor queue. If we are unwilling to abandon our commitment to these groups then the difficult question is whether any American program or system which includes large numbers of stigmatized groups can achieve the kind of "usefulness" or acceptance that characterize European efforts.

Stated differently, what we want to do is design an employment system that serves the core labor force and meets the needs of firms yet is permeable to poor people. If such a design can be accomplished, it will be worth a good deal, since such a broad-based system will meet an important need of the economy while at the same time avoid stigmatizing its weaker clients. However, designing such a system is far from easy.

An even more difficult obstacle is that the Swedish and German systems are effective in part because the role of the state in the economy is conceived differently than it is in the United States. As the discussion of health and safety regulation suggests, it is not just in the arena of employment policy that the interaction between private and public actors contrasts between the United States and Europe. Simply, it is much more natural for government to play an active role in Sweden and Germany than in the United States. This problem, of course, is intensified by the current American political climate, which can hardly be described as friendly to new social policy innovations.

A final issue concerns the role of employment security. We have seen that at the core of the Swedish and German employment policy systems is the notion of employment security, internalized in the case of Germany and relatively externalized in the case of Sweden. This security forms the basis of the relatively more flexible European internal labor markets. Indeed, the point that employment and training policy can help set the stage for flexible internal labor markets is the key lesson of this chapter. We observed in Chapter 4 that job security lies at the heart of the problem facing U.S. firms in restructuring their internal labor markets. Hence it is the possible role of job security in meeting the needs of firms that provides the best hope of interesting American companies in an employment policy and hence in making such a policy more central to the economy. However, it is far from clear how one provides job security in the American environment in which, at least until recently, employment at will has been the received doctrine and in which efforts to reduce employment levels are widespread.

These three themes will be at the core of Chapter 7, which will attempt to think through a role for the state that is plausible in the American setting, address the issue of job security, and attempt to remain aware of the need to integrate poor people into any policy effort.

7

A Renewed American Employment Policy

From a number of perspectives this seems to be a transitional period for the American labor market. The distribution of employment is shifting away from the traditional manufacturing firms into new manufacturing fields and into services. This raises important issues of labor market adjustment and explains the widespread concern with the plight of dislocated workers. White collar workers are also facing new adjustment difficulties, to a perhaps unprecedented degree, as firms reduce overhead staff. The underlying demographics of labor supply are shifting as the baby boom glut ends and middle-aged workers come to dominate the labor market. This also poses questions about the capacity of the market to respond to new needs. At the firm level there is a widespread sense of experimentation as innovations concerning participation, the organization of work, and the structure of pay are tried in many settings. In part these innovations are linked to new "nonunion" personnel practices for both blue and white collar work, but they are also being tested in traditional union settings. At the same time, however, other firms (and even sometimes the same firms) are testing another tack: aggressive employer militancy involving work rules and employment levels. The "commitment" strategy and the "concession" strategy seem inconsistent, but it is far from clear which will prevail.

This book offers an interpretation of these developments that centers on the dynamics of internal labor markets. Our argument is that the set of rules that firms use to organize work is the result of choice and that the choice can be understood as flowing from a weighing of the costs and benefits of alternative arrangements. We characterize the choices that firms perceive they face today as two major models, the industrial and the salaried internal labor market models, and two minor variants, the craft and secondary models. We lay out in some detail the costs and benefits of those alternatives. At the core of our argument is the proposition that much of the current flux is explained by a shift in the environment that has altered the relative advantages of the different structures. The confusion flows from an uncertainty concerning the best response. Although we cannot completely resolve this confusion, we do want to press the view that extending our theoretical and empirical understanding of internal labor markets aids significantly in understanding these developments.

The second aim of this book has been to build up an understanding of the possible role of an active employment policy in our economy. The expression "build up" is chosen with care. In our view (and Chapter 6 makes this point in detail) past efforts at employment policy have performed poorly. The reason has not been primarily administrative or financial—although these considerations exacerbated the problem—but conceptual. Employment policy has not been grounded in a deep understanding of how the labor market works. In the language of Chapter 6, employment policy has not been useful to firms as they make their human resource decisions. The consequence is that the government programs are marginalized and thus effectively blocked from reaching their goals.

To escape this trap, we must understand what problems employment policy might reasonably address and what strategies or entry points seem promising for making employment policy an attractive partner in a solution. Implicit in this approach is the view that if labor market policy is to succeed, it must swim with the current of events in the labor market. Each firm has its own employment policy, and that policy is based on a set of goals, incentives, and constraints. If the incentives offered by public policy are irrelevant to the firm's decision problem, unless public policy is coercive, it will not succeed. Hence public policy makers need a shrewd understanding of where the leverage points are in the system. In more abstract terms, we must understand how economic structures are shaped, how they work, and how they fit together before we can develop policies to alter them.

This view of employment policy might seem paradoxical in that it simultaneously calls for increased government involvement in the labor market, but an involvement that (we will argue) should be more attuned to private interests and more under the control of firms than past efforts. This view also rejects what Hugh Heclo has termed the social market economy view of the welfare state. Under that doctrine the labor market is left to generate whatever distribution of outcomes emerges from its assumedly efficient operation, and public policy either seeks to make amends afterward (through transfer payments) or alter the distribution of attributes that individuals bring to the labor market (through training programs). Our view is that such a strategy will fail because employers will view the remedial training programs as irrelevant to their needs and hence not participate. Furthermore, as a result of this marginalization, enrollment in such efforts is unavoidably stigmatizing. Our goal, therefore, is to ground employment policy in the needs of the labor market and, specifically, to find a way to make it useful to firms as they seek to solve the problems that are most salient to them. It is here, of course, that the argument about employment policy links to our efforts to extend the theory and empirics of internal labor markets. If employment policy can help resolve some of the uncertainties we identify within the firm, it is more likely to become better integrated into the economy and better utilized.

The Argument

To understand the evolution of internal labor markets and the case for public interventions, we sought to understand "the problem," and we did this from three perspectives: the individual, the market, and the firm. In the end we want to argue that these are three facets of the same theme.

Individuals and Markets

Survey data suggest that the American labor market has performed admirably in many respects, notably job generation. Furthermore, despite much popular and professional assertion to the contrary, the new jobs seem on average to be as high quality as those that they replace. There are, however, two circumstances in which serious problems not only persist but seem to be worsening. The first is the traditional focus of employment policy, persons with low earning levels. Working with a variety of data sources and several definitions and cutoff points, we showed that 8 to 15% of the labor force experiences low earnings over several years. These are substantial numbers and are clearly cause for concern. However, for reasons that will become clear, the analytical focus of the book is on other groups, and on the problems of firms, and we return to the problems of the disadvantaged when we take up our policy recommendations.

The second group of people in difficulty are "mainstream" workers, both blue and white collar, who lose their jobs through layoffs. Our very striking finding is that (in the "prime age group") 20% or more of these workers remain unemployed for long periods after losing their jobs, and another 6% withdraw from the labor force. The length of these unemployment spells is frequently beyond that which can be reasonably attributed to search behavior or the disincentive effects of unemployment insurance. Furthermore, among those who do find jobs, 30% take very substantial cuts in their earnings. Both findings seem robust in the face of various statistical controls we deployed and alternative data sets we examined. Taken together they suggest that the labor market does not do well in adjusting to shocks.

To understand the origins of this "adjustment problem," we shifted our perspective to the structure of the market. We develop a stylized description or model but one that captures the essential features that explain our findings. On the demand side are employers who organize work according to the principles of internal labor markets. This implies that employment is open mainly at the bottom rung of job ladders and that as workers gain seniority they are sheltered from outside competition. What made this system viable throughout the postwar period were large elastic supplies of flexible labor, youth and adult women, available for employment at the entry level. The ratio of entry to experienced labor was high. This meant that employers could expand or contract through adjustments at the bottom rungs of the internal ladder and that, in general, more senior workers were secure. However, one consequence of such an arrangement is that experienced workers who do lose their jobs are in difficulty because equivalent jobs elsewhere are closed to outsiders. Hence this system will be seen as performing well as long as rates of job loss are not so high as to pressure the weak adjustment mechanisms and as long as the ratio of flexible to experienced (inflexible) labor is high.

We argue that several developments threaten to undermine the viability of the traditional market structure. First, employment is becoming more volatile. This is partly due to the recent difficult macroeconomic climate, but there are also deeper reasons. We spent considerable effort exploring the impact of new technologies and, although it is not responsible to conclude that these technologies will reduce the level of employment, it does seem likely that they will substantially alter the distribution of jobs among firms and sectors and among workers possessing different skills. If the labor market was good at shifting experienced workers from one employer to another all would be well, but we have just argued that there is substantial difficulty in this respect. Exacerbating the problem is the second development, the changing demographics of the labor force. Both the absolute number and the fraction of employees who are middle aged will rise sharply in the next decade, and this is the group that has particular difficulty finding new employment and adjusting to change. Their inflexibility results from both the structure of internal labor markets and life-cycle considerations. Taking this all together, it seems that problems of adjustment and employment security loom large and are likely to grow in salience. When we turn to internal labor markets, we also find that job security is a central issue.

Firms and Internal Labor Markets

Central to our description of labor market structure and its difficulties is the concept of internal labor markets. Chapters 3 and 4 examine this institution in considerable detail. An internal labor market is the set of administrative rules by which firms structure employment. Much of the book's argument turns on changes and tensions in internal labor market arrangements. At its basic level, we argue that firms perceive several alternative ways of organizing work (i.e., several different internal labor market models). Each of these has its own strengths and weaknesses according to the objectives and constraints of firms, and we explore these. Hence we develop a theory of choice among alternative internal labor market systems. Its key contribution is the argument that alternative patterns are possible for accomplishing tasks and that it is possible to model the considerations that lie behind the firm's choice. From this we argue that several recent developments have placed considerable pressure on prevailing arrangements and have forced employers to face difficult choices. Although it is not clear which pattern will prevail, there are good reasons to believe that one model (which we term the "salaried" model) is perhaps the most desirable along several dimensions and that a substantial element of the employer community recognizes this. However, it is difficult to get "from here to there" because of a set of actual and perceived costs and uncertainties. It is here that the possibility of public employment policy emerges. Such a policy might be "useful" to firms by facilitating the transition while at the same time accomplishing other public purposes.

We term the two broad alternative ways of organizing work in internal labor markets the *industrial* and the *salaried* models. Each comprises a set of rules (concerning wages, promotion, training, internal deployment, and job security) that fits together in a logical way and forms a coherent system. This implies that pressures leading to changes in one area (say, internal deployment) will diffuse throughout the system and lead to changes elsewhere.

The industrial model of organizing blue collar work, which had its origins in the ideas of scientific management and industrial engineering, became the norm due to the unionization drives of the Great Depression and was solidified in the era of postwar prosperity. Work is organized into a series of tightly defined jobs with clear work rules and responsibilities attached to each classification. Wages are attached to jobs, and an individual's wage is determined by classification. Management's freedom to move individuals from one job to another can vary from situation to situation, but the typical case is that both promotions and lateral shifts are limited by seniority provisions and by requirements that workers agree to the shift. Finally, there is no formal job security, and it is understood that management is free to vary the size of the labor force as it wishes. However, when layoffs do occur, they are generally organized according to reverse seniority. Although this model became the dominant institutional form as unions grew, it should not be construed as limited to unionized situations. Because of fear of unions, government pressures for uniformity, and employer imitation, the model spread throughout the economy.

The salaried model combines a more flexible and personalistic set of administrative procedures with greater commitment to employment security. Although individuals have job descriptions, much as industrial employees have work rules, these descriptions are not intended to have legal or customary force. They are subject to revision by superiors and the employees are prepared to take on new activities as demanded. By the same token, the clearly defined job ladders and promotion sequences that characterize industrial settings are absent here. There is a considerably greater scope for merit considerations in pay setting, and the wages of two individuals in the same job can vary considerably.

The salaried model clearly characterizes much white collar work. The career patterns of most managers and many professionals who work in bureaucracies are accurately captured by the model. However, the salaried model is

not simply another way of describing white collar work. There have also always been a few American firms that have stood outside the mainstream industrial model for their blue collar workers. These firms are viewed as pointing
to alternative directions for blue collar employment.

The salaried and industrial models each entail distinctive costs and benefits.
The industrial model often implies considerable rigidity in wage structure and
the deployment of labor. However, it provides firms with flexibility in terms
of adjusting employment levels through layoffs. On the other hand, the salaried
model, with its attention to employment security, restricts the flexibility of the
firm concerning employment numbers. However, in return the firm gains a
measure of internal flexibility and commitment that may be lacking in the rival
system.

In the industrial model rigid job classifications and reliance on nonpersonalistic procedures "buy" worker acquiescence in the face of employment fluctuations. In the salaried model employment security is the central element of
the system. Once individuals pass a probationary period they can expect either
lifetime employment with the firm or that the firm will make extensive efforts
to avoid layoffs. This role that employment security plays in the two models
is very important to our argument. Workers are aware of the difficulties, just
described, of finding comparable new employment after layoffs. Hence they
will not readily forego the protections of the industrial model and provide the
flexibility and commitment of the salaried model without some level of assurances. At the same time, providing assurances is costly and risky, and this
makes it difficult for firms to move easily to a salaried model.

Much of the uncertainty of the current period reflects changes in the relative
costs and benefits, as perceived by firms, of the industrial and salaried models.
Indeed, much of the recent widespread innovations in human resource practices
can be interpreted as efforts to move from one model to another.

The industrial model is under extreme pressure from several sources. The
greatest source of tension flows from the nature of new technologies. First,
computer-based technology leads to pressures for altering traditional job classifications to encompass new and frequently broader ranges of tasks. This implies a one-time change in what has frequently become an unwieldy system of
organizing work. However, the pressures are deeper than this. A second characteristic of the new technologies is that they imply that job duties will continue
to shift over time as the flexibility inherent in the technologies interacts with
volotility in product markets. This implies that job classifications should *remain* loose and subject to change, and it is this thrust that is most inconsistent
with the premises of the industrial model. Additional pressures flow from the
perception that the industrial model cannot deliver the level of worker commitment and product quality that the salaried model can provide.

Employers face tension from a different source for white collar work. These
jobs are already organized along the lines of the salaried model. However, the
model is somewhat endangered as competitive pressures and the nature of new
technologies lead to white collar employment reductions and hence call the job
security aspect of that model into doubt. If these reductions are too severe,

employers may lose the commitment of their white collar employees, and other consequences (e.g., union organization) may follow.

Employers are therefore in a bind. In the case of blue collar work, many want to shift to a salaried model. However, macroeconomic uncertainty and unwillingness to permit labor to become too great a fixed cost leads them to fear that employment security is too high a price to pay. In the case of white collar employment they want to maintain the salaried model but at lower employment levels. However, it is not clear how to reduce employment without undermining the premises of the model. The central question is what are the alternative resolutions of these dilemmas. It is very unclear how events will play out, and this uncertainty explains the coexistence of very different tendencies in human resources, ranging from employer agression and concession bargaining to participatory systems.

For firms that do want to move in the direction of the salaried model for blue and white collar workers, one possible solution is to offer employment security (or a commitment to make every effort to avoid layoffs) to a core of more or less permanent employees, and surround that core with a periphery of temporary, contract, and part-time workers who enjoy less protection. The workers in the core will be willing to work under the salaried model and to provide both flexibility and commitment to the firm. The peripheral labor force provides the firm with a buffer against either macroeconomic—cyclical—downturns or labor force reductions necessitated by technical change. In a sense this core-periphery model is a strategy for having it both ways. It enables firms to achieve substantial internal flexibility with a highly trained and committed labor force while at the same time maintaining the ability to adjust employment levels at will.

Given these advantages, one would expect the core-periphery model to expand and, indeed, we present substantial evidence that it has for a wide range of skilled and unskilled work. Nonetheless, there are also good reasons to believe that there are limitations to this arrangement that restrict its ability to resolve the dilemma we have posed. We present evidence that the size of the labor force available for peripheral work will not increase substantially in the coming years and that for workers traditionally part of this group, particularly adult women, preferences are shifting against marginal work arrangments. Furthermore, there are limitations to the fraction of work that firms are willing to trust to a noncommitted work force. For these reasons the core-periphery model, while attractive to firms and destined to grow, has significant limitations. In addition, from a social perspective, serious consideration must be given to the implications of a greatly expanded "have-not" labor force.

An alternative resolution, pursued by some firms, is simply to force through "reforms" of internal labor market rules without any compensating concessions with respect to employment security. In the case of unionized blue collar work this takes the form of "concession bargaining," while large-scale white collar layoffs are the relevant analogy in that sector.

The current era is one of substantial employer strength vis-à-vis the work force, and it is far from clear that this strategy will not succeed. It may seem particularly promising in the short run. There are, however, also good reasons to believe that the long-term stability of this solution is problematic. We present evidence from a number of research efforts that product quality and productivity are influenced by the quality of shop-floor labor relations. Hence there may be substantial cost to this strategy. Furthermore, the forces that posed the problem in the first place—product market uncertainty and technical change requiring a flexible labor force—are ongoing and imply continuous adjustment and, while the concession strategy might work once, it is difficult to envision repeated successful applications in the same firm.

Perhaps the deepest source of uncertainty concerning the long-term viability of this strategy is that the current balance of power between management and labor is unlikely to persist. As working conditions worsen, it is likely that new opportunities for union drives will emerge. The historical analogy is the wave of employer militancy preceding and continuing into the early years of the Depression (which, in fact, represented a rejection of a 1920s version of the salaried model) and the subsequent unionization wave that followed. In blue collar employment we might expect renewed union strength in traditional areas as well as new organizing efforts. For white collar employment, an area of increasingly active but thus far not widely successful organizing efforts, there may be even greater chances for unions. As employees perceive that the implicit terms of the salaried model are violated, they are likely to become more open to organization. Indeed, interviews we conducted suggest that the human resource staffs in white collar settings, as well as in the more blue collar firms that currently are structured along salaried lines, are acutely aware of this possibility and constitute an internal lobby against employer militance strategies.

The foregoing arguments are not intended to predict the direction in which we can expect internal labor markets to evolve. We are in a period of considerable uncertainty and confusion in which competing forms coexist. Instead, the point is to describe analytically what some of the choices are and where they came from. In addition, we are interested in highlighting an opening for public employment policy. The salaried model has a great many attractions, both normative and practical. It would seem desirable that as large a fraction of the economy as possible evolve in that direction. However, there also seem to be significant obstacles, notably issues of employment security and the consequences to workers of labor market adjustment. As the earlier material on labor market adjustment demonstrated, employees have good reason to be highly risk averse in the face of any changes in the arrangements that provide a degree of job security. Hence, absent credible assurances, those working under the industrial model will resist giving up its limited protections while firms must fear that those employed in salaried settings will react strongly to cutbacks. By the same token, firms currently organized along the lines of the industrial model will be reluctant to provide the degree of security implied by a shift to a salaried model. This results both from the perceived costs and loss of flexibility in employment levels as well as from an ideological reluctance to forego the higher degree of managerial discretion inherent in the industrial model. Either the employer militancy strategy or marginal adjustments will seem the safer alternative. Hence, from both sides of the equation, workers and firms, the salaried model may seem too uncertain and too costly. The question is whether it is possible to envision ways in which public policy can assist in the transition.

Employment Policy

In our review of American employment policy to date we could not reach optimistic conclusions concerning its capacity to become a credible actor as the events described play out. We saw that if we include vocational education and community colleges along with the U.S. Employment Service and federal employment and training efforts aimed at poor people, the system is extensive. However, we also saw that it is stratified along class lines and that while some programs show net benefits, these gains are not large enough to make a substantial difference in peoples' lives. Furthermore, most components (the community colleges are a partial exception) are, at best, peripherally involved with employers, and the employer community tends not to take these programs seriously as an element of their human resource planning. Finally, the federal employment and training system is best seen as an extension of the welfare system, and this has substantial stigmatizing effects on its clients.

In the face of this (perhaps slightly overly harsh) assessment, what reason is there to believe that employment policy can play an important role in influencing the organization and reorganization of work within firms? Might not one believe that the opening described is illusory in the face of the irrelevance of government programs? To address this objection, we turned in some detail in Chapter 6 to the relationship between employment policy and internal labor markets in Germany and Sweden. In those nations there is a substantial interaction between public and private labor policy. The specifics of that relationship are suggestive, but the more important general lesson is that it is possible to conceive of and implement an employment policy that strengthens certain tendencies in internal labor market development.

In undertaking this comparative research it is very important to understand that we do not argue for the adoption of this or that program from across the Atlantic. A German or Swedish program that makes sense in that institutional context may be irrelevant here and, to assess this, one needs a fairly deep analysis of the context. Instead the point is to employ comparative analysis to sharpen our understanding and appreciation of the possibility of alternative institutional structures and patterns, and in particular the possibilities of a relationship between employment policy and characteristics of internal labor markets in different countries.

Much of the commentary concerning the labor market in Europe has emphasized its rigidity. Whatever the merits of this view concerning the external labor market—and we argue that the case is weaker than the debate would suggest—the *internal* labor markets in Sweden and Germany are surprisingly flexible. This flexibility is evident in the small number of job classifications, the freedom management enjoys in redeploying workers from one job or job family to another, and the very positive attitude of labor toward technical change. Furthermore, and this is important to the point we are making, employment policy plays a significant role in underwriting this pattern, albeit in different ways in each nation.

In Germany the vocational training system for youth—the so-called "dual" system—plays the double role of imparting broad general training and socializing the labor force into a respect for skill as the criteria determining work assignments. The upshot is a labor force able and willing to accept a variety of roles within the firm. An additional element of the German system is that legislation has rendered layoffs quite difficult. Since, as we have argued, job security is a powerful inducement for internal flexibility, this is an added explanation for the suppleness of German internal labor markets.

The Swedish pattern is different in that youth training is more akin to our vocational school system (although there is now some movement in the German direction). Furthermore, despite Employment Security Legislation, the reality is that layoffs are not difficult. The effect of the legislation is simply to require advance notification and some negotiations over which workers will be let go. Indeed, after accounting for the higher rate of temporary layoffs in the United States, the Swedish and American layoff rates are comparable. Instead of job security being based on a job entitlement, the key to the Swedish system is the welfare state, which cushions the cost of job loss, and the extensive set of job training programs that assist people in moving from one job to another. Put differently, in Sweden employment security is social and is based on a set of institutions external to the firm. In Germany the security is more firm specific and in that sense more limited.

None of the foregoing is intended to romanticize the two systems or to gloss over the genuine difficulties they face. It is unfair to attribute the currently high unemployment in Europe to the employment and training system: macroeconomic policy, world trade patterns, and perhaps collective bargaining play a far greater role. However, there are difficulties with both systems. The German dual, or vocational education, system has a degree of stratification and bureaucracy that often seems appalling to American eyes. Furthermore, there is widespread concern that the firm-specific employment security legislation discourages employers from expanding their work force. In Sweden even friends of the training system have criticized it for losing touch with emerging needs of the economy and for becoming too much of a social service agency and too little a labor market instrument. A series of reforms have been launched that address these concerns.

These difficulties should be taken seriously but do not detract from the point of the comparison. The lesson is that employment and training programs can indeed work successfully to solve some of the dilemmas inherent in internal labor market structure. A more concrete lesson is that there are important benefits to be gained from the provision of broad general training. In the case of both countries, although in different ways, labor market policy and training help achieve internal flexibility. As we have seen, this flexibility is highly valuable. The question for the United States, then, is how to construct a model that is relevant to our circumstances.

Employment Security and the Firm

Employment security has been central to much of the book's argument. At the same time—as we tried to make clear in our discussion in Chapter 4 of the core-periphery model—there is good reason for skepticism about the real meaning of the concept and whether it is realistic to expect firms to provide it. As we noted, for every IBM and Eli Lilly that have maintained the policy, there is a Kodak, Polaroid, and Data General that have retreated. Therefore, before turning to public policy, it is now time to be clearer about what employment security means and about whether an adequate, purely private policy is possible.

As we have implied throughout the discussion, employment security is not an absolute standard but, instead, represents a point on a continuum. If we think of one end of that continuum as a day labor shape-up in which there is no commitment beyond pay for that day's work and if we locate the other end by the practices of the very few firms that have made commitments not to lay anyone off regardless of circumstances, the relevant issue is at what point in between the two extremes a given firm falls. For example, historically the automobile industry has been more at the hire/fire end, although it does provide more security than is found in a shape-up, while IBM is closer to the other extreme (although not at it since its policies of forced transfers and incentive retirements amount to quasi-layoffs). One relevant question is where to locate a given firm, not whether that firm has achieved the "ideal-type" system.

A related complication is that, for the purposes of the salaried model, what is most central is that an employment security policy be perceived by the labor force as representing the "best efforts" of the firm. That is, the firm should be seen as making every effort to avoid layoffs, and it is the degree of effort (or cost), not the ultimate absence of layoffs, that represents the key test. Hence, if external events force some involuntary terminations, that in itself is not sufficient to obviate the firm's commitment to employment security nor necessarily to undermine the salaried model. Indeed, in some variants of the employment continuity idea the firm's responsibility is limited to actions—such as the introduction of new technology or outsourcing—over which it has control. Adverse shifts in the product market are not seen as the firm's responsibility and hence any resulting layoffs do not undercut the model.

Another important point concerns the challenge of critics who argue that employment security is a "good times" only policy. That is, many commentators believe that there is little more to the policy than the ability of firms that are profitable and growing to maintain a stable work force. There is obviously some truth to this view, given the bold claims of firms that they renounced as markets turn against them. However, to a substantial extent the criticism misses a deeper point. Employment continuity is, as we keep emphasizing, one aspect of a larger system. A firm that adopts an employment continuity policy must change how it does business along a number of dimensions, ranging from other personnel policies to (frequently) the interaction of design, manufacturing, and human resource strategy. The adoption of the salaried model and the new relationships among the elements of the enterprise signal a way of operating that extends beyond downturns or possibly beyond reductions in force. That is, a firm's inability to avoid all layoffs does not imply that the model is not viable. That determination rests on a broader assessment of all the elements in the system that constitute the firm's internal operations.

A final distinction, or theoretical point, involves stepping back from the operations of the firm and asking about alternative ways an economy can provide employment security. Obviously one option—the one we have emphasized thus far—is for the firm to maintain employment levels. This we term "internal" security or employment continuity. A second broad option is "external" or "social" employment security. In this model the emphasis shifts from maintaining employment at a given firm to assuring that when layoffs do occur the consequences are minimized. In the very extreme case, if there were no adverse economic or social consequences of job loss, the firm could establish a salaried internal labor market structure just as if the employer itself had provided the security. Such extreme security is, of course, highly unlikely but, as in the rest of the discussion, what is at stake is a matter of degree. Obviously, the notion of external security sets the stage for our (lengthy) analysis of public employment policy, and we will defer further discussion until then.

Can Employment Security Be Privately Provided?

We have established that employment security or stabilization programs need to be viewed in the larger context of the firm's internal labor market. We have also developed a number of additional distinctions aimed at clarifying the concept. What we want to do now is ask whether firms can reasonably be expected to develop and sustain effective employment continuity policies on their own. We have already admitted doubts on this score but, to make the discussion more concrete, we will report the results of a case study of a firm that aggressively sought to maintain its traditional no-layoff policy.[1]

The firm in question is one with a long commitment, put in place by the founder (who remains in a leadership position), to employment security. Virtually all staff described this commitment as one of the key "values" of the company. However, several years ago the policy came under severe pressure from two sources. First, the firm found itself drifting toward becoming a high-cost producer as technical change reduced unit labor requirements while staffing remained high. Second, sharp downturns in the product market resulted in several disastrous quarters. In response, the firm initiated a "transition" process. The goals of this effort were somewhat confused: in part it was aimed at rebalancing the labor force by altering the occupational distribution and in part it was intended simply to reduce employment levels. Regardless, the overriding purpose was to reshape the firm's human resource profile without resorting to layoffs.

Under the "transition" process individuals were "selected" if there was surplus staff in their location. In situations in which an entire line was shut down all employees were selected; in other cases specific people were selected by inverse performance ratings. Once selected, the person was exposed to various counseling and orientation sessions, given a chance (with company assistance) to find a new job within the firm, and provided support for outside job search. Retraining was offered to persons who could locate a job elsewhere in the firm. White collar labor (so-called "indirect" labor) could only turn down one job offer elsewhere in the firm, regardless of location, but blue collar workers were not required to relocate. If, after a given period of time, a person could not find a job elsewhere in the firm or a job she or he wanted to accept outside the company, they were placed in a pool and were expected to take on temporary work, part-time assignments, community service, and the like while they continued to search. In several locations when these pools threatened to become too large, the company also offered various plans to encourage resignations, such as bonuses and sweetened pensions.

The reason that this case is useful is that it enables us to draw lessons concerning the possibilities and limits of employment security policies at the firm level. The following seem to be the most important conclusions.

1. The policy entails very substantial resources and other organizational costs. Only a firm that is highly committed to such a policy is likely to undertake it. Although we were unable to quantify the costs of the program precisely, they were clearly very large. They include corporate staff who oversaw the program and collected data on it (at least four full-time staff for a 2-year period); staff in each plant (at least one and often more) who managed the program locally; substantial involvement required of line managers in selecting, counseling, and seeking to place individuals involved in the program; training costs, incentive retirement expenditures, and—doubtlessly the largest cost— continued salaries of individuals involved in the program who remained on the payroll as they looked for other work inside the firm or on the outside. Even one and a half years into the program there were still several hundred people on "hold" status who were collecting a salary but generally not contributing to the firm.

It is certainly possible to argue that some of these costs are offset by gains from the policy. At the concrete level, the firm saved on unemployment insurance taxes and recruitment costs. At the more abstract level, the firm was clearly organized along the lines of the salaried model and, as would be expected, executives rationalized the policy by referring to the positive impact on the morale of employees who were not directly involved. The problem, however, with these offsetting benefits is that they are very abstract. Either they are costs that are saved, and hence only appear on the bottom line by indirection, or else they are benefits that, when they do appear, will be difficult to attribute to the policy. By contrast, the costs are very real and quite attributable.

2. It is clear, at least to those who managed the transition process, that if a firm wishes to avoid crises in the future it must change in fundamental ways how it manages its business. In the past the central value driving this firm's manufacturing strategy was to assure that the product would be shipped with minimum delays. Plant managers were evaluated on their ability to meet virtually any volume requirements that might arise: "The cardinal sin is not being able to ship. Don't run out of capacity and don't fail to deliver on time." This incentive structure created a particular set of human resource practices. Overstaffing was obviously desirable, since it provided slack that could meet peak demands. As new products came on line, the tendency was to establish new production lines instead of risk disrupting production by integrating the new product into existing lines. This, in turn, led to a distant relationship between design and manufacturing divisions, since manufacturing needs could be met at the last minute by acquiring new bodies.

For the managers who participated in the transition process (and not all did, since many plants were unaffected and the engineering and sales divisions were only lightly touched), all of these assumptions were called into question. One manager commented:

> We learned a lot. For instance, take the four hundred contract people we had before. We were actually less productive with more people. Now we don't allow people to fill up all the space. We no longer see "bigness" as goodness. Before I ever hire another direct labor person I better be damn well convinced that I have a job for that person as long as I'm around. I don't want to have to go through this process again.

At a deeper level the senior managers responsible for the transition process are also attempting to introduce new practices. For example, staff from manufacturing now work with product design people in order to limit the duplication of staff required to bring new products on line. There are efforts to expand training expenditures in order to create a more flexible labor force as well as a rethinking of policies that move load from plant to plant in order to maintain employment. However, the politics of these reforms are difficult, as managers who participated in the transition process are true believers while others resist restructuring the firm.

With respect to our earlier discussion, what all of this implies is that a commitment to employment security requires restructuring the organization along a number of dimensions. This strengthens the point that employment security is not simply a "good times" or "bad times" policy but instead, at a different level, represents an alternative mode of planning and organization.

3. Even with a high level of commitment the firm cannot provide employment security. Despite the large expenditure of resources and extremely powerful company culture aimed at maintaining the security pledge in the end the firm was forced to rely on a number of devices that shifted insecurity into the external labor market. Although no layoffs were implemented, and in this sense the formal definition of security was maintained, the firm did withdraw employment from 1700 temporary and contract employees and also provided incentive retirements to another 1000 workers (retraining and redeployment involved a further 1500 employees).

The elimination of temporary and contract employment is clearly a layoff in the economic sense of the term, although the firm can argue that these were not regular employees. The incentive retirement case is more difficult, since the individuals voluntarily participated. Nonetheless, there was doubtless a concern that failure to participate would lead to adverse consequences (either layoffs or transfers to unacceptable locations), and some fraction of these separations must be seen as layoffs. In any case, despite the commitment of resources (and the underlying health of the product market), the firm was unable to maintain employment levels internally and had to shed labor. The subsequent fate of those who left is no longer of concern to the firm and becomes a matter of public policy. Firms on their own are limited in their ability to stabilize employment.[2]

What all of this suggests is not that job security is hopeless. A firm acting on its own can go some way down the road and in doing so accomplish a good deal. In the case described here the firm's obvious efforts enabled it to maintain the goodwill of the employees who were not part of the reduction, and hence the salaried model remained intact. It is clear that any fully mature policy must involve efforts by employers of the kind we have described. Nonetheless, without an effective public policy there is a real question about how many firms will show the degree of commitment and willingness to endure the costs outlined here and, as we have seen, even such firms cannot fully meet the issue.

In addition to the problems noted in the foregoing, an additional problem inherent in relying on firms to provide the necessary degree of security is that an important component of security must be the ability of workers to change employers successfully should the need arise. This ability rests in turn on general training (i.e., skills that are useful in other companies, not merely to the current employer), and virtually all analysts agree that firms will underprovide such training, since they fear that workers literally will walk away with the investment.

Hence the clear limitations of purely private strategies open the way for consideration of active employment policy, and it is to this that we will now turn.

Toward an American Employment Policy

The arguments developed in this book point to four goals for employment policy. The first three follow.

- *Enhance Prospects of Intrafirm Mobility for the Incumbent Work Force.*
  This is an important objective because, as the labor force becomes more mobile and flexible, it is better able to adapt to changing conditions without layoffs.

- *Improve the Efficiency with Which Interfirm Mobility Occurs*. It is not reasonable to expect that firms will never need to adjust the size of their labor force. We have seen that the American labor market does a poor job of moving experienced workers from one firm to another yet, without sufficiently hopeful mobility prospects, workers will remain attached to traditional forms of job protection.
- *Individuals in Persistent Labor Market Difficulty Need To Be Assisted*. For our purposes this assistance should take the form of employment and training efforts, although it is clear that other interventions, such as basic skills education, are also often necessary.

These three goals are reasonable objectives for an expanded employment and training system. However, they are limited, at least at a first approximation, to enhancing the mobility and employment prospects of individuals. Yet a major thrust of this book has been to argue that a pressing objective of public policy is to act as midwife to the shift from industrial to salaried internal labor markets (in much of blue collar work) and to the preservation of salaried internal labor markets in white collar settings. This, then, is a fourth objective. It is clear that there are other aspects of public policy, particularly regulatory efforts, that are as important as employment and training policy in this regard, and we are making no claim here that an effective employment policy is sufficient to accomplish the goal. Nonetheless, for the reasons we have developed at length, employment policy is important.

Employment policy can help achieve this fourth objective in several ways. First, as we have repeatedly argued, if a reasonable level of employment security can be maintained, the transformation will be eased. There are two forms employment security can take. Internal security can be provided by firms willing and able to stabilize employment. This is possible to an extent but is, as we have seen, quite difficult. External security can be provided if the penalties for job loss are not great. This can be accomplished by a combination of safety net efforts (unemployment insurance, extended health insurance, etc.) and by employment programs that can overcome the barriers to mobility between employers. The extreme European efforts can be interpreted as attempts to deploy public policy (laws prohibiting layoffs) to achieve internal security. By contrast, the suggestions in this book are aimed at using public policy to provide a higher degree of external security both because such external security has merit on its own terms and because it can provide the basis for reform of internal practices.

In addition to the direct provision of security, employment policy can be important if it creates indirect incentives to transform internal labor markets. If, for example, public support expands general training within firms this, in turn, will create pressure to utilize the new skills. The boundaries surrounding jobs may weaken and intrafirm mobility may ease. Over time the pressures and opportunities that derive from a highly skilled labor force may subtly move the internal labor market in the direction of salaried patterns.

The Employment and Training System

We have brought the discussion of employment policy full circle to its postwar beginnings. In the late 1950s and early 1960s the emphasis was on the problems of mainstream workers displaced by automation and trade. The first employment and training legislation—the Area Redevelopment Act and the Manpower Development and Training Act—was aimed at this group. Tight labor markets and the War on Poverty soon shifted the focus but, for the reasons we have laid out, it seems important to return to the earlier concerns. However, if we are to reemphasize these themes we want to do so with a difference and not simply play out again a familiar set of policy initiatives, strategies, and errors.

In thinking through the shape of policy two major issues emerge: the institutional structure in which that policy is embedded ("who does what to whom") and the programmatic content of the policy. It is our strong view that it is more important to focus on the creation of a credible system that on specific programmatic interventions. There are two reasons for this. The first is the relatively obvious one, that the needs of individuals are too varied to admit a single category of intervention, and there is also considerable variation in the tactics that are appropriate to different kinds of firms. The issue is whether a system can be put into a place that is flexible enough to shape programs to particular circumstances.

The second reason why it is important to emphasize the development of a strong system is more subtle but probably more important. We have argued that a central function of employment and training programs is to provide the labor force with sufficient security that on-the-job flexibility is forthcoming. Specific programs are too ephemeral, they lack "presence," and hence are unlikely to accomplish this objective. Instead, what is needed is the visible, concrete existence of an agency with the appropriate responsibilities that can be held accountable for meeting its objectives. This agency needs to have an active and vigorous presence at the local level and have at its disposal a variety of programmatic tools to meet different needs. Over time, as this system proves itself and gains credibility, it can meet the broad goals we have established.

There are, it is true, current discussions of programs (e.g., Individual Training Accounts) that bypass this question simply by making funds available to people to purchase their own training. In addition to being poorly targeted and hence wasteful (i.e., a substantial fraction of the funds would go to people who do not need them), the idea raises serious issues of quality control (consider the recent scandals regarding proprietary schools). Such a voucher system also provides no structure for maintaining any ongoing responsibility for the individual, either while they are "spending" their vouchers or after the training is complete. Without an organizational structure with a goal and accountability as well as with specific program components (e.g., counseling and placement), it is hard to believe that a program can achieve quality results, much less accomplish the difficult mission we have set of helping to re-create internal labor markets by providing a credible safety net.

Our discussion of the shape of an effective system will focus on four topics: eligibility, the structure of the system, financing the system, and staffing the system. After discussing these institutional issues, we will describe specific programmatic interventions that the system might deliver.

Program Eligibility

We have already described the consequences of an employment and training system that is means tested. It becomes perceived as part of the welfare system and mere participation has the effect of stigmatizing clients. Furthermore, firms—interested in recruiting people with a broad range of characteristics—will avoid the system or treat it as a charity. It is clear therefore that a public employment policy that seeks to play an important role in labor market issues cannot be limited to any one income group. As a practical matter, however, this does not mean universal coverage. The training system for high-level personnel seems to perform well, and there is no reason to expect that any new policy can or should supplant it. Indeed, the public employment policies of even the most activist European nations still do not extend into the top third or so of the occupational distribution. Our conclusion is that in the United States means tested eligibility should be eliminated and we should expect that the system will touch on noncollege-level occupations and perhaps a bit further. Even this more modest objective will greatly extend the system and make it a far more attractive instrument for the private economy.

What about poor people? They are the traditional constituency of the employment and training system. Furthermore, we took pains in Chapter 2 to demonstrate that their numbers are substantial and that their needs remain high on the list of priorities of any employment and training system. However, they seem to have dropped from view in our subsequent discussion, and suddenly we are considering broadening the system so that it is no longer aimed at those most in need. Is this not a perverse set of priorities? The answer goes to results. The current system "belongs" to poor people but does not (as we have shown) serve them well. A different system may have a broader constituency but, if the system as a whole is more effective, it will serve poor people better. The basic idea we propose is that a set of institutions provide training for a wide range of people, and the governmental (regulatory) authorities assure that poor people are included. The "graduates" of such training would not be stigmatized because of the broad client base. Poor people would blend in and at the next step in the system be treated no differently than anyone else.

There are practical objections to this scenario, the most serious of which is that many disadvantaged labor force participants require remedial services, especially basic education, that "mainstream" institutions may either be loath to offer or will provide in a set of tracks that have the effect of restratifying the system. It is here that there remains a continuing role for the range of community-based institutions that, in the past, have served as the backbone of the old employment and training system. It would be undesirable for these institutions to retain their training and placement functions since, by their very nature, they signal employers about the characteristics of their clients. However, they may effectively serve as preparatory institutions for the broader employment and training system that we envision.

The Employment and Training System

What institutional form should the employment and training system take? This question is particularly important given that we have emphasized the importance of the system *per se* (i.e., that an active, visible, administrative structure must exist in order to provide credibility to the policy). To repeat, we will discuss particular programmatic ideas and models, and many readers will find it easier to get excited about these than about a plea for what seems to be mere bureaucratic reform. Nonetheless, without the stable, visible, ongoing administrative agency, specific programs will come and go and make little impact on the broad themes we have raised and on large numbers of individuals.

In thinking through how to create a sound structure, one must choose between inventing new institutions or drawing on those already available. The former course may seem cleaner and has the advantage of giving greater freedom to the planners' imagination. However, this tactic loses the opportunity to gain the political support of existing and well-connected institutions. Furthermore, new institutional inventions rarely perform up to expectations.

Accepting this point, we still must ask where the system should be centered. In our view, the heart of the system must be at the level of local labor markets. With very few exceptions labor markets are local, and both workers and managers must see in their community an institution capable of addressing their needs. There are good arguments for loose linkages among these agencies— perhaps coordinated by state governments—and obviously federal money will bring with it a degree of federal oversight. Nonetheless, the bulk of the energy should go into building up the strong local presence of the system.

If we look at the existing landscape, three institutions seem to be appropriate players but, as things stand, each suffers from significant disabilities. Both logic and availability suggest that the Employment Service play an important role. The Employment Service is ubiquitous, and its placement and labor market information roles are clearly at the core of any policy. In Sweden the Employment Service runs the active labor market policy; in the United States there have long been calls to create a comparable role for the Employment Service. Indeed, in 1966 George Shultz headed a task force that suggested that the employment service become a "one stop manpower services agency."[3] The difficulty in America is not logic but performance. As we have seen, the reputation of the Employment Service is deservedly abysmal, and it seems unable to perform its mission for even low-level blue collar work. This raises serious questions concerning its capacity to play a constructive role in a program aimed at upper-level blue collar and low-level to mid-level white collar employees. Clearly, any effort to include the Employment Service in a new initiative must incorporate a wide-ranging reform of that institution.

Many would argue that the logical training providers are the community colleges. Among all the elements of the American employment and training system, these apparently perform best and have the great advantage of being potentially broad based and nonstigmatizing. The difficulty is that there is considerable state to state variation in quality. This, of course, raises the problem that has plagued all programs of this sort: what is the appropriate balance between federal and local control? The War on Poverty (and, to a lesser extent, CETA) were federal efforts that drew on local providers, but with substantial central regulation. The Job Training Partnership Act creates strong state power and largely eliminates federal oversight. There is no easy answer, but it may be that a new federal/state governance structure able to assert and exert quality control is necessary.

Given our focus on local labor markets the Private Industry Councils (PICs), initiated under CETA but greatly strengthened by the JTPA, would seem appropriate to play a central role. What gives the PICs a potentially distinctive mission (in contrast to the Employment Service, which also has local offices) is that the PICs are tripartite, including representatives from government, business, and labor. Hence they are best positioned to achieve the sort of corporatist control and commitment that characterize European models. A PIC that reached its potential could organize a labor market around a set of objectives concerning employment security, placement, and training. The rub is again practical. The great majority of PICs contain third-level business representation, limited union participation, and far too many government officials. It is a rare PIC that has begun to conceive of its role, much less act on it, in any but the most pro forma terms.

The true administrative power for employment and training at the local level is the so-called Service Delivery Agency, which houses the staff that administers the JTPA grant. Typically, this agency is under mayoral control and is the successor to the former CETA administrative agency. The staff of this agency generally constitutes the most experienced group of employment and training professionals in an area. Most PICs depend on this staff and, while there are exceptions, it would be naive to expect most PICs to develop substantial independent expertise.

In the end, the best option seems to be to strengthen PICs and to rely on the combination of a strong PIC and Service Delivery Agency. This agency would (as is done now) develop financial agreements with training agencies, particularly community colleges, to provide services.

As noted, the placement function of the Employment Service should be central yet, as constituted, the Employment Service is unable to deliver quality services, and none of the (internal to the Employment Service system) administrative reforms of the past two decades have changed this. This implies that one major organizational change is warranted: placing local Employment Service offices directly under the control of the employment and training agency we have described. JTPA, in fact, recognizes that the two institutions should work together and attempts to accomplish this by requiring that the PIC approve the annual plans of local offices. However, as a practical matter, this is pro forma, since local office heads report to a central state Employment Service agency and that central agency has discretion over the distribution of resources and over personnel decisions. The only way to improve the Employment Service and to integrate it into the Employment and Training System is to alter radically the power and reporting relationships.

With the exception of shifting control over the Employment Service and elimination of income based eligibility limits, the arrangement described in one sense does not represent much of a departure from the current structure. The minimal interpretation of the recommendations is that existing structures simply be greatly expanded, professionalized, and given new tools and resources. However, what seems to be a difference in degree would become a difference in kind. To see the contrast between the current situation and the setup we envision, under the new system it would be a natural response for a firm to call our agency to seek help with a training issue, to recruit new workers, or to plan for a reduction in employment, and it would be equally natural for workers to turn to the agency for retraining or job placement assistance. Similarly, other local actors (e.g., mayors and economic development officials) would regard the agency as a major player to be brought into a wide range of issues. Instead of being an obscure bureaucratic backwater, the agency would be as visible and well known as any city department other, perhaps, than the school system. In short, a well-financed, locally based agency that provides services to a range of income groups and occupations, with control over the Employment Service, good ties to community colleges, and a range of programmatic tools, could become a visible and active presence in a way in which the Employment and Training System never has in the past. As such, it could go a long way toward fulfilling the mission that we have set for the employment and training system.

Financing the System

It is clear that we envision a substantially expanded employment and training effort and that this in turn will require increased funding. Normally one would expect resources to be derived from general revenue and, doubtlessly, a substantial portion will be. However, there is a strong case to be made for consideration of a training payroll tax.

Such a scheme would levy a percentage tax on firms based on the value of their payroll. It would be undesirable to increase the tax burden on labor, since that would create a disincentive to expand employment. However, such a tax need not have this effect. Several states have already reduced the unemployment insurance tax by a given amount (in California by a half a percentage point) and replaced it with a training tax. Federal legislation could mandate such a system nationally.

The advantage of a training tax (with or without a reduction in Unemployment Insurance taxes) are several. Given that the very existence of a stable and credible training system has significant programmatic value, the identification of dedicated and relatively stable revenue becomes programmatically important. In the past the roller-coaster budgets of training programs have destroyed, not enhanced, the sense of a institutionalized system that can reliably deliver services.

The second advantage of the payroll tax is that it enhances firms' and unions' identification with the training system. How this would work is illustrated in many states where the politics of unemployment insurance is such that the employer community and unions take a proprietary attitude toward funds and are active players in policymaking concerning any disbursements into nonunemployment benefit purposes. Given that an important goal is to tie the training system and the employer community more closely together, giving employers a financial stake in the system makes good sense.

The final advantage of payroll tax funding is that it can set the stage for some interesting program designs. In particular, a fraction of the funds can be returned to firms in return for enhanced training and mobility prospects for incumbent workers. The goal here is to encourage firms to provide more general training (versus very specific job-related training) and, in doing so, to make the labor force more mobile both internally and externally. Typically, firms are reluctant to provide such training for fear of losing the investment as workers leave. However, the arrangement proposed here avoids this disincentive, since the firms would pay the tax regardless and from the firm's perspective there would be no reason not to reclaim a portion of the tax for internal training. We will have more to say about the implementation of this proposal.

Staffing the System

We have already noted that one characteristic of the remedial Employment and Training System is the tremendous institutional instability of service providers. Organizations come in and out of existence, and there are no clear career lines for staff. Since one of our major objectives is to create a visible and stable presence, it will be important to alter these past patterns. In part this can be accomplished by greater reliance on more stable institutions, notably community colleges. In part it will be necessary to raise salaries, establish career development programs, and generally treat employment and training staff as most professional civil servants are treated. This is clearly not a striking or dramatic recommendation nor one likely to generate enthusiasm, but it is an important component of system building.

The Content of Employment Policy

As we have emphasized, the most important task is to build a credible system. If such a system were in place its managers would find no shortage of interesting programmatic ideas. These might range from remedial education followed by job training for the economically disadvantaged to vigorous use of the training tax program previously outlined in order to enhance mobility prospects of incumbent workers. In some respects the programs would seem little different from those currently in place while, in other instances, they would represent innovations. What would be most different would be the sum of the parts. Under the system we envision that strong, well-funded, professionalized local agency would be able to deliver, and coordinate, a range of services. Ultimately this agency would become powerful enough to organize the local market in the sense of providing, directly or indirectly, a considerable amount of training and placement services and thus having a noticeable impact on the flow of labor. It is foolish and undesirable to expect that the agency could in any sense manage or dominate labor market flows, but the fact that the agency is a significant player will go a long way toward meeting our objectives.

What are examples of programs that such an agency could sponsor? Whatever programs are organized must share the ability to provide general skills and inter-firm mobility. Although we have not emphasized youth employment as a policy issue, it is at this point that a revitalized training policy should begin. If youth received more effective training either prior to labor market entry or upon entry, they would gain a deeper skill base which in turn would enhance the prospects of later mobility and leave them less vulnerable to shifts in the demand for their skills. The point here is not to design a "youth program" to reduce youth unemployment, although that is a legitimate concern, but rather to improve the entry process in a way that upgrades the skill base of the labor force and hence makes it more flexible and mobile.

One approach toward accomplishing this is to improve school based vocational education programs. There is much to recommend this strategy, given the enormous investment in such programs already in place. However, we have seen that vocational education has minimal payoff. Among the sources of the disappointing performance of school-based training are the stigmatization inherent in programs geared to a small minority of school graduates, the difficulty such programs have in staying in touch with shifting technologies, and the related issue of long-term commitments to often-obsolete equipment and courses. For these reasons, it is worth considering alternative ways of improving entry-level job skills. In the end, as a realistic matter, the vocational education system will have to be a partner in any policy initiative, but it is important to have a clear sense of where we would like to go.

The obvious starting point for such an effort is the German apprenticeship program. As we have seen, there are two highly desirable aspects of this model. First, youth training is tightly integrated into the economic needs and calculus of firms, and this makes for better quality training and a highly ordered and unwasteful entry process. Second, because the training is deep, it provides employees with a genuine skill base that can form the foundation of a career. A third characteristic is the near universality that imbues the credential with credibility, avoids stigmitization inherent in separate narrow vocational tracks, and insures that the system has a substantial impact on the structure of the economy. Taken as a whole, the key lesson is that the provision of high-quality general training provides the basis for a more adaptable labor force than that which characterizes the United States.

The characteristics of the model that are the hardest for most American observes to swallow are bureaucractic rigidity (with a central agency defining

acceptable occupations and prescribing a uniform curriculum) and, too frequently, highly firm-specific training. In fact, however, these are not the big-
gest problems facing any attempt at transplantation. One key difficulty is the
early tracking implicit in the system. It is unlikely that American colleges will
accept high school degrees in which a large fraction of the final 3 years is spent
outside school in firms. This means that a literal adoption of the system implies
an early stratification of youth in college and noncollege streams (as, in fact,
is done in Germany). Such tracking would run into widespread opposition.

A second problem flows from the decentralized character of American education. Because of local control a national program is not possible. However,
in a geographically mobile labor market educational credentials need to have
some commonly understood content or they are not transportable. It is true that
the quality and even content of a high school degree today is far from uniform,
but the introduction of such a substantial deviation from accepted practice may
pose problems.

These difficulties suggest that the best chances for adopting features of the
German model lie in some combination of an additional apprenticeship year
after high school for youth who do not continue to college and a less stringent
partnership between business and high school for enrolled youth. The Swedes,
for example, are considering adding an additional vocational year for high school
graduates who will use that period for apprenticeships in firms. However, perhaps the most relevant example comes from Britain.

Britain, whose educational system is more akin to ours (and where traditional union-based apprenticeship programs have virtually collapsed), has established a Youth Training Scheme that draws heavily on the German example.
Under this system all youth, on leaving school, are entitled to subsidized employment in a firm. The placement is intended to provide training by rotation
through a variety of occupations and, in some versions of the scheme, the
equivalent of a day a week over the course of a year is spent in more formal
education. Although many of the specific activities involved in this effort seem
hasty and a simple stopgap response to high unemployment, when viewed from
another angle it does indeed represent an effort to alter the training and entry
process fundamentally.

Closer to home a few communities have experimented with new approaches. Perhaps the best-known example is the Boston Compact, a program
under which businesses in Boston guarantee jobs to all youth who graduate
from high school. As part of this effort, many firms work with schools throughout the year, providing a variety of assistance as well as summer job placements. Most experts regard this as the most successful example of so-called
business/school partnerships, and it has had a substantial impact on reducing
youth unemployment among school graduates. However, it is too early to judge
the program's impact on subsequent career mobility.

Given that such a system holds promise, there remain a series of very difficult issues in making it work. The respective roles of firms, unions, and
schools in the design and management of the system is one example. Further-

more, given past performance and a history of extreme bureaucratic aggressiveness, it is highly desirable to prevent the vocational education system from capturing such an effort, yet this will not be easy. Striking the proper balance between specific and general training is yet another challenge. Nonetheless, these obstacles are not sufficiently daunting that an effort to deepen and broaden the skill base of entry workers should not be undertaken.

Enhancing mobility prospects (as well as having some impact on youth unemployment) by building a more mature entry process does seem promising. However, the major effort is to find ways to secure adult employment. This will require enhanced training (and, when necessary, placement) efforts for the incumbent work force.

Providing general training for incumbent employees will be a difficult objective to accomplish because, perhaps surprisingly, expanded general training goes against the grain of many firms' personnel practices. We have already noted one reason why this is true: firms fear that any investments they make in general training are insecure since, by definition, worker mobility is enhanced. This difficulty is compounded because the rigid wage structure that characterizes many internal labor markets makes it hard for firms to be "paid" for the general training through lower wages for workers who are receiving it.[4] There are additional reasons why such training has historically been underprovided. Training for jobs that do not yet exist implies sharing with the labor force information on future plans for technological innovations. Reluctance to do this has been a major obstacle for some of the joint union-management training programs to be discussed shortly, and it extends into nonunion settings. In addition, line managers—who usually have to approve released time and sometimes budgets—fail to see the payoff for themselves, since they lose staff and budget from production and do not gain any immediate output increases. Finally, the experience of several training projects suggests that on the employee side there is often fear and reluctance to step into unknown occupational areas.[5]

These reasons, as well as more mechanical ones such as the tendency of companies to reimburse employees after the fact and not before, help explain why the most prevalent form of general training assistance—tuition remission policies—is usually extremely underutilized. Nonetheless, for all of the reasons we have developed, it is important to find ways to expand general training for incumbent workers.

One promising strategy is to support whenever possible the initiation and expansion of joint union-management training programs. There are a number of notable examples of such agreements, particularly the ones between the Communications Workers of America and both AT&T and the regional phone companies and the agreements between the United Auto Workers and Ford and GM.[6] These programs can take a variety of forms but usually involve some source of joint funding and joint administration. However, in some cases the union manages training on its own. The orientation and content of the programs can also vary. There are examples of very general training in which workers receive support for taking courses in local community colleges on topics related to their work but not tied to any specific occupational goal. More specific training occurs when employees are trained in emerging fields that are highly likely to be relevant to foreseeable job openings. Finally, other efforts are organized in the context of employment reductions and are aimed at finding new jobs for workers suddenly in distress.

There are a number of ways in which public assistance can help expand the scope of these efforts. Increasingly, for example, Title III dislocated worker funds from JTPA are used to underwrite programs partially, but other possibilities include technical assistance, funding of pilot efforts, tuition remission at community colleges, and moral suasion directed toward reluctant parties. The central objective is to help support existing efforts and diffuse the model into sectors not yet active.

Promising as these programs are, they are clearly only a relatively small part of the story simply because the scope of union coverage is narrow and is getting smaller. It is more difficult to devise promising models for expanding general training in nonunion settings. At this point the outlined training tax scheme becomes relevant. The key difficulty in such an effort, of course, is assuring that the training represents a net addition and not simply a substitution for on-the-job training that would have otherwise occurred. Indeed, it would be impossible to monitor this directly short of requiring firms to provide detailed accounting of their past and current training expenditures; this would be overly burdensome and would ultimately remain unreliable. Instead, the best strategy seems to be to require some level of match by the firm and then collect data to assure that this subset of the training budget (the tax return plus the match) is spent on general training. This could be operationalized as training not required for performance of the individual's current job. The training could occur in the firm, in local community colleges, or in other training institutions. The local labor market agency described previously would be responsible for administering this program and monitoring the training. This definition is not watertight, and there would remain considerable slippage; nonetheless, widespread underprovision of general training suggests that this modest redirecting of the already existing unemployment insurance tax is worth undertaking.

It is not possible to administer a training tax/subsidy program like the one outlined before in all firms because the cost of administration and monitoring would be prohibitive. A firm size cutoff is therefore necessary. This, however, raises a difficult problem, because a strong case can be made that it is in small firms that the greatest underprovision of general training occurs. Several studies have shown that training is underprovided in small firms for two reasons.[7] First, these firms often are simply unable to devote management time to human resource issues. They are early in their product life cycle or operate in more competitive environments and hence have more pressing product development and product market concerns. Second, small firms lack an extensive internal labor market and hence will be even more concerned than large firms that any resources devoted to training will be lost as workers leave.

Given these considerations, it makes sense for a consortium of small firms, along with the public authority, to sponsor training jointly at an external institution. The role of the training agency is crucial here as a catalyst to bring the firms together, to develop an accurate assessment of common training needs, and to help finance and organize the program. If most of the relevant firms in the area participate, it is not unreasonable to expect some financial participation by the firms, since they will be protected from "free riders." A logical extension of such an approach, although one with more radical implications, is to create a common labor pool so that workers who are temporarily redundant in one firm will be loaned to another. Arrangements of this kind seem common in Japan, and there are a few examples in the United States.[8] Such a model would require a set of firms that share relatively similar skills but tend to be at different points on the product cycle or the business cycle. It would not work if all firms needed to divest themselves of employees at the same time. However, whether or not this particular extension is viable, the general model of industry-centered joint training agreements with a strong placement component has considerable promise.

Turning to other efforts at adult training and placement, in recent years an important thrust has been efforts to assist the victims of plant closings and large-scale layoffs. These are the dislocated workers to whom we paid such close attention in Chapter 2. Programs for this group have been sponsored under the auspices of Title III of JTPA, under the Trade Adjustment Assistance Act, and under various union-management agreements of the sort described for CWA and the UAW. By now we have a reasonable body of data on what works for whom.[9] Indeed, this knowledge goes back even further and includes some of the earlier retraining efforts aimed at displacement, such as the Armour Automation program in the 1960s. The general lesson from these efforts is that success is strongly age related, with older workers faring poorly, that placement is at least as important as retraining, that a major issue is teaching workers who have labored for years in sheltered markets how to function in an external market (Shultz and Weber speak of "a sense of mobility"), and that hastily designed last-minute programs usually fail. (Again from Shultz and Weber: "the most artfully conceived plan only has significance to the displaced worker when the parties are committed to the intensive administration of the program over a prolonged period of time.")[10]

The typical program today centers around a worker assistance center that provides counseling, placement, and training services for laid-off workers who are searching for employment elsewhere. Although these efforts often ameliorate the situation of the displaced, they suffer from being reactive. They are typically triggered by a plant closing or large-scale layoff. The crisis nature of the intervention, the short time usually available (even if advance warning is practiced), and the institutionally ad hoc nature of the response all limit the effectiveness of such efforts. This is not to imply that such efforts are not important; when a layoff or closing occurs, a response is necessary, and our training agency should take an active role. However, the most effective response will have been the prior training and placement efforts that will have created a more flexible and mobile labor force and hence make the last-minute responses less desperate.

These points notwithstanding, in addition to the worker assistance center approach, there are several other creative policy responses to layoffs that have been sporadically tried but that deserve diffusion. The first two seek to reduce (although not avoid) layoffs. Several states have experimented with part-time unemployment insurance under which firms can reduce a full-time employee to part-time work, and the worker can collect unemployment insurance for the lost hours. This, of course, would reduce the number of workers permanently separated, since the firm can attain the appropriate reduction in hours without laying people off. As already noted, such a scheme is less attractive in U.S. settings than it is in Europe because many American layoffs end in recalls anyway. Furthermore, the seniority system may create a disincentive for more senior employees to accept reduced hours given that their full-time jobs are relatively secure and the brunt of adjustment falls on younger employees. Furthermore, in many cases the firm's technology may make part-time work cumbersome, and the fixed costs (e.g., benefits) associated with each body employed may make two part-time employees more expensive than one full-time worker. Nonetheless, this plan has been intensively used by a number of employers (Motorola is often cited as making the greatest use in Arizona and California[11]), and its slow diffusion may be attributable to the limited number of states (12 as of 1986) that permit it and the fact that most employers, even in those states, are not fully familiar with the possibilities.[12]

Second, it is worth considering the implications of the paradox that firms that are laying off one category of employees are often at the same time hiring in another area. For example, a company may be reducing its ranks of middle managers and blue collar production workers but expanding employment of technicians and salespeople. There are several reasons for this paradox. First, and most obvious, the firm may believe it impossible, too expensive, or too time consuming to train a blue collar worker to be, for example, an effective salesperson. Second, except at the most senior levels (and senior executives are generally unconcerned with the details of personnel actions), different managers who do not connect with each other are responsible for the two actions.

A worthwhile experiment would be for the training agency described previously (which has as part of its function keeping in touch with the actions of firms in its area) to offer retraining subsidies to firms that are willing to retrain workers due to be laid off for other jobs within the firm. Such a subsidy would not be aimed at featherbedding or keeping on unneeded workers, and there would be a need for a check, such as requiring that after training the employee change occupations. Not all laid-off employees, or even a majority of them, can be saved in this way, since the hiring may not be sufficiently extensive and since in many cases the retraining will be impractical (it would be less impractical if our earlier recommendations for more extensive general training for incumbent employees were taken up). However, firms frequently underestimate the recruitment, training, and socialization costs of new employees, and a training subsidy tied to layoff prevention would tip the balance again maintaining employment levels in a number of cases.

Getting from Here to There

What reason is there to believe that expanded public policies will find a friendly reception in the current political climate? We have devoted considerable energy to arguing that product market, technological developments, and demographic developments will increase uncertainty in labor markets and will force the issue of job security onto the agenda. We have also argued that the constituency for such efforts is broader than that which previously existed for training policy because firms, increasingly finding difficulty in reorganizing work and in maintaining an incumbent labor force, will become receptive to a public policy that helps meet their needs.

A more forceful argument against the pessimistic view is that the evolution of policy in this area is often a long-term affair and that ideas that seem utopian at their inception gain, with changing circumstances and local experimentation, a legitimacy and constituency and often success. Consider, for example, the history of unemployment insurance, a policy that today is taken for granted.[13] Although European nations, by the first decade of the twentieth century, had introduced a form of insurance, based on union-managed funds on the Continent and managed by the government in England, the idea of a compulsory insurance system was anathema in America. Concerned social policy experts, particularly those associated with the American Association for Labor Legislation, sought to use the European experience to place unemployment insurance on the American agenda. However, the business community and politicans were opposed, and even the head of the American Federation of Labor, Samuel Gompers, believed as late as 1921 that "anyone who advocates compulsory unemployment insurance simply aggravates the evil of unemployment instead of helps those it is . . . desired to aid."[14]

However, as circumstances changed so did the possibilities of reform. Some elements of the business community experimented with company-based unemployment insurance schemes, the General Electric Swopes plan being the most famous, other firms (e.g., Kodak) also organized similar efforts. Some unions, notably those in the needle trades, organized industry-based plans. Finally, some states—with Wisconsin in the lead—passed unemployment insurance plans. Many of these efforts were flawed in their design or failed in the face of rising unemployment. However, even in the 1920s, before the urgency caused by the Depression, the idea of unemployment insurance gained increasing support and moved to center stage. The combination of intellectual discussion, growing business support of at least some versions of plans, changing union attitudes, local experimentation and, finally, brutally changed circumstances brought a new social policy to fruition.

With this history in mind how can we interpret current developments? Employment security and employment policy are indeed important emerging issues. It is possible to discern three thrusts or tendencies along these lines.

First, some firms are working on their own to maintain or expand their commitments to employment security. As noted, from the firm's perspective— and in terms of the salaried internal labor market model—an absolute no-layoff pledge is not required, and few companies (Lincoln Electric is often cited for making the pledge) make this commitment. However, many other employers are attempting to make employment continuity part of their human resource planning.[15] It is certainly the case that in the professional personnel literature there is a growing recognition of the issue. It should be no surprise that these companies are utilizing many of the techniques—peripheral work forces, ex- panded internal training, broad job classifications—that we have discussed. However, also for the reasons we have examined at length, it is very difficult for firms on their own to maintain such a policy. Still, there is strong evidence that the issue is on the corporate agenda, and interest in employment stabili- zation is strong.

Second, we have already noted that at the level of union-management ne- gotiations employment security has become a (if not *the*) central issue. Some of the joint training agreements described in this conclusion are the fruits of these agreements, and it is now a typical pattern to bargain to expand training and gain security in return for eased work rules. The most recent such example in a major contract is the agreement between the U.A.W. and Ford which attempts to fix employment levels for the life of the contract. However, as promising as these agreements are, they are subject to the same difficulties that a firm acting on its own faces in providing employment continuity. Put dif- ferently, the agreements accomplish a good deal but still must be buttressed (and diffused) by public policy.

Growing public policy efforts represent the third thrust. Quite surprisingly, employment policy has been reborn late in the Reagan Administration. Much of the current discussion of welfare reform centers on increasing the role of job training to reduce dependency. We have explained why a training system limited to, or focused largely on, welfare recipients is problematic, but the growing interest still represents a real opportunity. In addition, expansion of training programs for dislocated workers, consideration of extending health in- surance to laid-off workers, advance notification of layoffs and plant closings, and improvements in the Trade Adjustment Assistance Act are all lively items on the policy agenda. Indeed, a Department of Labor task force chaired by former undersecretary Malcolm Lovell recently recommended expansion of these efforts, and the theme has been taken up by the new Democratic Senate. Again, the problem is that these efforts thus far have been conceived as relatively narrow reactions to layoffs, not as establishing a system with the kind of proac- tive and continuing employment and training policy we have advocated. None- theless, the opportunity is real.

Each of the foregoing three impulses are flawed in some way, yet it is also important to recognize that each also represents an opening in the direction we advocate. The policies outlined in this chapter are aimed at extending and building on each of these tendencies. As we have repeatedly emphasized, policy in this area cannot succeed in a vacuum. It must proceed from perceived needs and build on existing interests. What we have suggested is a series of initiatives that fill in some gaps, provide incentives to move in a particular direction, diffuse best practices, and underwrite some risks. It is not unrealistic to believe that such a strategy will succeed, given the growing salience of the issues that concern us and the foundation of efforts along the three lines just described.

Another way to conceive of the policy we propose is that we want to link together a series of initiatives that are now proceeding independently. Some firms are experimenting with employment continuity in their efforts to transform internal labor markets. Some unions are working with employers to develop job security and training programs. In many localities public/private partnerships have emerged around issues such as education and economic development. At the local and the federal levels, interest in various aspects of job training is growing. Our analysis suggests that all of these initiatives emerge from common impulses and are part of a similar set of concerns. Our proposal is to create a set of programs and an administrative structure that can take link the different efforts together in ways appropriate to specific local needs and circumstances. None of the initiatives listed here are likely to succeed fully on their own. However, as part of a larger effort, a good deal can be accomplished.

In the end the question of how best to create an effective employment policy must be the subject of concentrated work devoted exclusively to that task. This book does not provide such a map but, instead, shows whether the trip is necessary and the nature of the destination. Our fundamental argument is that employment policy and, indeed, any public policy, must be grounded in an understanding of the institutional environment in which it must operate. Most of this book, therefore, was devoted to understanding some of the key institutions in the labor market. Special emphasis was placed on internal labor markets and the employment policies of firms because we believe that these offer a window for understanding much of the current ferment in human resources and industrial relations. Throughout the book we have also sought to include white collar work in our framework and hence avoid the common trap of commenting only on the evolution of blue collar unionized work. For all these reasons, the book has as much to say about internal and external labor markets as about public policy. It is hoped that it will be read with both tracks in mind and that, in the end, we can emerge with a better understanding of how the world works and how we might shape it.

APPENDIX TO CHAPTER 2

One issue raised in Chapter 2 is whether the earnings losses that we attribute to unemployment are, in fact, due to job loss or whether we are picking up the effects of other considerations. In principle, we would like a control group of otherwise identical people who had not been laid off and hence be able to compare the subsequent earnings of the laid-off and not laid-off groups. Of course, such a control group is not available, so we will check our results using two different statistical procedures.

In our first test we estimate an earnings regression for individuals in the Current Population Survey who *had not* experienced any layoffs. This regression will include information on the personal characteristics (education, work experience, sex, race, region of residence, marital status) of the individuals. We then use this regression to predict the earnings of the individuals in the dislocated workers sample. If a dislocated individuals's earnings, after controlling for these personal characteristics, is below that of a similar *nonlaid-off* person (i.e., if the regression overpredicts the earnings of an individual in the dislocated worker's sample) then there is some presumption of earnings loss due to unemployment.

Our interest in this exercise is to check and see if the earlier estimates of earnings losses are in the ballpark. In Table App. 2.1 we present the earnings loss estimates for both the original procedure and for the new procedure. The results are reassuring, since the regression procedure produces larger estimates of earnings losses. This means that our earlier estimates erred in the conservative direction. An additional implication of the fact that the control group procedure produces higher estimates of loss than does the simple comparison is that the job losers did not have inappropriately high prelayoff wages. The central point, however, is that the major qualitative conclusions we reached earlier concerning the magnitude of earnings loss are not altered by this different procedure.

An Alternative Data Source

The evidence we have presented thus far may seem quite persuasive in demonstrating the adverse consequences of involuntary unemployment. We have seen that a substantial percentage of the sample do not find any work and that among those who are reemployed a large fraction experience considerable loss of earnings.

There still remains, however, the nagging issue of whether those individuals

Table App. 2.1 Estimates of Earnings Loss for Two Estimation Procedures

	Percent Loss in Original Procedure	Percent Loss in Regression Procedure
Loss of 25% or more	32.1	45.9
Loss of 10 to 25%	13.7	14.0
Plus or Minus 10%, or no change	22.8	14.2
Gain of 10% or more	31.2	25.7

Source: January 1984 Current Population Survey. Regression estimates based on equation applied to members of the two outgoing rotation groups who had not experienced layoffs. The dependent variable is weekly earnings in the current job. The independent variables were education, race, marital status, labor market experienced (age-education-6), sex, and eight regional dummy variables.

laid off differ in some important but unobservable respect from the others who keep their jobs. In principle, if such differences exist and they are large, they might explain our results. The data we have worked with thus far cannot address this question as effectively as can a longitudinal data set (although the synthetic comparison group we constructed took us some way on this question). Hence we will return to the Panel Survey on Income Dynamics. The sample size is substantially smaller than those with which we have been working, but this is partially compensated by our ability to control for these unmeasured differences.

The basic procedure is to estimate equations that relate an outcome (say earnings) in year $t + 1$ up to year $t + 5$ to unemployment experienced in year t, the individual's age, and the individual's prior values for the same outcome in the years prior to unemployment, that is, years $t - 1$, $t - 2$, and $t - 3$. (This model is stated in econometric notation in footnote 1, which also provides a fuller description of the data and other technical issues.)[1] For example, we examine annual earnings in 1977 as a function of unemployment experienced in 1975–76, the individuals' ages, and their annual earnings in 1971, 1972, and 1973. The variable that interests us is whether unemployment in 1975–76 results in a reduction in earnings in subsequent years.

The key to this procedure is that the prior values of the outcome variable (i.e., preunemployment earnings) provide us with a natural control for those ideosyncratic characteristics (ability, motivation, etc.) that would affect earnings in all periods. Hence if the person was problematic (had a serious but unobservable problem in the sense of not being measured in the data we are using), this would be captured by the preunemployment earnings variable, and the unemployment variable itself would not misleadingly proxy the person's low productivity.

Table App. 2.2 presents the results for this procedure. Our earlier discussion suggested that many people experience relatively short spells of unemployment but that the individuals who experience long spells account for much of the measured unemployment rate. This line of thinking suggests that we may want to capture unemployment more finely and examine the impact of

Table App. 2.2 Impact of Unemployment by Length of Unemployment Spell

Dependent Variable	1977	1978	1979	1980	1981
Men					
Annual earnings					
U_1	−.011	−.040	−.092	−.162	−.215
U_2	−.373	−.385	−.046	.080	−.299
U_3	−1.845[a]	−1.153[a]	−.927[a]	−1.248[a]	−.742[a]
Wage rate					
U_1	.054	−.002	−.067	−.040	−.138
U_2	−.210	−.328	−.022	.067	−.238
U_3	−.782[a]	−1.187[a]	−.673[a]	−1.105[a]	−.427
Weeks worked					
U_1	−.046	−.031	−.026	−.100[a]	−.058[a]
U_2	−.150[a]	−.064	−.016	.004	−.047
U_3	−.437[a]	−.107[a]	−.100[a]	−.041[a]	−.166[a]
Women					
Annual earnings					
U_1	−.589	.642	1.092[a]	.486	.153
U_2	−.676	.759	−.001	.588	.455
U_3	−1.017[a]	−.685[b]	−.973[a]	−.887[a]	−.828[a]
Wage rate					
U_1	−.020	−.265	.114	−.236[a]	−.062
U_2	−.040	−.116	.106	.013	−.489[a]
U_3	−.158[a]	−.258[a]	−.329[a]	−.134	−.037
Weeks worked					
U_1	.117	.150	.050	.133	.017
U_2	.068	.105	.210	−.173	.136
U_3	−.439[a]	−.063	−.386[a]	−.404[a]	−.592[a]

[a]Significant at the 5% level or better.
[b]Significant at the 10% level.
The sample is limited to individuals between the ages of 24 and 53 in 1971, who had not retired by 1981, and who had no permanent disability, and who had worked during 1971–75. The unemployment variables takes on the value of "1" if the person experienced the indicated amount of unemployment in 1975 or 1976 and "0" otherwise. The sample includes both individuals who did and did not experience any unemployment. Additional variables in the equation include age and the dependent variable (i.e., annual earnings, wages, or hours) for 1971, 1972, and 1973.
Note: U_1 = 1 to 10 weeks of unemployment.
U_2 = 11 to 20 weeks of unemployment.
U_3 = 21 or more weeks of unemployment.

different amounts of unemployment. The coefficients presented in Table 2.13 are for variables that measure the amount (if any) of unemployment the individual experienced during 1975–76. As our procedure requires, the sample includes people who experienced unemployment as well as people who had no unemployment in 1975–76. We present results for three dependent variables: annual earnings and the two components of annual earnings, wage rates and weeks worked.

The results for short-term spells of unemployment are generally negative, implying that there is an adverse effect on earnings, wages, and weeks worked. However, the coefficients are generally not significant. It is not hard to understand why short spells are of uncertain impact. Although the nature of the sample excludes new entrants and reentrants (since a person had to work in the 3 years prior to the unemployment spell in order for us to record the control variables), a certain amount of voluntary job changing—which could be expected to lead to higher wages—can be accompanied by brief unemployment. More significantly, many short-term unemployment spells are due to temporary layoffs in which the individual returns to the prior employer. As we saw in Chapter 2, roughly 70% of all U.S. layoffs are of this character. (Although most layoffs are temporary, they do not account for much of the total unemployment in the economy. This reason is the same as in our earlier discussion: many short spells are dominated by the fewer long spells.)

There is no such uncertainty about the impact of long spells of unemployment. For both men and women the impacts are very substantial, often reducing earnings by half. (Because of the nature of the specification, the coefficients on the unemployment variables can be approximately interpreted as percentage reductions in earnings for a positive value of the variable.) If anything, these results are so substantial as to raise concern that we are capturing more than just the impact of unemployment and that our procedure fails to control completely for the special characteristics of those who are jobless. However, it is hard to believe that results of this magnitude, generated by a procedure designed to control for unobservable characteristics, and which are consistent with the findings for the other data set, can be explained away by "unmeasured" personal characteristics.

It is also worth noting that these results are consistent with the earlier findings in another respect. Recall that the earnings loss in the Current Population Survey sample was not dependent on how long ago the job was lost. In other words, there was no "catch-up" effect in which initial loss was made up. It therefore seemed that people faced permanently lower earnings. The same pattern holds in these results: there is very substantial loss several years after the event.

The Correlates of Being a Loser

At the end of Chapter 2 we presented a number of tables examining the relationship among several variables (e.g., occupation, industry, and tenure) and the chances that an individual who was laid off was a loser in the sense of remaining unemployed or experiencing a large earnings loss. We noted that it would be worthwhile to check the results of the simple tables against a more sophisticated procedure in which we control for the simultaneous effects of the several variables.

To do this we estimate three regression models, one for the probability that an individual is a loser (as previously defined) and then one for each of the components of loser [i.e., the probability that an individual finds a new job and (for those who did find a job) the probability that the job pays 25% or more less than the lost employment]. Each model is estimated with a technique (logit) appropriate for probability equations. The results presented in Table App.

Table App. 2.3 Determinants of the Probability of Becoming a Loser

	Dependent Variable		
	Loser	*Find*	*Loss*
INTERCEPT	.31**	−.403**	−.106
EDUCATION	−.018**	.026**	−.011**
AGE	−.001**	−.002**	.001**
SEX	.045**	.010	.011
RACE	.109**	.194**	.003
MARITAL	−.068**	.073**	−.040**
BC	.103**	−.084**	.051*
MAN	.025	−.017	.016
CONST	−.020	.123	.032
BC X MAN	−.012	.020	.025
BC X CONST	.039	.143	.043
TENURE1	.022	.024	.035*
TENURE2	.045**	.018	.067**
TENURE3	.085**	.014	.126**
SAME	—	—	−.232**
YRLOST	−.201**	.274**	.017

Source: January 1984 Current Population Survey. The dependent variables are defined in the text. The independent variables are defined as follows: EDUCATION is years of education completed; AGE is age in years; SEX is a dummy variable that is "1" if male; RACE is a dummy variable that is "1" if nonwhite; MARITAL is a dummy variable that is "1" if married; BC is a dummy variable that is "1" if the lost job was in a blue collar occupation; MAN is a dummy variable that is "1" if the lost job was in a manufacturing industry; CONST is a dummy variable that is "1" if the lost job was in the construction industry; TENURE1 is a dummy variable that is "1" if tenure on the lost job was 2 or 3 years; TENURE2 is a dummy variable that is "1" if tenure on the lost job was 4 or 5 years; TENURE3 is a dummy variable that is "1" if tenure on the lost job was 6 years or more; SAME is a dummy variable that is "1" if the three-digit industry code on the new job is the same as the three-digit industry code on the lost job; YRLOST is a dummy variable that is "1" if the job loss occurred between 1979 and 1982. In the third column the sample is limited to individuals who found a job. In all equations the sample is limited to the nonagricultural civilian work force. The asterisks indicate that a variable was significant at the 5% level or better.

2.3 are transformed coefficients[2] and should be interpreted as increments to the probability of each outcome associated with a given variable. For example, each year of education reduces the probability of being a loser by 1.8 points when evaluated at the mean. Since the mean probability of being a loser is .38, this means that if the person had an additional year of education, his probability of being a loser would be .362. Similarly, being a man increases the probability of being a loser from .38 to .425.

The patterns in Table App. 2.3 confirm in virtually all respects the earlier discussion. The personal characteristic variables behave as expected, although the impact of sex is attenuated when the variable loser is decomposed into its component parts. It is clear that occupation plays an important role, and neither industry nor industry-occupation interactions are of significance. High-tenure workers face no special difficulty finding a job but, when they are employed, they are more likely to suffer an earnings loss. As expected, finding a job in the same firm/industry reduces the chances of losing earnings. Finally, the longer ago one lost the job, the more likely one is to be reemployed. However, length of search does not result in any impact on the wage of the job that is found. This is consistent with our earlier discussion that job losers accept the first job that is offered.

APPENDIX TO CHAPTER 6

Microevidence of Policy Costs in Sweden

In this appendix we will examine evidence to see what merit there is to the argument that employment policy has "rigidified" the labor market. Our evidence in this section will be drawn from Sweden. There are two reasons for this choice. First, better and more consistent data and secondary studies are available for Sweden than for Germany. Second, as noted, the German model is less applicable to the United States than the Swedish approach. The strong legislative barriers to layoffs do indeed make Germany a more rigid labor market than is conceivable in U.S. terms. As noted, there are substantial benefits to this—the chief of which is the internal flexibility we have emphasized— and our argument strongly suggests that U.S. policies should move along a continuum further in the German direction. However, in assessing costs through measures of external market fluidity, Sweden seems a more appropriate laboratory.

Much of the criticism of Swedish-style policy is couched in vague and often ideological terms. However, it is possible to discern two lines of argument concerning the possible negative program effects. The first is that the programs have reduced workers' incentives to be mobile, to change jobs in search of better wages and opportunities. To the extent that this is true, growing employers will be unable to recruit the skilled labor they need and, over time, the labor force will be increasingly misallocated. The second criticism concerns the behavior of firms. If it is unreasonably costly to lay off employees in the face of declining demand or technical change then, among other responses, firms will be reluctant to hire new workers. Hence an employment policy aimed at protecting work may end up reducing opportunities. We will take up each of these two criticisms in turn.

The Impact of Employment Policy on Job Changing

An important aspect of the case against extensive employment policies is the argument that such programs reduce the willingness of the labor force to change jobs and otherwise exhibit the mobility that many feel is necessary for a well-functioning market. The basis for concern is evidence that mobility has decreased. For example, the percentage of the labor force age 25 to 54 who changed jobs at least once during the year fell from about 11% in 1966 to just over 8% in 1985; for 55 to 64-year-olds the decline was even steeper (by contrast, among 16 to 24-year-olds the rate of job changing has gone up).[1] Other data are consistent with the sense of declining movement: the rate of cross-county geographic migrations has fallen from 2.5% or more, which prevailed in from the middle 1960s to the early 1970s to 2.0% or less, which has characterized the period from the middle 1970s onward.[2] (Of course, we have also seen that this trend is not special to Sweden; in Chapter 2 we presented data showing a decline in U.S. mobility over time.)

The difficulty with the easy interpretation that these trends indicate increasing rigidity in the Swedish labor market is that job changing and mobility are the outcome of both supply and demand forces. The advocates of the rigidity hypothesis view these results as flowing from changes in supply behavior (which, in turn, is induced by government employment and welfare policy), but it is equally possible that they result from demand conditions. In particular, the slow growth of the Swedish economy provided relatively few opportunities for job changing. The trick, of course, lies in distinguishing between these two competing explanations.

The most thorough effort to examine the underlying determinants of Swedish mobility is the research of Bertil Holmlund based on longitudinal data tracing a sample of the Swedish labor force over the 1970s.[3] Holmlund shows that in contrast to the data on actual job changes, data on intentions show no secular decline in the willingness of people to change jobs. For example, the percent of the Swedish labor force who engaged in a search for new employment while holding another job remained steady for men throughout the 1970s and actually increased for women, and the percentage of the labor force who intended to change employers also held steady throughout the 1970s.[4]

Furthermore, in regression estimates of quit equations, which include demand variables, supply variables, and policy variables (e.g., a variable representing the implementation of the employment security law), the overwhelmingly most powerful determinants of quit behavior is demand: vacancies and new hire rates. Furthermore, by comparing equations estimated for different time periods, Holmlund is able to study whether structural changes in quit behavior have occurred and his only finding of significance is that women have, over time, become more attached to the labor force, although they remain as willing as before to change employers. Holmlund is quite clear in his conclusion that declining Swedish mobility is due to weakness on the demand side, not to any decreased willingness on the part of the labor force to change employers.[5]

It will be recalled from our earlier discussion of the solidarity wage policy that employers sometimes complain that limited wage differentials reduce incentives for skill acquisition. The previous discussion of quit behavior addresses this point, but various other bits of evidence also suggest that the complaint is not well founded. For young people (age 16 to 24), the group for whom investment in skills is most crucial, there has been no secular decline in job changing or mobility.[6] In addition, enrollments (supply behavior) in school training programs track demand very well. For example, the degree that trains technicians and lower-level engineers—4-year technology degree in gymnasiums (high schools)—is completely subscribed, while there are vacant spaces is such low-demand vocational fields as consumer education, clerical, and general operative.[7] Finally, Swedish unions have been aggressive in trying to increase firm commitments of resources to training. As part of the last round of wage negotiations, unions bargained for so-called "renewal funds," a pool of money based on a 10% profits tax that firms would be required to set aside and administer (in a manner codetermined with unions) for training and research and development.

An additional piece of evidence that the Swedish labor market (as opposed to the macroeconomy) has performed well is that annual surveys of Swedish employers show no secular increase in reported labor shortages. In fact, the percentage of employers who report that labor shortages represent an obstacle to expansion fell from over 30% in the early 1970s to below 20% in the early 1980s.[8] This is not consistent with the argument that bottlenecks have developed due to the unwillingness of employees to change jobs.

The Impact of Policy on the Hiring and Layoff Policies of Firms

The second major possible difficulty generated by active employment policy, and particularly by measures aimed at job security, is that firms may perceive such a large marginal cost of reducing employment levels that they respond by restricting hiring rates. A phenomenon of this sort is often cited as an explanation for slow European versus American job growth.

This argument can be at least partially tested by examining data on layoff, hiring, and quit rates in Swedish and American firms. The best available comparable data is presented in Table App. 6.1.

Each of the series presented in Table App. 6.1 are, of course, highly cyclical, and so year-to-year comparisons across the two countries are not valid unless the cycle is synchronized. The column containing the manufacturing production index provides such a rough control.

Turning first to the new hire rates and the quit rates, the overall pattern of the data do not suggest that the pattern of accessions and turnover in Sweden differs in very substantial ways from that in the United States. Although U.S. new hire rates are generally above those in Sweden, the difference is not of a sufficient magnitude to suggest radically different structural features in the two economies, particularly given the generally stronger production performance in the United States. There is certainly nothing in these data to support a conclusion that Swedish industry has failed to hire as a result of the institutional features of the labor market.

A very similar conclusion would be drawn from the quit series. Again, while the rates are generally lower in Sweden than in the United States, the differentials are not substantial and would not seem to support a conclusion that Swedish workers, once employed, refuse to leave their employers in search of better jobs.

Table App. 6.1 Comparison of Swedish and American Hiring and Turnover Rates in Manufacturing (Monthly Rates per 100 Workers)

	Manufacturing Production Index (1975 = 100)		New Hires		Quits		Layoffs		
	Sweden	United States	Sweden	United States	Sweden	United States	Sweden	United States (1)	United States (2)
1969	82	94	3.8	3.7	2.9	2.7	0.24	1.2	0.36
1970	87	91	3.5	2.8	2.9	2.1	0.24	1.8	0.54
1971	88	93	2.3	2.6	2.1	1.8	0.36	1.6	0.48
1972	89	101	2.5	3.3	1.9	2.3	0.30	1.1	0.33
1973	96	110	2.7	3.9	1.9	2.8	0.22	0.9	0.27
1974	101	109	3.0	3.2	2.2	2.4	0.16	1.5	0.45
1975	100	100	2.2	2.0	2.0	1.4	0.15	2.1	0.63
1976	99	110	1.9	2.6	1.8	1.7	0.12	1.3	0.39
1977	94	117	1.3	2.8	1.5	1.8	0.15	1.1	0.33
1978	93	124	1.4	3.1	1.3	2.1	0.16	0.9	0.27
1979	99	129	2.2	2.9	1.7	2.0	0.17	1.1	0.33
1980	100		2.1	2.1	1.8	1.5	0.11	1.7	0.51

Source: Swedish data from National Statistical Board, rounded up to nearest decimal. U.S. data from Employment and Earnings Various Years. Manufacturing production index from OECD Main Economic Indicators.

The major difference between the two countries lies in the striking difference in the layoff series. It is apparent from the first two layoff columns that the Swedish rate is substantially below that of the United States. However, this difference is to a certain degree deceptive. In the United States a large percentage of layoffs are temporary and end in a recall by the employer. Such temporary layoffs are not used in Sweden; the common response to a downturn in demand that is perceived as temporary is to reduce hours. The extent to which layoffs in the United States end in recalls varies over the cycle, but a good average estimate is that 70% of layoffs have this character.[9] The second column of U.S. layoffs makes this correction. We see that U.S. layoff rates are still above the Swedish rates, but the differential is sharply reduced.

In summary, it is hard to examine these data and conclude that Swedish employers are hamstrung by the labor market policies we have described. Although there are differences in the patterns in the data, the adjustment flows within firms seem to operate in roughly similar ways. If we sum Swedish layoffs and quits and U.S. permanent layoffs and quits we find that while flows out of U.S. firms are higher than in Swedish one, the gap is relatively modest. The average difference of these sums over the entire period is that U.S. outflows are only 0.17 workers per 100 per month higher than Swedish outflows. (This translates into 2 workers per 100 difference per year which, using the 1980 Swedish figures as a base, means that annual turnover in the United States is 8% higher than in Sweden.)

Firms may prefer the American "mix," since they might wish to avoid quits (which may be by their best workers) and favor layoffs, but it is difficult to argue that the labor market flows are of a different order of magnitude in the two nations.

A final point concerning employment levels in manufacturing is that Sweden, in the face of the adverse economic climate of the 1970s, was in fact able to restructure its key industries. Between 1974 and 1982 employment in shipbuilding, a major export industry that was badly hurt by heightened competition, fell by over 44%, and employment in basic metals fell by 36%.[10] These employment reductions were achieved despite an industrial policy that tended in the 1970s to prop up ailing industries.

The foregoing material demonstrated that at the level of the microfunctioning of labor markets there is little evidence that active employment policy, at least as practiced in Sweden, impedes efficiency. There are more questions that might be raised concerning the German model, given its greater emphasis on within-firm job security, but even here the benefits are substantial. For example, in addition to the gains in internal flexibility that we have already discussed, there is some evidence that the job-matching system in German is more effective than in the United States and hence a disturbing recent phenomenon in U.S. labor markets—increasing numbers of unfilled vacancies coexisting with large stocks of unemployed workers—has not emerged in Germany. This so-called "Beveridge curve" relating the unemployment rate to the vacancy rate has shifted out in the United States but has not done so in Germany.[11]

Some Recent Complications

The last decade has not been a happy one for European economics, and those of Sweden and Germany have been no exception. This has had consequences for many of the systems and structures described here. In a slow growth economy with a surplus rather than a shortage of labor, many programs simply work less effectively. The balance seems to shift away from active policies and toward efforts aimed either at stockpiling unemployed workers (e.g., the youth teams in Sweden) or at reducing the labor force (the various early retirement and disability pensions programs of both Germany and Sweden). These are not efforts likely to inspire a great deal of enthusiasm or support.

A second problem is that when a labor market policy is tightly integrated into the economy, a shift in the economic base may render the labor market policy less functional, and perhaps even dysfunctional. The policies are likely to change much more slowly than the economy because of the nature of political bureaucracies, the peculiar problems of training programs (e.g., heavy fixed investment in equipment and staff skills), and the simple difficulty of tracking change. Hence, programs may find themselves losing their base in the economy and be in serious difficulty. These observations explain why, if one has followed developments closely in Europe, the discussion in this chapter has a slightly anachronistic air. Europeans are not as enamored of their employment and training system as one might expect, given the foregoing description. It is under attack, in Sweden and Germany, not simply by those who feel that it impedes labor market flexibility but also from its natural constituency who believe that many of the programs and strategies have been rendered somewhat ineffective by labor market developments. And, it is precisely these labor market developments that impart the out-of-date flavor to some of the earlier discussion. For example, in a manner similar to our description of recent trends in American internal labor markets, there seems to be a loosening of the structure of German internal labor markets. Recent legislative changes have made it easier for firms to implement fixed-term labor contracts and to employ part-time workers. Even prior to the legislation these developments accelerated: between 1972 and 1981 placements by the employment service into fixed-term jobs of less than 3 months increased from 12.7% of placements to 21.1%; between 1980 and 1983 employer listings of fixed-term contracts increased from 25.4% to 33.9%; and temporary help (or personnel leasing) increased by 250% between 1975 and 1981.[12] The portion of the economy in which the "classic" patterns hold may be shrinking. In a sense this is equivalent to the rise of the core-periphery model, which we have described for the United States. A related development in Germany is the rising eligibility threshold required to gain access to training opportunities. The required number of prior weeks of continuous work has been increased.

This point is even more clear in Sweden than it is in Germany. Recall that the function of Swedish labor market policy has been to use the employment exchange and training programs to provide the level of security necessary to "grease" the bargain struck between Swedish employers and unions. In recent years, however, the programs have experienced increasing difficulty in accomplishing this. This explains why direct job creation and unemployment insurance have grown in importance in the repertoire of AMS. Direct job creation is, however, generally not an attractive strategy. It provides few services of use to firms, it is vulnerable to charges that people remain on the rolls and are not available for "productive labor," and it is expensive in an era of growing concern with fiscal deficits. Concomitant with the shift in the composition of labor market programs[13] has been a growing volume of criticism against labor market policy.

The criticisms of the labor market policies generally take one of three forms. Many observers note that the employment exchange has not been able to penetrate into the better jobs in the economy. Instead, it serves the less skilled workers and the firms that offer relatively unskilled jobs. Furthermore, once this reputation develops it takes on a momentum of its own, since a stigma comes to be attached to workers who are referred by the employment service. This is a dilemma that faces all social programs of this type: how to serve those most in need without stigmatizing clients by labeling them as weak. A second, related, criticism of the employment exchange is that it has become too service oriented, too much like a social work agency. Hence staff expend the bulk of their time and resources on those most in need and are satisfied to place them into one of the many available treatment programs. The consequence is that the labor market function (rapidly filling vacancies with the best available candidate) receives short shrift.

The effectiveness of labor market training also seems to have declined over time. For example, whereas during 1966–70 66.9% of all laid-off workers had found a new job within 5 months, by 1976–80 that figure had fallen to 50.4%.[14] Results of this sort are highly sensitive to cyclical variables as well as changes in benefits such as unemployment insurance and pensions. Nonetheless, there is a general sense, supported by some (although far less than one might like) econometric work that there is a negative time trend in the effectiveness of retraining.[15]

The other criticisms are more straightforward. The growing reliance on job creation is seen, particularly by the business community, as creating rigidities and reducing work effort (the irony here is that the greater expansion of these programs occurred during the period in which the "bourgeois parties" were in power). Finally, the administration of the agency has been increasingly viewed as rule ridden and rigid. This sort of criticism is hardly surprising for such a visible program, but the fact that it is frequently made is symptomatic of the more general dissatisfaction with the agency. In addition, the complaint is increasingly heard from municipal officials who, faced with growing unemployment, would like to use labor market funds for local economic development. This urge tends to be opposed by central officials who fear it will lead to further immobility of the labor force and protectionism, the twin bêtes noires of Swedish economic policy.

How is one to interpret the growing difficulties facing Sweden's vaunted labor market policy? One possible plausible conclusion is that the economic base has changed in ways that make it difficult for the labor market policy to play the same role that it has in the past. In particular, white collar employment has increased relative to blue collar jobs. In addition, within blue collar work there is a growing emphasis on the importance of technical skills. Historically, the employment exchange has placed people into middle- and lower-level blue collar jobs, and the AMU training centers have provided training in these areas. Hence the system is now less able than in the past to provide security, since there is a mismatch between the needs of the economy and the capacity of the labor market policy. Furthermore, it is not easy to fine-tune this match out of existence. There is a major reputational problem to overcome before white collar workers or employees are willing to use the employment service, since the stigma associated with it can be self-reinforcing. In the meantime other institutions may develop that compete with the government's labor market policy in providing the necessary amount of job security. For example, some white collar unions and the SAF (employers' association) have joined to form "The Security Council" (Trygghetsradet), an institution that is jointly funded to provide counseling, placement services, and early retirement support for unemployed white collar workers. The blue collar LO is also establishing a similar institution. These are legal because they are nonprofit, but it represents a clear challenge to AMS. Even as such, however, they differ from U.S. models in that they represent union-management cooperation.

The AMS administration has recognized that it faces a serious challenge and has taken a number of innovative steps. It has attempted to alter the orientation of the employment exchange in the direction of serving firms by emphasizing rapid filling of vacancies instead of providing services to clients. This has the potential of "creaming" (service to the best off), but it does represent a clear attempt to alter the perception of the institution. Indeed, as we noted earlier, it is an attempt to strengthen the original mission of serving "core" labor force members. It has also split the AMU off as a separate institution (it was formerly jointly administered by AMS and the Board of Education) in order to permit greater flexibility in the provision of training services. It has urged the government to place less reliance on direct job creation and put more emphasis on fiscal stimulus during future downturns. Finally it has attempted to decentralize policymaking and to give municipalities more power.

These efforts to turn AMS around represent a fascinating story of (attempted) bureaucratic renewal but to pursue it would take us too far afield. For our purposes the point to understand is that a labor market policy historically was well integrated into the economy, and "useful" in our terms has to a certain extent lost its way as the underlying economic base shifted. The functional requirements, the need for an underwriting of the security pledge, remain constant, but the means of implementing it are now in doubt. However, it remains true that the central features of both the German and Swedish models are still in place and that as a "national system" they can still be distinguished from that of the United States.

NOTES

Chapter 1

1. In regressions in using annual data for 1968–84 we included the Federal Reserve Board index of capacity utilization as a cyclical control and a time trend to measure any upward secular shift. The time trend was positive and statistically significant in equations for the entire labor force 16 years and older as well as for equations estimating the unemployment rate of males aged 25 to 54.

2. This argument was first put forth by George Perry in his article "Changing Labor Markets and Inflation," *Brooking Papers on Economic Activity*, 1970, No. 3, pp. 411–441. However, the argument has lost force in recent years as the fraction of the labor force composed of teenagers has declined and women's unemployment rates have moved closer to those of men. If anything, the unemployment rate should now be declining if these demographic factors (as well as the increased educational level of the labor force) are taken into account.

3. Mary Corcoran and Martha S. Hill, "Reoccurrence of Unemployment Among Adult Men," *Journal of Human Resources*, Vol. XX, No. 2 (Spring 1985), p. 168.

4. Martin S. Feldstein, "Lowering the Permanent Rate of Unemployment," a study prepared for the Joint Economic Committee of Congress (Washington, D.C.: U.S. Government Printing Office), September 18, 1973, pp. 11–12.

5. George Akerloff and Brian Main, "An Experience Weighted Measure of Employment and Unemployment Durations," *American Economic Review*, Vol. 71, No. 5 (December 1981), pp. 1003–1011.

6. Using different methodologies, two recent studies have, in fact, concluded that durations of unemployment are increasing. This implies that an important fraction of the secular increase in unemployment can be explained in these terms. See Hal Sider, "Unemployment Duration and Incidence: 1968–82, *American Economic Review*, Vol. 75, No. 3 (June 1985), pp. 461–472, and Lawrence Summers, "Why Is the Unemployment Rate So Very High Near Full Employment?" *Brookings Papers on Economic Activity*, No. 2 (1986), pp. 339–396.

7. Carl Rosenfeld, "Job Search Among the Unemployed," *Monthly Labor Review* Vol. 100, No. 1 (November 1977), pp. 39–42.

8. This point was first made in James Tobin, "Inflation and Unemployment," *American Economic Review*, Vol. 62 (March 1972), pp. 1–18.

9. Katherine Bradbury and Lynn Browne, "Black Men in the Labor Market," *New England Economic Review* (March/April 1986).

10. Surprisingly, very little of the economic literature that attempts to assess the extent and nature of discrimination has used the substantial courtroom-generated evidence to examine the issues. One problem, however, is that many cases are settled out of court and hence the information is not publicly available. Nonetheless, this would appear to be a fruitful research direction.

11. William Julius Wilson, *The Declining Significance of Race* (Chicago: University of Chicago Press), 1978.

12. See Charles Killingsworth, "Structural Unemployment in the United States," in Jack Steiber, ed., *Employment Problems of Automation and Advanced Technology* (London: McMillan), 1966, pp. 128–156.

13. The other categories are "frictional" unemployment, which refers to joblessness due to people changing employment or moving in and out of the labor force, and "demand deficient" unemployment, which is another term for Kensyian unemployment (i.e., joblessness that can be relieved by macropolicy).

14. For a range of criticisms, from quite different perspectives, see Michael J. Piore, "The Importance of Human Capital Theory to Labor Economics, A Dissenting View," *Proceedings of the 26th Annual Meetings of the Industrial Relations Research Association,* Madison, Wisconsin, 1974, pp. 251–258; Samuel Bowles and Herbert Gintis, *Schooling in Capitalist America* (New York: Basic Books), 1976; and James Medoff and Katherine Abraham, "Experience, Performance, and Earnings," *Quarterly Journal of Economics,* Vol. XCV, No. 4 (December 1980), pp. 703–736.

15. Richard Lester, *Manpower Planning in a Free Society* (Princeton, N.J.: Princeton University Press), 1960, pp. 3–5.

16. See, for example, Eli Ginzberg, *Manpower Agenda for America* (New York: McGraw-Hill, 1968), and Sar Levitan, Garth Mangum, and Ray Marshall, *Human Resources and Labor Markets* (New York: Harper & Row), 1972.

Chapter 2

1. For example, Bennett Harrison and Barry Bluestone construct an index of job quality that identifies a wage cutoff in the 1970s, characterizes jobs with wages below this as "low quality," and then asks how many jobs in the 1980s had inflation-corrected wages at or below this level. This procedure combines a possible downward shift in the overall average with a possible increase in the fraction of jobs in the bottom of the distribution. Both developments are of concern, but analytically they are very different and one cannot tell from their work which factor explains their findings. Barry Bluestone and Bennett Harrison, "The Great American Job Machine; The Proliferation of Low-Wage Employment in the U.S. Economy," paper prepared for the U.S. Congressional Joint Economic Committee, December 1986.

2. For a careful analysis see Katherine Bradbury, "The Shrinking Middle Class," *New England Economic Review* (September/October 1986), pp. 41–55.

3. See James Medoff, "The Structure of Hourly Earnings Among U.S. Private Sector Employees," mimeograph, Harvard University Economics Department, December 1984.

4. The evidence for this is reviewed in the first footnote of Chapter 1.

5. This point is also made by Lawrence Summers, "Why Is the Unemployment Rate So Very High Near Full Employment?" *Brookings Papers on Economic Activity,* No. 2 (1986), pp. 339–396.

6. In fact, people who had lost work due to other reasons—seasonal jobs ending, failure of a self-operated business, and "other," were also asked the questions. However I have excluded these people from the sample since their situation is different from the others in important respects.

7. That is, if the three-digit occupation code for the prior job was 351, 270, or 271, the individual was classified as automobile or steel.

8. For example, among 30- to 35-year-old males (presumably the most employable group), 24.7% of those who had been laid off over a year ago and who had a year or less of tenure were without work compared to 32.2% of those with 5 years or more of

tenure. This is a difference in the hypothesized direction, but not a very great one. Among 36- to 55-year-old males the respective figures were 24.7% and 26.3%, hardly any difference at all. If we look at those laid off less than a year prior to the survey, the corresponding figures by tenure class for the 30- to 35-year-old males were 53.0% and 46.7% without work, and for women of the same age and tenure groups the corresponding percentages without work are 46.5% and 49.2%.

9. For a discussion of sources on layoffs, see Carol Utter, "Labor Turnover in Manufacturing, The Survey in Retrospect," *Monthly Labor Review,* Vol. 105 (June 1982), pp. 15–17.

10. These figures are taken from David T. Ellwood and Lawrence H. Summers, "Poverty in America: Is Welfare the Answer or the Problem?," mimeograph, Harvard University, Kennedy School of Government March 1985. pp. 12–15.

11. In 1980, prior to the Reagan cuts, Medicaid expenditures were $6.7 billion, food stamps $8.6 billion, and housing $4.0 billion. The basic welfare program, AFDC, was $12.5 billion, general assistance $1.4 billion, and supplemental security income $5 billion. Ellwood and Summers, *op. cit.,* p. 14.

12. The panel survey oversampled low-income groups but, for the purposes of the tables in the text, a weighting factor was applied to make the data nationally representative.

13. If we limit the female sample only to those who work (or work plus look) full time and full year, then we can get a lower bound on our estimates. These limitations are too restrictive, since they ignore constraints due to low earnings (e.g., women who would want to work full time but can earn too little to pay for child care). Furthermore, low earnings of part-time workers are a legitimate source of concern. Nonetheless, it is worthwhile exploring the lower bound. The panel survey collected data on female unemployment hours only for a 7-year period (1975–81) and, hence, we are restricted to those years. Using the same procedures as before, we find that if we use the male earning standard (which is more justified for this full-time sample), 7.3% of women who were in the labor force full time fell below the cutoff for 3 or more of 7 years, and if we use the female earnings standard, the figure is 2.0%.

Chapter 3

1. These data were compiled by Lawrence H. Summers, "Why is the Unemployment Rate So Very High Near Full Employment?," *Brookings Papers on Economic Activity,* Vol. 2 (1986), p. 353, and are taken from the Bureau of Labor Statistics *Handbook on Labor Statistics.*

2. See, for example, Bennett Harrison and Barry Bluestone, *The Deindustrialization of America* (New York: Basic Books), 1982, and Marc Bendick and Judith Devine, "Workers Dislocated by Economic Change: Do They Need Federal Employment and Training Assistance?," in National Commission on Employment Policy, Seventh Annual Report (Washington, D.C.: U.S. Government Printing Office), 1981, pp. 175–226.

3. For further discussion of this point, see Paul Osterman, *Getting Started, The Youth Labor Market* (Cambridge, Mass.: MIT Press), Chapter 6. Another convincing paper on this point is David Ellwood, "The Spatial Mismatch Hypothesis: Are There Teenage Jobs Missing in the Ghetto?," in Richard Freeman and Harry Holzer, eds., *The Black Youth Employment Crisis,* National Bureau of Economic Research, (Chicago: University of Chicago Press), 1986, pp. 147–191.

4. This issue is discussed at length in Michael J. Piore, *Birds of Passage; Long*

Distance Migrants in Industrial Society (New York: Cambridge University Press), 1979.

5. Lloyd Reynolds, *The Structure of Labor Markets* (New Haven, Conn.: Yale University Press), 195.

6. Paul Osterman, *Getting Started; The Youth Labor Market,* (Cambridge, Mass.: MIT Press), 1980.

7. Lloyd Ulman, "Labor Mobility and the Industrial Wage Structure in the Postwar United States," *Quarterly Journal of Economics,* Vol. LXXIX, No. 1 (February 1965), pp. 73–97.

8. Richard B. Freeman, *The Market for College Trained Manpower* (Cambridge, Mass.: Harvard University Press), 1971.

9. Donald Cullen, "The Interindustry Wage Structure, 1899–1950," *American Economic Review* (June 1956), pp. 353–369. Sumner Slicter, "Notes on the Structure of Wages," *Review of Economics and Statistics,* 1950 (quoted in Krueger and Summers); and Alan B. Krueger and Lawrence H. Summers, "Efficiency Wages and the Inter-industry Wage Structure," mimeograph, Harvard University Department of Economics, February 1986.

10. William T. Dickens and Lawrence Katz, "Industry and Occupation Wage Patterns and Theories of Wage Determination," mimeograph, University of California, Berkeley, February 1986.

11. Richard B. Freeman, "The Effect of Demographic Factors on Age/Earnings Profiles," *Journal of Human Resources,* Vol. XIV, No. 3, (Summer 1979), pp. 289–318.

12. Daniel J.B. Mitchell, "Shifting Norms in Wage Determination," *Brookings Papers on Economic Activity,* Vol. 2 (1985), p. 585.

13. George A. Akerloff and Brian G.M. Main, "An Experience Weighted Measure of Employment and Unemployment Durations," *American Economic Review,* Vol. 71, (December 1981), pp. 1003–1011.

14. Herbert Simon, *Administrative Behavior* (New York: Macmillan), 1947.

15. Richard Lester, *Hiring Practices and Labor Competition* (Princeton, N.J.: Industrial Relations Section), 1954, p. 36.

16. Osterman, *op. cit.,* Howard Wial, untitled PhD dissertation on the youth labor market, Department of Economics, MIT.

17. Katherine Abraham and James Medoff, "Length of Service and Promotions in Union and Non-Union Work Groups," *Industrial and Labor Relations Review,* (April 1985), pp. 408–420.

18. Peter Doeringer and Michael J. Piore, *Internal Labor Markets and Manpower Analysis* (Lexington, Mass.: D.C. Heath), 1971.

19. Paul Osterman, "White Collar Internal Labor Markets," in Paul Osterman, ed., *Internal Labor Markets* (Cambridge, Mass.: MIT Press), 1984, p. 172.

20. Ulman, *op. cit.*

21. In that debate David Lilian intially argued that, contrary to conventional wisdom, shifts in demand patterns across sectors were as important as fluctuations in aggregate demand for explaining the level of unemployment over the cycle. In rebuttal, however, Katherine Abraham and Lawrence Katz demonstrated that in the presence of industries that grew at steady but different rates, aggregate demand shifts could explain the patterns in the data. Furthermore, they employed vacancy rate data to support their contention that aggregate demand remains the major explanation of cyclical movement in the unemployment rate. However, this research is focused on within-business cycle movements. Neither paper resolves the question of whether the positive time trend in unemployment is understandable by a widening employment dispersion over time. In-

deed, Abraham and Katz include variables in their estimation equations that are intended to purge the results of long-term effects. David Lilien, "Sectoral Shifts and Cyclical Unemployment," *Journal of Political Economy*, Vol. 90, No. 4 (August 1982), pp. 777–793; Katherine G. Abraham and Lawrence F. Katz, "Cyclical Unemployment: Sectoral Shifts or Aggregate Disturbances?," *Journal of Political Economoy*, Vol. 94, No. 3 (June 1986), pp. 507–522.

22. For a review of the empirical literature see Wassily Leontief and Faye Duchin, *The Future Impact of Automation on Workers* (New York: Oxford University Press), 1986. It is possible, of course, for firms to search for capital savings innovations. The classic argument concerning the direction of the U.S. bias is found in H. Habbakkuk, *American and British Technology in the Nineteenth Century; The Search for Labor Saving Inventions* (Cambridge, England: Cambridge University Press), 1962.

23. *Business Week,* September 10, 1984.

24. W.E.G. Salter, *Productivity and Technical Change* (Cambridge,: Cambridge University Press), 1960.

25. Paul Osterman, "The Impact of Computers Upon the Employment of Clerks and Managers," *Industrial and Labor Relations Review*, Vol. 39, No. 2 (January 1986), pp. 175–186.

26. Michael J. Piore and Charles F. Sable, *The Second Industrial Divide* (New York: Basic Books), 1984.

27. *New York Times,* March 4, 1986, p. D5.

28. Steven Wheelwright and Robert Hayes, "Competing Through Manufacturing," *Harvard Business Review*, Vol. 63 (January–February 1985), p. 108.

29. *Wall Street Journal*, April 14, 1986, p. 20.

30. *Business Week*, June 9, 1986, p. 70.

31. Nicholas Basta, "New Life for Steel," *High Technology* April 1986), p. 47.

32. *Ibid.,* p. 48.

33. For example, General Electric plans to reduce its work force by 25% over the next 4 years, AT&T envisions similar cuts, Kodak has recently launched a series of layoffs and other work-force reductions, Ford has announced plans to trim its white collar labor force by 25%, and so on. A recent report in *Business Week* concluded "CIM's [computer integrated manufacturing] primary benefits come from automating the flow of information through a factory. That eliminates not only direct labor but also the bulk of costs—usually in the area of 45%—attributed to indirect labor, middle management, and other overhead." *Business Week*, June 16, 1986, p. 101.

34. Between 1973 and 1985 manufacturing employment grew at a weak annual rate of 0.3% while output grew by 1.9% per year. Since 1982, manufacturing's share of GNP increased while its share of employment fell. See *Economic Outlook: United States, 1986* (Paris: OECD), pp. 73 and 82.

35. These figures are calculated from Wassily Leontief and Faye Duchin, *The Future Impact of Automation on Workers* (New York: Oxford University Press), 1986, p. 13.

36. Leontiff and Duchin, p. 15.

37. Joseph A. Schumpter, *Business Cycles*, Vol. 2 (New York: McGraw-Hill), 1939, p. 515.

38. Leontiff and Duchin, p. 31.

39. For interesting evidence see Haruo Shimada and John-Paul McDuffie, "Industrial Relations and 'Humanware'; A Study of Japanese investment in Automobile Manufacturing in the U.S.," mimeograph, Keio University and Sloan School of Management, December 1986.

40. Office of Technology Assessment, *Computerized Manufacturing Automation,* U.S. Congress, G.P.O., April 1984, p. 53.

41. H. Allan Hunt and Timothy L. Hunt, *Human Resource Implications of Robotics,* (Kalamazoo, Mich.: Upjohn Institute), 1983, p. 51.

42. Vincent E. Giuliano, "The Mechanization of Office Work," *Scientific American,* Vol. 247 (September 1987), p. 163.

43. National Commission on Employment Policy, *Computers in the Workplace; Selected Issues* (Washington, D.C.: U.S. Government Printing Office), 1986, p. 38.

44. Cited in *Business Week,* June 16, 1986, p. 102.

45. Leontiff and Duchin, p. 41.

46. For men this age group accounted for 50.1% of the 1980 civilian labor force and for women 52.8%.

Chapter 4

1. The literature on internal labor markets is growing quite extensive. The two classic articles are Clark Kerr, "The Balkinization of Labor Markets," in E. Wight Bakke, ed., *Labor Mobility and Economic Opportunity* (Cambridge, Mass.: MIT Press), 1954, pp. 92–110, and John T. Dunlop, "Job Vacancy Measures and Econmic Analysis," in National Bureau of Economic Research, *The Measurement and Interpretation of Job Vacancies,* (New York: Columbia University Press), 1966. The 1972 book by Peter Doeringer and Michael Piore, *Internal Labor Markets and Manpower Analysis* (Lexington: D.C. Heath), 1972, brought the concept to the center of modern discourse.

2. This term is used loosely to exclude what might be termed the secondary labor patterns. That is, we are not interested here in understanding the low-wage/high-turnover sector in which many youth, immigrants, minorities, and women find themselves. This sector of the labor market is, of course, of central importance to issues of poverty and low income.

3. A complete description of these additional models as well as an effort to develop a general theory about how firms choose among internal labor market alternatives can be found in Paul Osterman, "Choice Among Alternative Internal Labor Market Systems," *Industrial Relations,* Vol. 26, No. 1 (February 1987), pp. 46–67.

4. For an historical account of the emergence of this model see Sanford Jacoby, *Employing Bureaucracy* (New York: Columbia University Press), 1985.

5. For example, unemployment insurance is structured to encourage layoffs and to discourage part-time employment.

6. For an account of the spread that links it to more general institutions of macroeconomic "regulation" see Michael J. Piore and Charles Sabel, *The Second Industrial Divide* (New York: Basic Books), 1984.

7. Katherine Abraham and James L. Medoff, "Length of Service and Layoffs in Union and Non-Union Workgroups," *Industrial and Labor Relations Review,* Vol. 38 (October 1984), pp. 87–97.

8. Harry C. Katz, *Shifting Gears* (Cambridge, Mass.: MIT Press), 1984, p. 44.

9. Rosabeth Moss Kanter, *Men and Women of the Corporation* (New York: Basic Books), 1978, p. 132.

10. For evidence that merit is important in these settings see Paul Osterman, "White Collar Internal Labor Markets," in Thomas Kochan, ed., *Challenges and Choices Facing American Labor* (Cambridge, Mass.: MIT Press), 1985, pp. 175–192.

11. For a discussion of welfare capitalism see David Brody, "The Rise and Decline of Welfare Capitalism," in David Brody, *Workers in Industrial America; Essays on the*

Twentieth Century Struggle (New York: Oxford University Press), 1980, pp. 48–81.

12. Theodore E. Grosskopf Jr., "Human Resource Planning Under Adversity," *Human Resource Planning,* Vol. 9, No. 1 (1986), p. 45.

13. For example, in the 1969–72 downturn 12,000 employees were transferred to new sites and 5000 were retrained for new careers (*ibid.*). For a description of these practices see Leonard Greenhalgh, Robert McKersie, and Roderick Gilkey, "Rebalancing the Workforce at IBM: A Case Study of Redeployment and Revitalization," MIT Sloan School Working Paper No. 1718-85, October 1985.

14. In the dual labor market literature it is conventional to distinguish between primary and secondary firms. We are using the term secondary in a different sense, to refer to unstable, high-turnover-job families within so-called primary firms. See Osterman, "Choice of Internal Labor Markets," *op. cit.*, for a further discussion of these issues.

15. For a more detailed description of wage determination in these settings see John T. Dunlop, *Wage Determination Under Trade Unions* (New York: Augustus Kelley), 1950; and Daniel J.B. Mitchell, *Union Wages and Inflation* (Washington, D.C.: Brookings Institution), 1980; and Peter Doeringer and Michael J. Piore, *op. cit.*

16. In the union context these were identified by Arthur Ross as "orbits of coercive comparision." See Arthur Ross, *Trade Union Wage Policy* (Berkeley: University of California Press), 1948.

17. Although it is also true that a substantial part of our trade gap is due to trade with nations whose wages are not that different from ours. See Arthur Neef, "International Trends in Productivity and Labor Costs in Manufacturing," *Monthly Labor Review,* Vol. 109 (December 1986), pp. 12–17.

18. Harry Braverman, *Labor and Monopoly Capital* (New York: Monthly Review Press), 1974.

19. An excellent review of this literature is found in Paul Attewell, "Work and Deskilling," *Work and Occupations,* Vol. 14, No. 3 (August 1987), pp. 323–346.

20. The following discussion is based on a case study of a one of the new regional operating companies.

21. Harry C. Katz, *op. cit.*, p. 39.

22. *New York Times,* March 13, 1986, pp. D2.

23. Steven M. Miller and Susan R. Bereiter, "Modernizing to Computer-Integrated Production Technologies in a Vehicle Assembly Plant: Lessons for Analysts and Managers of Technological Change," mimeograph, Carnegie Mellon University, paper presented to National Bureau of Economic Research Conference on Productivity Growth, November 1985, p. 3.

24. Haruo Shimda and John-Paul McDuffie, "Industrial Relations and 'Humanware'" Sloan School of Management Working Paper #1855-88, December 1986, p. 60.

25. *Ibid.*, p. 57–60.

26. John Krafcik, "Learning from NUMMI," working paper, International Motor Vehicle Program, MIT, 1986, note 33.

27. Michael J. Piore and Charles F. Sabel, *The Second Industrial Divide* (New York: Basic Books), 1985.

28. Michael J. Piore and Charles F. Sabel, *op. cit.*, p. 261.

29. The following description of the General Electric case is drawn from Steven Wheelwright and Robert Hayes, "Competing Through Manufacturing," *Harvard Business Review* (January–February 1985), pp. 99–101; Garrett Young, "G.E.: Dishing Out Efficiency, *High Technology,* Vol. 5 (May 1985); and Harvard Business School

Case, "G.E. Dishwasher Automation, Project C.," (Richard E. Walton, author), 1984.

30. The quote is from Ray Rissler and is drawn from "G.E.: Dishing Out Efficiency," *op. cit.*, p. 33.

31. This example is drawn from interviews conducted by the author.

32. Thomas G. Gunn, "The Mechanization of Design and Manufacturing," *Scientific American*, Vol. 247, September 1982), pp. 114–130.

33. Paul Osterman, "The Impact of Computers Upon the Employment of Clerks and Managers," *Industrial and Labor Relations Review*, Vol. 39, No. 2 (January 1986), pp. 175–186.

34. Wassily Leontief and Faye Duchin, *The Future Impact of Automation on Workers* (New York: Oxford University Press) 1986, p. 13.

35. *Business Week*, September 16, 1985, p. 34.

36. John Fay and James Medoff, "Labor and Output Over the Business Cycle," *American Economic Review*, Vol. 75 (September 1985), pp. 638–655; Ray C. Fair, "Excess Labor and the Business Cycle," *American Economic Review*, Vol. 75 (March 1985), pp. 239–245.

37. *Business Week*, May 29, 1985, p. 51.

38. In the 1920s Andrew Gordon notes that [Andrew Gordon, *The Evolution of Labor Relations in Japan; Heavy Industry 1853–1955*, (Cambridge, Mass.: Harvard University Press), 1985, p. 155]:

> Bad times, combined with the . . . weakness of unions . . . gave managers the power to almost fire at will [and many did] but negotiations over layoffs and union willingness to strike over jobs, even in a depression, remained characteristic of Japanese labor relations. In the late 1920's this tension over job security led some companies to exercise caution or even moderation when faced with the need to fire, so as to avoid labor disputes. This sort of interaction would eventually produce far greater job security when the balance of power shifted to favor labor two decades later.

The key to shifting this balance came with the American occupation at the end of World War II. The occupation decrees reestablished and empowered unions. Two watershed events occured in the late 1940s when management at the Japanese National Railroad and Toshiba announced large-scale layoffs. In both instances major strikes (the Toshiba one lasted 55 days) forced retraction of the plan and issuances of no-layoff pledges. Yet even this victory was short lived; the early 1950s witnessed a management offensive that—combined with restrictive macropolicy—succeeded in remaking the Japanese industrial relations system. Management accepted and broke major strikes, including a 113-day mine strike and a 173-day steel strike. A series of layoffs (including a 20% layoff at Toshiba) was announced and carried out. More important, however, union shop floor job control (along American lines) was destroyed and union rights (e.g., union/management councils and large numbers of union officers within the plant) were eliminated. The wage system was also changed from one based on need (age and family circumstances) to one more linked to productivity (seniority, education, and sex). However, when firms established increased flexibility and the principle of management control they in turn compromised on the job security issue, and that comprise became what we now think of as the "timeless" Japanese system.

39. Some marketing researchers argue that promotions increase volatility in product markets by increasing peaks and troughs and by spreading consumer loyalty across a broader range of brands. See Tod Johnson, "The Myth of Declining Brand Loyalty," *Journal of Advertising Research*, Vol. 24 (February/March 1984), pp. 9–17.

40. William Qualls, Richard Olshavsky, and Ronald Michaels, "Shortening the

Product Life Cycle—An Empirical Test," *Journal of Marketing*, Vol. 45, No. 4 (Fall 1981), p. 80.

41. A poll by Opinion Research Corporation found that for managers the percent who rated their company favorably declined from 82% in the 1977–74 period to 68% in the 1980–84 period. For clerical workers the figures were 58% and 50%, while for hourly employees the figures were 48% and 44%. Cited in Richard S. Belous, "Two-Tier Wage Systems in the U.S. Economy," Congressional Research Service Report No. 85-165, August 1985, p. 30. The quote is from a survey by Hay Associates and is reported in the *Behavioral Sciences Newsletter*, Book XVI, No. 6 March 3, 1987), p. 3.

42. *New York Times*, April 26, 1986, p. D1.

43. See Sanford Jacoby, *op. cit.*

44. *Wall Street Journal*, April 7, 1986.

45. For example, the fraction of contracts that include two-tier arrangements have declined in the past year.

46. J. R. Norsworthy and Craig Zabala, "Worker Attitudes, Worker Behavior, and Productivity in the U.S. Automobile Industry, 1959–76," *Industrial and Labor Relations Review*, Vol. 38, No. 4 (July 1985), pp. 544–557.

47. Harry Katz, Thomas Kochan, and Kenneth Gobeille, "Industrial Relations Performance, Economic Performance, and QWL Programs: An Interplant Analysis," *Industrial and Labor Relations Review*, Vol. 37, No. 1 (October 1983), pp. 3–17.

48. Thomas Weiskopf, Samuel Bowles, and David Gordon, "Hearts and Minds: A Social Model of U.S. Productivity Growth," *Brookings Papers on Economic Activity*, No. 2 (1983), pp. 381–450.

49. Bureau of National Affairs, "Collective Bargaining Negotiation and Contracts, Vol. 18, March 13, 1986, p. 461.

50. For a description of this agreement see Peter Cappelli, "Competitive Pressures and Labor Relations in the Airline Industry," *Industrial Relations*, Vol. 24 (1985), pp. 316–338.

51. These interviews are reported in greater detail in Paul Osterman, "White Collar Internal Labor Markets," in Paul Osterman, ed., *Internal Labor Markets* (Cambridge, Mass.: MIT Press), 1984, pp. 163–190.

52. Garth Mangum, Donald Mayall, and Kristin Nelson, "The Temporary Help Industry: A Response to the Dual Labor Market," *Industrial and Labor Relations Review*, Vol. 38, No. 4 (July 1985), p. 603.

53. See *Business Week*, January 1, 1985, p. 63, and the *San Jose Mercury News*, December 7, 1985.

54. *San Jose Mercury News*, April 17, 1984. The U.S. Immigration and Naturalization Service launched a heavily publicized series of raids in response to the saturation of this area's labor force with undocumented workers.

55. *Business Week*, February 25, 1985, p. 93.

56. The first figure was provided by the Association in private correspondence. The second figure was reported in the *New York Times*, October 24, 1985.

57. Max Carey and Kim Hazelbaker, "Employment Growth In the Temporary Help Industry," *Monthly Labor Review*, Vol. 109, No. 4 (April 1986), p. 42.

58. Mangum, *et al.*, *op. cit.*, p. 601.

59. Magnum, *et al.*, p. 608.

60. Magnum, *et al.*, and Mayhall and Nelson. This figure is based on a point-in-time employment level of roughly 430,000 multiplied by five. The multiplication factor was determined by a survey in California in which the authors found that for every

person currently working on the rolls of the agencies, they interviewed four others were on the rolls at some point during the year.

61. *Business Week,* December 15, 1986, p. 53. Contingent employment is defined as leased, temporary, home work, subcontracted work, and involuntary part-time work.

62. Garth Mangum, Donald Mayhill, and Kristin Nelson, *op.cit.*

63. The current stylized view of the Japanese labor force is that roughly 30% of employees are covered by the lifetime employment system while the remainder either work in firms without such a system (many of whom are subcontractors to larger firms who provide security) or are employees in firms that provide lifetime security to "members" but not to others. These "nonmembers" are frequently women or older workers.

64. *The Employment and Unemployment of Women in OECD Countries* (Paris: OECD), 1984.

65. Thomas J. Nardone, "Part-Time Workers, Who Are They," *Monthly Labor Review,* Vol. 109, No. 2 (February 1986), p. 18.

66. Bernard Ichniowski and Anne Preston, "New Trends in Part-Time Employment," Proceedings of the Industrial Relations Research Association, Spring 1986.

67. Martin Gannon presents evidence from three surveys of temporary clerical workers that between 66% and 85% of them were below age 30. See Martin Gannon, "A Profile of the Temporary Help Industry and Its Workers," *Monthly Labor Review,* Vol. 97, No. 5 (May 1974), pp. 44–49.

68. In 1983 the participation rates of men 65 and older was 17.4% and for women it was 7.8%, in 1960 the respective rates were 33.1% and 10.8%; and in 1970 they were 26.8% and 9.7%.

69. Brody, *op. cit.*

70. Kenneth Arrow, "Models of Job Discrimination," in Anthony Pascal, ed., *Racial Discrimination in Economic Life* (Lexington, Mass.: D. C. Heath), 1972.

Chapter 5

1. The current requirement for JTPA services is that an individual's income fall below the poverty line or that the person receive welfare.

2. There are numerous reviews of the evaluation literature. See, for example, Charles Betsey, *et al., Youth Employment and Training Programs, The YEDPA Years* (Washington, D.C.: National Research Council), 1985; Burt Barnow, "The Impact of CETA Programs on Earnings: A Review of the Literature," *Journal of Human Resources,* Vol. 22, No. 2 (Spring 1987), pp. 157–193; Howard Bloom, "Estimating the Effect of Job Training Programs Using Logitudinal Data: Ashenfelter's Findings Reconsidered," *Journal of Human Resources,* Vol. XIX, No. 4 (Fall 1984), pp. 545–555; and Laurie Bassi and Orly Ashenfelter, "The Effect of Direct Job Creation and Training Programs on Low-Skilled Workers," in Sheldon Danziger and Daniel Weinberg, eds., *Fighting Poverty* (Cambridge, Mass.: Harvard University Press), 1986, pp. 133–151. Virtually all of the studies reviewed in the material cited estimated the impact of employment programs on earnings as the dependent variable and find results in the range cited in the text. A recent study of CETA by David Card and Daniel Sullivan instead examined the impact of the program on the probability of employment. They found that participation in CETA training programs raised the probability of employment by between 3 and 5 percentage points (e.g., prior to participation a trainee had about a .85 chance of having a job; after participation the probability was between .88 and .90). Given that the typical job held by a trainee after participation paid $5800, this translates into an earnings gain from participation of $100–$300 per year on average. See "Measuring

the Effect of Subsidized Training Programs on Movements In and Out of Employment," National Bureau of Economic Research, Working Paper No. 2173, February 1987.

3. There are, of course, individual success stories or even programs as a whole that are more successful than average. But the point raised earlier about key importance for public policy of expected average effects must be kept in mind.

4. These data and the following information on TJTC are taken from John Bishop and Kevin Hollenbeck, *The Effects of TJTC on Employers,* (Columbus, Ohio: National Center for Research in Vocational Education), November 1985.

5. *Ibid.* p. 48.

6. *Ibid.*, p. 70.

7. Thomas Bailey, "An Assessment of the Employment and Training System in New York City," in Charles Brecher and Raymond Horton, eds., *Setting Municipal Priorities, 1988* (New York: New York University Press), 1987.

8. Charles Mallar, Stuart Kerachsky, and Craig Thornton, *Evaluation of the Economic Impact of the Job Corps Program,* Third Follow-up, Mathematica Policy Research, Princeton, N.J., 1982.

9. Manpower Development Research Corporation, *Summary and Findings of the National Supported Work Demonstration* (Cambridge Mass.: Ballinger), 1980.

10. See, for example, Paul Osterman, "The Politics and Economics of CETA Programs, *Journal of the American Planning Association* (October 1981), pp. 434–446.

11. Jim Darr and Erik Butler, "Reexamining the Federal Experience with Youth Employment; What Are the Managerial Lessons?," paper prepared for the National Research Council, December 1984, pp. 49–50. The low estimate is derived from the *Employment and Training Reporter,* the high estimate from a poll of members of the National Youth Practioners Network.

12. Bureau of National Affairs, *Personnel Policies Forum Survey No. 140,* p. 22.

13. The statement is by Freiher von Reitzenstein and is cited in John A. Garraty, *Unemployment In History* (New York: Harper & Row), 1978, p. 131.

14. William Beveridge, *Unemployment: A Problem of Industry* (London:McMillan) 1930; this summary is based on Garraty, *op. cit.* p. 139.

15. See Terry Johnson, Katherine P. Dickinson, and Richard West, "An Evaluation of the Impact of ES Referrals on Applicant Earnings," *Journal of Human Resources,* Vol. XX, No. 1, (Winter 1985), pp. 117–138.

16. For a good review of the changing role of the employment service and some of the issues this raises see Stanley Ruttenberg and Jocelyn Gutchess, *The Federal-State Employment Service: A Critique* (Baltimore: Johns Hopkins University Press), 1970.

17. Richard Lester, after arguing that the employment service should be at the center of an employment and training system, went on to note that (in the early 1960s) only 30% of all placements made by the service were nonfarm jobs of over 3 days duration. Lester, *op. cit.,* p. 71.

18. National Commission on Employment Policy, Seventh Annual Report, *The Federal Interest in Employment and Training* (Washington, D.C.: U.S. Government Printing Office), 1981, p. 65.

19. The best review of this debate is provided by W. Norton Grubb and Marvin Lazerson, *American Education and Vocationalism* (New York: Teachers College Press), 1974.

20. In 1938 Roosevelt complained that "Much of the apparent demand for the immediate extension of the vocational education program under the George-Dean Act appears to have been stimulated by an active lobby of vocational teachers, supervisors

and administrative officers in the field of vocational education who are interested in enrollments paid in part in Federal Funds." Quoted in Edward Krug, *The Shaping of the Modern High School,* Vol. I (New York: Harper & Row), 1964, p. 311.

21. Stanley Ruttenberg assisted by Jocelyn Gutchess, *Manpower Challenge of the 1970's: Institutions and Social Changes,* (Baltimore: Johns Hopkins University Press), p. 17.

22. The most recent summary of this literature is provided by the National Research Council, *High Schools and the Changing Workplace* (Washington D.C.: National Research Council), 1984.; see also John Grasso and John Shea, *Vocational Education and Training: Impact on Youth* (New York: Carnegie Foundation for the Advancement of Teaching), 1979.

23. I am grateful to Norton Grubb and Jerry Karabel for sharing with me drafts of their very insightful work in this area. My analysis has been influenced by their views.

24. Fred L. Pincus, "Customized Contract Training in Community Colleges: Who Really Benefits," paper presented to the 1985 American Sociological Association, Washington, D.C., p. 2.

25. *Ibid.*

26. Pincus, *op. cit.,* p. 6.

27. When asked by the Opinion Research Corporation what kind of school they would attend if they continued their education (and 40% of adults indicated an intention to pursue further education), 26% of the adults indicated a preference for vocational-technical schools and 21% for community colleges. The *Boston Globe,* October 20, 1985, p. 16.

28. Wellford W. Wilms and Stephen Hansell, "The Dubious Promise of Postsecondary Vocational Education: Its Payoffs to Graduates and Dropouts in the U.S.A.," *International Journal of Educational Development,* Vol. 2, (Spring 1982), pp. 43–60.

29. According to the General Accounting Office, among Title III participants in 1985, 88% were 22 to 54 years old, 78% had a high school degree or more, 60% were male, and 69% were white. The comparable figures for Title II—the main training program for the disadvantaged—were 57%, 61%, 48%, and 54%. See General Accounting Office, *Dislocated Workers; Local Programs and Outcomes Under the Job Training Partnership Act;* Washington, D.C., March 1987, p. 39.

30. A good recent review is provided in the Task Force Report to the Secretary of Labor on Plant Closings (The Lovell Report) (Washington, D.C.: U.S. Government Printing Office), 1987. For a good description of a program see Gary Hansen, "Ford and the UAW Have A Better Idea: Joint Labor Management Approaches to Plant Closings and Worker Retraining," *Annals of the American Academy of Political and Social Science,* Vol. 475 (September 1984), pp. 118–174.

31. Mathematica Policy Research, Inc., *An Impact Evaluation of the Buffalo Dislocated Worker Demonstration Program* (Princeton, N.J.), March 1985, p. vi.

32. Stanley H. Ruttenberg assisted by Jocelyn Gutchess, *Manpower Challenge of the 1970s: Institutions and Social Changes* (Baltimore: Johns Hopkins University Press), 1970, p. 53.

33. Statement by Thomas Donahue, Executive Assistant to the President, AFL-CIO in National Commission on Employment Policy, *Labor's Views on Employment Policy* (Washington, D.C.: U.S. Government Printing Office), July 1978, p. 30.

34. *New York Times,* October 20, 1985, p. 1.

35. Gary Burtless, "Are Targetted Wage Subsidies Harmful? Evidence From a Voucher Experiment," *Industrial and Labor Relations Review,* Vol. 39, No. 1 (October 1985), pp. 105–114.

36. Peter Doeringer, David Gordon, and Penny Feldman, "Low Income Labor Markets and Manpower Programs in Boston," mimeograph, Kennedy School, Harvard University, Mass.; Peter Doeringer and Michael J. Piore, *Internal Labor Markets and Manpower Analysis* (Lexington Mass.: D.C. Heath), 1971.

37. George Johnson, "Do Structural Employment and Training Programs Influence Unemployment?" *Challenge* (May/June 1979), p. 56.

Chapter 6

1. These are OECD data and are taken from Paul Ryan, "Human Resources, Job Training and Industrial Restructuring in OECD Countries," Mimeograph, Kings College, Cambridge, England, September 1981, p. 50.

2. Thomas Rohlen, *Japan's High Schools,* (Berkeley: University of California Press), 1983.

3. Shun'ichiro Umetani, "Background Paper for Japan/ARSDEP Study Tour on In-Plant Training," mimeo, Tokyo Gakugei University, October 1980, p. 34.

4. David Soskice, "Industrial Relations and The British Economy," *Industrial Relations,* Vol. 23, No. 3 (Fall 1984), pp. 306–322.

5. Robert Cole, *Work, Mobility, and Participation: A Comparative Study of American and Japanese Industry* (Berkeley: University of California Press), 1979.

6. The three tracks are *Hauptschule, Realschule,* and *Gymnasium.* The first two typically conclude with an apprenticeship, while the latter is the path to university. Germany has experienced an educational inflation similar to ours and hence, on the one hand, the *Hauptschule* is increasingly seen as a dead-end and, on the other hand, a growing number of *Gymnasium* graduates, faced with a decline in public sector employment, are returning for an apprenticeship.

7. A skilled blue collar worker is called a *Fachabeiter* and a skilled white collar worker *Angestellte.*

8. Karen Schober, "Youth Employment In Germany," in Beatrice Reubens, ed., *Youth At Work* (Totowa N.J.: Allanheld Osmun), 1981, pp. 5–23. And, in fact, the share of apprenticeships in small firms is growing. Between 1973 and 1982 handicraft's share of apprenticeships increased from 35% to 39.7%. This represented an increase of 200,000 new slots compared to an increase of 70,000 slots in industry and commerce. Stephen F. Hamilton, "Apprenticeship as a Transition to Adulthood in West Germany," paper presented to the American Educational Research Association, Cornell University, p. 41. The statistics are drawn from *Bundesminister fur Bildung und Wissenschaft, Grund-und Strukturdat, 1983/84* Bad Honnef, Bock, 1984, p. 84.

9. Schober, pp. 5–38.

10. It is very difficult to measure the costs of informal on-the-job training and the benefits (and quality) of output produced by the trainees.

11. Paul Osterman, *Getting Started; The Youth Labor Market* (Cambridge, Mass.: MIT Press), 1980.

12. David Ellwood, "Teenage Unemployment: Permanent Scars or Temporary Blemishes," in Richard Freeman and David Wise, eds., *The Youth Labor Market Problem* (Chicago National Bureau of Economic Research: University of Chicago Press), 1982, pp. 349–390; Osterman, *op. cit.*

13. Anders Bjorklund and Inga Persson-Tanimura, *Youth Employment In Sweden,* The Swedish Institute for Social Research (Stockholm), January 1983.

14. For a description of this pattern see Osterman, *op. cit.*

15. In large part this is due to the Swedish wage structure, which rules out youth

jobs. One consequence of this, however, is that youth unemployment is in fact a major problem and has forced the government to create so-called "youth teams" which are public service employment jobs for youth and are operated by the municipalities. As we will discuss later, this is one of the more controversial aspects of Swedish labor market policy.

16. Currently, the vocational program consists of a series of fields ("lines") that follow the 9 years of compulsory education and are generally 2 years in length, although a few may last 4 years. These are school based, although there is provision for some "work-study." However, there is a growing perception that the programs are failing because in the dynamic occupations they cannot keep pace with technical change (i.e., cannot update equipment and curriculum) and in many cases lose qualified staff to better paying private employment. These are the fundamental problems facing all school-based vocational education in an environment in which skill content changes. The proposed Swedish solution will be a final year (after formal graduation) of plant-based training. The debate in Sweden concerns exactly the issues that make the German model so distinctive: Who will control the "admission" of students into various fields (i.e., the hiring into training positions)? Will firms be required to provide all the training slots that are demanded? Who will control training content? How will efforts to turn the program into a source of cheap labor be met? These issues are inherent in any vocational education model that emphasizes firm-based training, yet the fact that Sweden, with a balance of economic power very different from Germany's, is willing to raise these topics in order to reform vocational education is further evidence that school-based models of the sort employed in the United States are not viable.

17. Minor exceptions include elements of the Appalachian regional development programs, which provided migration assistance, and migration assistance in the Trade Readjustment Assistance Act.

18. In Sweden unemployment insurance is available to the two-thirds of the labor force that belong to an unemployment society. To receive benefits it is necessary to have been employed for at least a year, including 12 weeks of the year preceding unemployment. Payments last for 300 days (450 days for workers between 55 and 65) and the replacement ratio varies between 60 and 90% (depending on previous wage), with most people receiving toward the upper end. For people not eligible for unemployment insurance or whose benefits have run out, the second-tier program, cash assistance, provides a flat daily payment (100 SEK, or 24% of the average manufacturing wage in 1984) and lasts for 150 days up until age 55, 300 days from age 55 to 60, and without limit after age 60. See Bjorklund, *op. cit.*, and Sven Olsson "Welfare Programs in Sweden," Institute for Social Forskning, University of Stockholm, 1985.

19. In 1980 72% of the Swedish labor force belonged to a unemployment insurance fund. In addition to fund membership for at least 12 months, receipt of unemployment insurance depends on having worked for 5 out of the past 12 months. In 1984 57.3% of unemployed workers received unemployment insurance, 10.1% received KAS (the second-level cash assistance program, which is means tested), and 32.5% received no support. It is not clear whether the individuals who receive no support are being supported by other welfare state transfer programs. Because of the nature of the benefits scheduling the replacement rate (the percent of the wage that is replaced by unemployment insurance) varies with duration of unemployment. For those unemployed 1 month, the after-tax replacement rate is 0.49; it rises to 0.62 for those unemployed 6 months. For KAS the comparable figures are 0.19 and 0.24. On an annual basis, if after 6 months or so the person returns to work, the replacement rate is higher because the lower income during unemployment reduces marginal tax rates. The few studies

that have been done do not provide any evidence that unemployment insurance payments increase duration of unemployment spells. All of these data (and more!) are contained in the excellent study by Anders Bjorklund and Bertil Holmlund, "Unemployment Compensation in Sweden," IUI, 84-05-07, December 1985.

20. Twelve states permit short-work unemployment insurance payments. However, evaluations of the program in the two states with the longest experience, California and Arizona, suggest that the take-up rate is very low. See Stuart Kerachsky, Walter Nicholson, Edward Cavin, and Alan Hershey, "An Evaluation of Short-Time Compensation Programs," *Proceedings of the Industrial Relations Research Association* (Madison Wis.,: IRRA), 1986, pp. 424–432.

21. The two most significant of these are "bottleneck training," which provides government subsidies for in-plant training in shortage occupations, and the "recruitment subsidy," which is simply a subsidy to firms if they hire additional workers beyond "planned" levels. The bottleneck program's premise is that if the firm accepts government assistance for on-the-job training of skilled workers then, as part of the bargain, it will be more responsive to the employment office's requests that it hire referrals. The program got off to a slow start but is now popular among employers and trains for roughly 9000 positions per year. I know of no evaluation that examines either displacement effects (would the company have provided the training anyway?) or whether the bargain with the employment office is made and kept. The recruitment subsidy program is much like our Targeted Jobs Tax Credit in that it aims to provide subsidies to incremental employment. Unlike our program it is not limited to specific target groups and it is not an entitlement but, instead, is administered at the discretion of the local employment office. A recent evaluation of this program concluded that 30% of the program positions were pure windfall profit (the company would have hired the people anyway), and 52% of the positions represents earlier hires than would have otherwise occurred. The remaining positions were evidently not classifiable but there was also some evidence that the employment offices were able to use the subsidies to affect which people were hired (in 30% of the hires the firms indicated that their decisions as to whom to hire were influenced by the program). These figures are based on interviews with companies and hence probably represent an upper bound on the program's effectiveness, given the tendency of firms to exaggerate the effect of subsidies in interviews with the dispensers of those subsidies. See Lena Eriksson, "Erfarenheter Au Rekryteringsstodet," AMS Report, March 8, 1985.

22. *Labor Market Training 1985* [Stockholm: National Labor Market Board Research Division (Fredrik Winter)] 1985-01-09, pp. 12–13.

23. The discussion in this paragraph follows that of Wolfgang Streeck, "Qualitative Demands and the Neo-Corporatist Manageability of Industrial Relations," *British Journal of Industrial Relations,* Vol. 14 (1981), pp. 149–169.

24. The foregoing description of the powers of the Works Council is taken from Wolfgang Streek, *Industrial Relations in West Germany* (New York: St. Martin's Press), 1984, pp. 110–112.

25. What is not clear is how to apportion the respective fractions of local wage settlements. In an insightful paper Robert Flanagan argues that wage drift over the 1970s accounted for 40 to 50% of the earnings of blue collar workers and 25 to 40% of the earnings of white collar employees. However, he does not examine the extent to which what seems to be drift is really mechanical adjustments to the national agreement. See Robert Flanagan, "Efficiency and Equality in Swedish Labor Markets," in Barry Bosworth and Alice Rivlin, eds., *The Swedish Economy,* (Washington, D.C.: The Brookings Institution), 1987, pp. 125–184.

26. An extensive discussion of Swedish wage setting is provided by Robert Flanagan, David Soskice, and Lloyd Ulman, *Unionism, Economic Stability, and Income Policies* (Washington, D.C.: The Brookings Institution), 1983.

27. Flanagan, *op. cit.*

28. Arndt Sorge and Malcolm Warner, "Manpower Training, Manufacturing Organization and Workplace Relations in Great Britain and West Germany," *British Journal of Industrial Relations*, Vol. 18, No. 3, pp. 318–333.

29. Marc Maurice, Francois Sellier, and Jean-Jacques Silvestre, "The Search for a Societal Effect in the Production of Company Hierarchy: A Comparison of France and Germany," in Paul Osterman, ed., *Internal Labor Markets*, (Cambridge, Mass.: MIT Press), 1984, pp. 231–270.

30. Gert Hartmann, Ian Nicholas, Arndt Sorge, and Malcolm Warner, "Computerized Machine Tools, Manpower Consequences, and Skill Utilization: A Study of British and German Manufacturing Firms," *British Journal of Industrial Relations*, Vol. 21, No. 2 (July 1983), p. 229.

31. Sorge and Warner, *op. cit.*, p. 329.

32. Paul Windolf, "Industrial Robots in the Automobile Industry: New Technology in the Context of German Industrial Relations," paper prepared for the International Automobile Conference, Berlin Science Center, August 1984, p. 8.

33. Peter Lawrence, *Managers and Management in West Germany* (New York: St. Martin's Press), 1980, p. 134.

34. For evidence that seniority is important in both union and nonunion settings in America (albeit more so in union shops) see Abraham and Medoff *op. cit.*

35. Werner Sengenberger, "West German Employment Policy: Restoring Worker Competition," *Industrial Relations*, Vol. 23, No. 3 (Fall 1984), p. 324.

36. The information in this paragraph and the entire description of Swedish internal labor markets is based on personal interviews conducted with Swedish employers (in manufacturing, finance, and service industries), union leaders, academics, and government personnel.

37. See Richard Freeman, *The Market for College Trained Manpower*, (Cambridge, Mass.: Harvard University Press), 1971. There is a regular cycle in the United States of complaints about shortages and surpluses of engineers. The downside of the cycle is being played out once again as the high-technology industry contracts and defense spending come under attack in Congress.

38. A good recent example is strong teacher resistance to the various merit proposals put forward by recent educational reform commissions.

39. Paul Windoff, *op. cit.*, p. 34.

40. The discussion of these early retirement schemes closely follows the excellent presentation found in Gert Bruche and Bernd Reissert, "Manpower and Regional Adjustment Policies: The Case of West Germany," International Institute of Management, Berlin Science Center, November 1984.

41. OECD, *The Employment and Unemployment of Women in OECD Countries*, (Paris: OECD), 1984.

42. The key eligibility requirement is that in order to receive stipends for training an individual must have contributed to the unemployment insurance system for a number of years.

43. Evidence on this is presented in the section on the consequences of alternative systems.

44. This estimate is based on internal AMS data found in the regular reporting system and compiled in a quarterly report labeled "Tabell K." In the first quarter of

1985 267,000 jobs were listed with the employment service, of which 32% were filled by individuals sent by that exchange. The comparable percentages (or penetration rates) for the second quarter were 22% and for the third quarter 22%. For 1984 the penetration rate for each of the four quarters was 15%, 17%, 19%, and 28%. These figures must be regarded as estimates for several reasons. First, they are based on openings listed with the employment service and while the law requires complete listing, in fact the requirement is not actively enforced. This suggests an upward bias to the estimates. Second, the estimates do not include what might be termed blanket listings [e.g., employers who engage in mass recruitment by listing an examination (such as civil service) or mass interviews with the employment service]. It is not clear what the direction of bias is here, since the employment service does send clients to these employers. Finally, the number of employment service clients who get these jobs is based on a survey of employers to capture the identification number of new hires which, in turn, is matched against the identification number of employment service referrals. This probably leads to an underestimate of the penetration rate because it is now possible for clients to collect job listings without registering with the employment service and hence the employment service would not match their identification number against a referral. Taken as a whole, we must view these figures as simply order-of-magnitude estimates.

45. The most careful study of this question concludes that "It is thus difficult to make it seem credible that the number of persons with functional impairments or disabilities should have increased, thereby causing the number of employment handicapped also to rise." This conclusion is based on evidence such as the decline in occupational accidents and automobile accidents. The only offsetting factor may be an increase in drug and alcohol problems. See Eskil Wadensjo, "Labor Market Policy Towards the Disabled in Sweden," Swedish Institute for Social Research, University of Stockholm, September 1984, mimeograph p. 22.

46. "Labor Market Policy Under Reconsideration," EFA, Arbetsmarknadsdepartementet, Stockholm, 1984, p. 36.

47. In 1970 the labor force participation rate of 65 to 70-year-olds was 28.9% for men and 8.7% for women. By 1983 the rates had declined to 12.0% and 4.1%, respectively. For men aged 55 to 64 the rates declined from 85.4% to 77.1% over the same period, although there was an increase for women of this age group. *Ibid.*, 18.

48. For a review see Michael Bruno and Jeffrey Sachs, *Economics of Worldwide Stagflation* (Cambridge, Mass.: Harvard University Press), 1985.

49. For example, the series of papers published by the OECD on labor market flexibility and the general view that European labor markets are too rigid has in turn been attacked by the European Trade Union Institute in their report "Flexibility and Jobs: Myths and Realities," Brussels, 1986.

Chapter 7

1. The following material was developed jointly in a case study with Thomas Kochan and John-Paul McDuffie.

2. These conclusions are strengthened by another case: the difficulties of the U.A.W.-Ford agreement in the Rawsonville plant, which we discussed in Chapter 4. Recall that the agreement included a Ford commitment to stabilize employment, the use of temporary workers to underwrite that, and the consequent union agreement to alter work rules. Despite these agreements employment is falling as Ford continues to outsource production. Once again, the evidence is very clear that it is difficult for a firm under pressure to maintain job security agreements.

3. Quoted in Charles Meyers, "Critical Issues in National Manpower Policy," in Stanley M. Jacks, ed., *Issues in Labor Policy* (Cambridge, Mass.: MIT Press), 1971, p. 14.

4. This point is made in Paul Ryan, "Job Training, Employment Practices, and the Large Enterprise: The Case of Costly Transferable Skills," in Paul Osterman, ed., *Internal Labor Markets* (Cambridge, Mass.: MIT Press), 1984, pp. 191–230.

5. In the case study of the high-technology firm referred to earlier the company had difficulty recruiting sufficient employees willing to undergo retraining, despite very high job security assurances.

6. Useful discussion of these and other agreements is provided by Ernest J. Savoie, "Current Developments and Future Agenda in Union-Management Cooperation in Training and Retraining Workers," *Labor Law Journal*, Vol. 36, No. 8 (August 1985), pp. 535–547, and Ronnie J. Straw and Margaret L. Hilton, "Training for Employment Security and Personal Growth: The CWA Approach," paper presented to the Twentieth Atlantic Economic Conference, Washington, D.C., August 31, 1985.

7. These studies are reviewed in Patricia Flynn Pannell, "Employer Response to Skill Shortages: Implications for Small Business," Proceedings of the Small Business Research Conference, Vol. II (Waltham, Mass.: Bentley College), 1981.

8. See John Gennard, "Job Security: Redundancy Arrangements and Practices in Selected OECD Countries," mimeo, Directorate for Social Affairs, Manpower, and Education (Paris: OECD), September 1985.

9. Much of this material is reviewed in a recent report by the Congressional Office of Technology Assessment, *Technology and Structural Unemployment; Reemploying Displaced Adults* Washington, D.C. U.S. Government Printing Office, Office of Technology Assessment), 1985.

10. See George P. Shultz and Arnold Weber, *Strategies for the Displaced Workers* (New York: Harper & Row), 1966.

11. Stuart Keraschsky, Walter Nicholson, Edward Cavin, and Alan Hershey, "An Evaluation of Short-Time Compensation Programs," *Proceedings of The Thirty-Eighth Annual Meetings* (Madison, Wis.: Industrial Relations Research Association), 1986, pp. 424–432.

12. Keraschsky, et al., *op. cit.*

13. The account that follows is based on Daniel Nelson, *Unemployment Insurance, the American Experience 1915–1935* (Madison, Wis.: University of Wisconsin Press), 1969.

14. Quoted by Nelson, *op. cit.*, p. 72.

15. For a recent survey of the field see Work in America Institute, *Employment Security In A Free Economy* (New York: Pergamon Press), 1985.

Appendix to Chapter 2

1. The equation takes the form $Y_{t+x} = \beta_1 U_t + \beta_2 \text{Age}_{t+x} + \beta_3 Y_{t-1} + \beta_4 Y_{t-2} + \beta_5 Y_{t-3} + e$, where Y is either annual earnings, the wage rate, or annual weeks of work, depending on the model. This model is a fixed-effects approach to examining the impact of an "intervention" on subsequent outcomes. The data are from the Panel Survey on Income Dynamics. Unemployment is measured for two interview years, 1975 and 1976. Subsequent earnings, and so on, are for 1977 to 1981 (separate equations are run for each year), and the preintervention earnings, wages, and weeks variables are for 1971, 1972, and 1973. Separate equations are estimated for men and women and, in both cases, the sample is limited to those who were between 25 and 53 years old in 1971.

This eliminates retirement as a possible outcome. In addition, the individual must have had some earnings in 1973 and must not have been permanently disabled. Individuals who report themselves as having had 9999 hours of unemployment during 1975 or 1976 are eliminated. All variables are estimated in natural logs except for the unemployment variables.

2. In a logit specification $\partial Y/\partial X = \beta(P)(1 - P)$, and we evaluate this expression at the mean of P.

Appendix to Chapter 6

1. Anders Bjorklund, "Policies for Labor Market Adjustment in Sweden," Industrial Institute for Economic Research, Working Paper No. 163, Stockholm, 1986, p. 41.

2. Bertil Holmlund, *Labor Mobility* (Stockholm: The Industrial Institute for Economic and Social Research), 1984, p. 35.

3. Holmlund, *op. cit.*

4. *Op. cit.*, pp. 77 and 96.

5. He writes, "First, it is clear that the weakened demand for labor in the 1970s is a major explanation of the decline in quit rates. Also important are indirect cyclical effects. . . . Since recently hired workers are those who are most likely to quit there are indirect mobility decreasing effects from a reduction in vacancies. There has (also) been a secular increase in average plant size in manufacturing industry, implying a growing importance of internal labor markets. One important structural shift pertains to women whose firmer attachment to the labor force is revealed as lower quit intentions. This change, however, does not necessarily reflect a reduced willingness to *move between jobs* [italics in original]; most likely it primarily indicates a decreasing frequency of labor force transition." Holmlund, *op. cit.*, pp. 110–111.

6. Anders Bjorklund, "Policies for Labor Market Adjustment in Sweden," Stockholm, Industrial Institute for Economic and Social Research, 1985, p. 41.

7. These statements are based on data provided to me by the Ministry of Education on 1984–85 enrollments in each of the 25 lines or tracks available in the gymnasiums. Among those tracks with enrollments of 3000 students or more (the smallest tracks include fields such as music, aesthetics, and woodwork. Agriculture and operations maintenance have enrollments in the range of 2000), those that had a surplus of applicants over spaces were nursing, economics, technology, electrotechnical communications, motor engineering, food manufacturing, social service, and social science. Those with a surplus of space relative to applicants were distribution and clerical, consumer, construction, and workshop (operative).

8. Johannesson, *op. cit.*, Figure 7.

9. This is based on David M. Lilien, "The Cyclical Pattern of Temporary Layoffs In U.S. Manufacturing," *Review of Economics and Statistics*, Vol. LXII, No. 1 (February 1980), pp. 24–30. Lilien estimates that temporary layoffs accounted for 60 to 78% of all layoffs during 1965 to 1976.

10. Lennart Erixon, "What's Wrong With The Swedish Model? An Analysis of Its Effects and Changed Conditions," Institute For Social Forskning, University of Stockholm, 1985, p. 76.

11. See OECD, *Economic Outlook: Germany, 1984/85* (Paris: OECD), 1985, p. 35. These data are somewhat controversial, however, because Germany vacancy statistics are administratively collected by the employment service and firms are required to list vacancies. As incentives change the reporting rates vary over time.

12. Werner Sengenberger, "Employment Security: Redundancy Arrangements and

Practices in West Germany," A Report Prepared for the OECD, Munich, January 1985, p. 27.

13. For more details on this shift see Jan Johannesson and Inga Persson-Tanimura, *Labor Market Policy Under Reconsideration* (Stockholm: Swedish Ministry of Labor), 1984.

14. P-A Edin, "Individuella sysselsattningskonsekvenser av nedlaggningar," Working Paper No. 119, Svenska Handelshogskolan, Helsinki, 1984, quoted in Anders Bjorklund, "Policies for Labor Market Adjustment in Sweden," IUI, 1985, p. 19.

15. In another study Anders Bjorklund and Robin Moffitt conclude that there is a positive average return to training but the marginal return is negative. This implies that too many people are in training programs. However, the sample size is very small and so caution is necessary. See Bjorklund and Moffit, *op. cit.*

INDEX